THE RORSCHACH TECHNIQUE:
AN INTRODUCTORY MANUAL

Bruno Klopfer

UNIVERSITY OF CALIFORNIA AT LOS ANGELES

Helen H. Davidson

THE CITY COLLEGE OF THE
CITY UNIVERSITY OF NEW YORK

THE RORSCHACH TECHNIQUE
An Introductory Manual

Harcourt, Brace & World, Inc.

NEW YORK : CHICAGO : SAN FRANCISCO : ATLANTA

Preface

The Rorschach Technique by Klopfer and Kelley, first published in 1942, has long served as an introductory text for students of the subject. For advanced workers who are interested in validation problems and problems of personality theory and who are specializing in the various fields of application of the technique, there are available also *Developments in the Rorschach Technique, Vols. I and II,* by Klopfer, Ainsworth, Klopfer, Holt, and others, published in 1954 and 1956, respectively. The aim of the present practical *Introductory Manual* is to integrate fundamental information from *The Rorschach Technique* with refinements from the *Developments* volumes and to eliminate material not essential for the student who wishes to learn the Rorschach technique only as part of his training in clinical psychology or in a related area.

After a brief history of the Rorschach technique and a discussion of the underlying theories and of the problems of the method, this book devotes itself to a thorough explanation of the processes involved in administering the Rorschach examination and in scoring and interpreting the responses. Case studies, scored on the new Individual Record Blank, and many scoring examples illustrate the proper application of the technique.

The two case studies in the body of the text, of individuals who are not clinical cases in any sense, demonstrate the value of the Rorschach technique as a psychodiagnostic method for the understanding of normal people and their development. They reflect not only the use of the interpretative hypotheses cited in the text but also the myriad problems that make up the normal person—with all his imperfections and areas of incompleteness. In the Appendix the case of a disturbed child with borderline intelligence provides a basis for comparison with the normal cases.

Dr. Mary Ainsworth, Mr. Jay Efran, Miss Adele Kramer, Mrs. Edna Meyers, and Dr. Marvin Spiegelman, as well as the subjects of the case studies, have made significant contributions to this volume. The authors gratefully acknowledge their assistance and wish to thank also the countless other colleagues who have aided and encouraged them in the preparation of this manuscript.

BRUNO KLOPFER
HELEN H. DAVIDSON

Contents

THE RORSCHACH TECHNIQUE:
AN INTRODUCTORY MANUAL

Chapter One

BACKGROUND
OF THE RORSCHACH TECHNIQUE

WHAT is known today as the Rorschach technique was formally presented to the world in 1921 with the publication of the monograph *Psychodiagnostik,* by Hermann Rorschach [13]. In this remarkable work written in German, the 37-year-old Swiss psychiatrist included his selected ink blots, his clinical findings, and the theoretical bases for his investigations. So penetrating and far-reaching were Rorschach's insights that, in the main, the original concepts put forward in the slim volume are still in use, as are the ten slightly asymmetrical patterns which today are part of the standard equipment of all psychological diagnosticians.

Rorschach himself described how these patterns were produced and selected:

A few large ink blots are thrown on a piece of paper, the paper folded, and the ink spread between the two halves of the sheet. Not all figures so obtained can be used, for those used must fulfill certain conditions. In the first place, the forms must be relatively simple; complicated pictures make the computations of the factors of the experiment too difficult. Furthermore, the distribution of the blots on the plate must fulfill certain requirements of composition or they will not be suggestive. . . .
Every figure in the series has to fulfill certain special requirements as well as these general ones, and each, as well as any whole series, must be thoroughly tried out before it can be used as apparatus for the test. [13, p. 15]

Rorschach's final set of cards, standardized on the population of a hospital in which he served as chief psychiatrist, was the result of ten years of untiring personal research and exploration. The ten cards were selected from among thousands of trial blots.

Many psychologists before this time had been fascinated with ink blots and were conducting their own investigations on the significance of the responses made by individuals to the stimulus. Rorschach's "test" was the culmination of over twenty years of experimentation with ink blots in Europe and in America. Most of the research preceding and contemporary with his own, however, considered the use of ink blots as a method for studying visual imagination through the analysis of the content of the subject's responses. It is a testament to Rorschach's genius that he was able to go beyond this limited usage and to postulate that, in addition to content, a consideration of the formal and structural aspects of a subject's reactions to random forms could reveal that subject's basic personality.

Early Work with Ink Blots

The first recorded discussion of ink blots came about accidentally. Justinus Kerner was working in a laboratory in Tübingen, Germany, in a period marking the beginnings of modern psychology and psychiatry. Quite by chance, he began to be aware of the many objects to be seen in ink blots. His deepening interest and attention were set down in *Kleksographien,* published in 1857 [9].

Kerner did not quite grasp the possibility of a relationship between ink-blot perceptions and personality diagnosis. He noted, however, the difficulty of interpreting ink blots according to a preconceived plan and called attention to the interplay between the objective material and the projective responses of a subject.

In 1895 Alfred Binet, of intelligence test fame, suggested that ink blots might be used in the investigation of visual imagination for the study of personality traits [4]. About a year later Dearborn of Harvard published an article [5] in which he described how to make both black and white and colored ink blots and suggested ways of using ink blots in experimental psychology.

Dearborn later [6] reported an experiment with 12 sets of 10 blots each, which he administered to a group of subjects, mainly Harvard students and professors. His observations foreshadowed Rorschach's own rationale when he wrote:

> Why one subject should see in a blot a "cabbage head" and the next an "animal with his mouth open," or why a professor should be reminded by a blot of "half a sweet pea blossom" and his wife of a "snake coiled round a stick," of course no one can at present pretend to explain. . . .

It is clear that, as a general principle, the experience, and especially the early experience, of the subject has important influence. [6, p. 190]

And again,

In particular would it be interesting to know to what degree, if at all, the fixed ideas, delusions, and changed emotional conditions of what the Germans term conveniently *der Wahn,* influence and subvert the repro- ductive imaginations of the persons who are the victims of these obses- sions and delusions, fixed into their mental natures deep as life. [6, p. 190]

The turn of the century saw continued efforts to make use of ink blots. Kirkpatrick [10] had youngsters respond to ink blots, in conjunc- tion with other tests. He suggested that age was a factor in the quality of response. Pyle, in his "Examination of School Children" [12] several years later, concluded that ink blots tested the quickness of the associa- tion process.

In 1910, Whipple published an important contribution [15] to the developing field. His was the first series of standardized ink blots to appear. His *Manual,* in addition, was the first comprehensive review of work done to date by ink-blot experimenters. From the vantage point of Whipple's manual, it is easy to note that this early work had an emphasis quite different from that of the Rorschach period and afterwards. Very little attention was as yet being paid to the possible relationship between personality characteristics of the subject and their actual responses. The blots were still being considered largely in terms of the light they shed on imaginative processes.

The next decade revealed still further insights into the value of ink blot testing. F. C. Bartlett [1] of the University of Cambridge used blots as part of the testing equipment in a study of perception and imagination. On the basis of results from 36 subjects, he concluded that blots were able to point up the interests, and perhaps the occu- pations, of his subjects.

In 1917, Cicely Parsons [11], of the University College of South Wales, studied 97 young children, using some of Whipple's standard blots. She arrived at several formulations as a result. She found a high percentage of animal and human responses; differences resulting from sex; gradations in the type and quality of description depending on age. Parsons pointed out that, although the goal of her own work had been to measure imagination, the results indicated possibilities for pointing out significant individual differences.

Both Bartlett and Parsons, in their analyses of the content of responses, were pointing the way toward the later formulations of Hermann Rorschach. It remained for Rorschach, with his psychiatric and
scientific background, to broaden the bases of interpretation.

The Record Grows

Hermann Rorschach was born in Zurich, Switzerland, on Novem-
ber 8, 1884. By the time he had been graduated from medical college
in 1910, a good deal of preliminary work with ink blots had already
been published. His own interest in the field developed in 1911, and
throughout the years of his short life that interest was paramount. His
work in psychiatric hospitals gave him broad opportunity to explore
and test. Rorschach's own psychological approach was built on a global
view of personality and the interrelationships of its aspects. This was
evidenced in *Psychodiagnostik* in which the responses of a subject to
the blots, judged in formal categories, provided the basis for what
Rorschach considered an objective method of total personality diagnosis. Rorschach was the first to develop a workable method (sometimes called a "shorthand") for handling the complex response
patterns.

Rorschach's first published monograph was also the last to appear
during his life. On April 2, 1922, Rorschach died. He had been working on some amplifications and differentiations in technique, the results of which were published in a posthumous paper prepared by
Emil Oberholzer, a co-worker of Rorschach's [14].

In 1924, the first publication on the Rorschach method appeared in
English. This was a translation of the Rorschach and Oberholzer paper which presented a thorough analysis of a Rorschach record and
demonstrated the task of the Rorschach worker in scoring and interpretation [14].

Shortly afterward David Levy, who had trained with Oberholzer,
introduced the Rorschach method into the United States. Samuel
Beck, influenced by Levy, also studied under Oberholzer, and became
the first American psychologist to publish material about the method
[2, 3]. Hertz [8] followed soon after, exploring the methodological
aspects of the Rorschach.

During this first period of development, the Rorschach pioneers encountered stubborn resistance, particularly in the United States. The

psychiatrists, who would have welcomed a method which could give them a more complete and more objective understanding of their patients, were deterred by the cumbersome method of scoring and tabulation of the Rorschach technique; they were even more troubled by the fact that it was almost impossible to discover how a Rorschach interpreter arrived at his findings. The psychologists, on the other hand —academic psychologists as well as psychometricians—doubted the scientific value of a method which seemed to be applied in a rather subjective and experimentally uncontrolled manner.

As an understanding of the Rorschach technique grew in scope, however, its followers grew in number. Their job was one not only of administration and refinement of the method, but of public education and public relations as well. Thus, from 1934 on, Bruno Klopfer sought to advance the ideas and technique of the Rorschach method through study groups, in courses, and from the lecture platform. He also interested himself in refining the techniques of scoring. With others, he helped found and edit the *Rorschach Research Exchange,* which first appeared in 1936. Three years later, the Rorschach Institute was organized as a clearing house for research and as a training center.

The success of the ink-blot technique stimulated the development of the entire field of projective techniques, each instrument in turn emphasizing special aspects of character organization and personality structure. In recognition of the growth of interest and the expansion of research relative to all projective tests, the Rorschach Institute in 1948 became the Society for Projective Techniques. Its publication, now called the *Journal of Projective Techniques,* publishes material not only on the Rorschach but on other projective techniques, such as the Thematic Apperception Test (TAT).

The Rorschach Technique Today

To date, the widest application of the Rorschach is in the field of mental health in public and private institutions and practice. New possibilities for the Rorschach continue to emerge, however.

The second World War, for instance, with its pressing demands for methods of selecting personnel, stimulated the development of group techniques for administering the Rorschach. Best known of these is that devised by Molly Harrower-Erickson [7]. In the Harrower-Erickson technique, subjects write their responses from projected slides of the ink blots. A multiple-choice method of response has also been developed. Group Rorschachs are now given not only in the armed services but also in industry and in hospitals and clinics.

Many areas of research have been stimulated and aided by the Rorschach technique. The Rorschach has enriched studies in the developmental aspects of perception, has broadened knowledge of intellectual functioning, has improved analysis of behavior under stressful situations. It has contributed to an understanding of such various personality deviants as juvenile delinquents, alcoholics, stutterers, and schizophrenics. The Rorschach has achieved a significant place in child guidance work. The Rorschach has been able to shed light on the effectiveness of psychotherapy. It has stimulated a new approach to the study of culture-personality interrelationships. At present, it seems that Rorschach findings may contribute as much to the development and refinement of personality theories as personality theories have contributed to the development of Rorschach hypotheses.

Testimony to the value that the Rorschach has today exists in the fact that most of the countries in the five continents have practitioners in the field who keep in constant communication through national and international organizations. The Rorschach is internationally the dominant method used in the field of projective techniques.

The Ten Standard Ink Blots

Let us look briefly at the basic Rorschach material. The ten blots that Rorschach developed consist of nearly symmetrical ink blot designs, each printed and centered on a piece of white cardboard about $6\frac{3}{4} \times 9\frac{1}{2}$ inches in size. Each ink blot design has its unique characteristics originally indicated by Rorschach in his *Psychodiagnostik* [13, p. 52]. Other qualities have been noted since his time, including important factors in the succession from one card to the next. Each blot, therefore, because of its individual properties of form, color, shading, white spaces, and the like, tends to provoke typical responses. These unique properties bestow upon each blot its own character, with which the Rorschach student becomes more and more familiar as he works with the cards. This familiarity aids in understanding the reactions of subjects to blots because it forms a backdrop against which the individual variations in responding may be noted.

Card I

Card I is a fairly large over-all black-gray blot with four rather conspicuous white spaces. If one looks closely, small black spots may be observed outside the large blot material. The large black-gray area is easily subdivided into three parts: the center area and the two side areas. The first reaction of many people to this card is to use the whole blot and to see in it some winged creature. More imaginative or less constricted subjects use the whole blot in many different ways, sometimes projecting human movement onto it. Observing any of the smaller portions or using the white spaces by themselves is less frequent. However, it is not unusual for the white spaces to be used as part of a concept which involves the entire blot ("a pumpkin face," for example).

In addition to the winged creature, the blot lends itself to the perception of human beings, especially a female figure in the center area. Persons who are concerned about their bodies may perceive a pelvis or some other anatomical concept in the entire blot. Sometimes individuals choose one of the smaller portions of the blot (top center) to see "hands," or "baby birds." Profiles are sometimes seen around the edges of the blot.

Card II

Card II is the first blot that has color (red). It differs from Card I also by being less compact. Card II consists of two large grayish black areas; connected with them above and below are three red spots. It should be noted that the colored spots are connected with the rest of the blot material in such a way that it is difficult for a subject to ignore them. Some subjects react to this by becoming disturbed.

This blot facilitates responses that use the large black or the red areas separately rather than taking in the entire blot material. Only subjects who have organizational interest and ability, or who are overwhelmed by the impact of the black and red mixture ("fire" and "blood"), use the entire material for a response.

There are three other interesting blot areas in Card II: the white spaces in the center, the small area above it, and the lower red area; the latter two are often associated with sexual responses.

Both human and animal figures are seen in the black areas of this card, the animal figures being very frequently seen in action.

Card III

Card III consists of two distinct black-gray areas joined together by a lighter gray portion. Between these two areas is a definitely shaped red spot, and above them are two other red spots. In contrast to Cards I and II, the shapes of these blot areas are clearly separate and highly suggestive.

Most people react first to this card by using all the black portion to see human figures in action. If human figures are perceived, they are interesting for analysis in terms of sex, clothing, and the kind of action that is involved. If the red spots are not ignored, the center one is frequently seen as a bow tie or butterfly. The two top red portions suggest a variety of concepts. It is unusual for a subject to attempt to use both the black and red areas for one concept.

Card IV

The blot material of Card IV appears massive, compact, yet indistinct in shape. This card is black-gray all over and highly shaded. Because of its massive structure and dense shading, it appears ominous to some people. Thus monsters, giants, gorillas, or peculiar-looking people are seen sitting or approaching, or the blot looks like a dense forest with mountains and lakes. The frequency of the giant, ape, or monster type of response has prompted some clinicians to refer to this card as the "father card." They believe that attitudes toward paternal authority are revealed because of the combination of masculine aggression and dependent needs related to shading.

Subjects who are prone to select details for their responses may perceive the large side areas as "boots," or the top side areas as "snakes" or a "female figure diving." Two other areas that are easily delineated are the lower center portion and the small top center area, frequently associated with sexual responses.

The shading of the card, if not disturbing to a subject, may suggest furriness; in that case the blot is frequently seen as a fur rug.

Card V

Card V, because of its definite outline and nearly allover blackness, is an easy card for most subjects. It therefore offers subjects who have been disturbed by the earlier cards an opportunity to recover.

The most frequent response to the entire blot material is a winged creature such as a bat or a butterfly, often seen in action. The side extensions are sometimes seen separately as animal heads or human legs; otherwise, the content of this card varies greatly.

For some subjects, the blackness of the card is disturbing. This phenomenon is sometimes referred to as "black shock."

Card VI

Card VI is known as the "sex" card because the upper part is interpreted by many as a phallic symbol. The shading qualities of the card are also distinctive and, more than in any other card, evoke responses involving the use of shading. The most frequent such response is a fur rug. A "totem pole," a "bedpost," or a "lamppost" are other responses in which the shading plays an important part because of the suggestion of highlights on turned wood. As in Card IV, the shading, combined with sexually symbolic areas, is particularly disturbing to some subjects.

The card is frequently seen as a whole. Often, however, the upper and lower portions are perceived as separate units.

Card VII

In contrast to Cards IV, V, and VI, Card VII may be described as light and airy. The entire blot is light gray in color with only a very small darker area in the bottom center portion. Perhaps because of this quality, plus the fact that the bottom center area suggests a female sex organ, the card has been labeled by some the "mother card." In children between the ages of four and eight, the bottom center area more frequently evokes the image of a house with smoke coming out of the chimney, and in this way carries the same mother symbolism. Also, the outline of the two upper side portions of the card suggests women or children more often than men.

This card facilitates a response to the entire area of the blot, often involving the perception of human figures in action, especially if held upside down. The light gray color and the shading elements of this card suggest "clouds," "smoke," or "maps."

Card VIII

Card VIII is the first in a series of three entirely colored cards; however, the colors are pastel shades instead of the bright red of Cards II and III. It is rather small and consolidated; yet there are several definite and distinct areas in it: the bluish gray or greenish gray top, the blue center, the pink and orange bottom, and the two pink side portions.

The pink side areas are of such definite shape that almost everyone sees in them animal figures in movement. The other areas are used in many different ways, if they are not disregarded altogether.

Since the animal figures are so obtrusive, it is rather difficult to use the entire blot material for a concept unless it be in the nature of an heraldic emblem with the animals as an integral part of the design.

The color aspects of the blot, if not ignored, are frequently used in a concept such as a "colored butterfly," or as an "anatomical chart."

Card IX

In contrast to Card VIII, Card IX is large, vague in outline, with no clearly distinguishable small portions, and with the colors all running into one another. The structure of the blot, the mixed-up colors, and the shading make it difficult for some subjects either to respond to the card as a whole or to choose parts of it for a response. As a result, this is the card most frequently rejected.

Responses to this card are extremely varied and therefore, from an interpretative viewpoint, extremely worthwhile. The more usual, but by no means frequent, responses to this card are: "witches" in the top orange portion; "a human head" in the outer bottom pink area; and, since the atomic bomb, "an atomic explosion" (with the card held upside down).

Card X

Generally, at first glance, Card X looks like an artist's palette full of colors. This card has more colors than any other, and they are distributed on many more separate areas than in other cards. It is, therefore, difficult for many subjects to see the blot as a unity unless in a response such as "an artist's palette" or "an underwater scene." However, since the blot areas are so separated, subjects tend to use the separate parts on this card even if they do not do so anywhere else.

Three responses are very frequently given to parts of the card: "a green snake or worm" to the longish green area in the bottom center (a response which combines the shape and color of the area); "crabs" to the outer blue; and "a rabbit's head" to the small detail between the "snakes."

This card facilitates a considerable number of animal responses, many in action. Human beings are rarely seen except in the large pink side areas, where they may be perceived as sucking on something.

References

1. Bartlett, F. C. "An Experimental Study of Some Problems of Perceiving and Imaging," *Brit. J. Psychol.*, 1916, 8, 222–266.

2. Beck, S. J. "The Rorschach Test and Personality Diagnosis: I. The Feeble-Minded," *Amer. J. Psychiat.*, 1930–31, 10, 19–52.

3. ——. "The Rorschach Test as Applied to a Feeble-Minded Group," *Arch. Psychol.*, 1932, No. 136.

4. Binet, A., and Henri, V. "La Psychologie Individuelle," *L. Année Psychologique*, 1895–96, 2, 411–465.

5. Dearborn, G. V. "Blots of Ink in Experimental Psychology," *Psychol. Rev.*, 1897, 4, 390–391.

6. ——. "A Study of Imaginations," *Amer. J. Psychol.*, 1898, 9, 183–190.

7. Harrower-Erickson, M. R., and Steiner, M. E. "Modification of the Rorschach Method for Use as a Group Test," *J. Genet. Psychol.*, 1943, 62, 119–133.

8. Hertz, M. R. "Concerning the Reliability and the Validity of the Rorschach Ink-Blot Test." Unpublished doctor's thesis, Western Reserve University, 1932.

9. Kerner, Justinus. *Kleksographien.* Tübingen, Germany, 1857.

10. Kirkpatrick, E. A. "Individual Tests of School Children," *Psychol. Rev.*, 1900, 7, 274–280.

11. Parsons, C. J. "Children's Interpretations of Ink-Blots," *Brit. J. Psychol.*, 1917, 9, 74–92.

12. Pyle, W. H. "A Psychological Study of Bright and Dull Pupils," *J. Educ. Psychol.*, 1915, 6, 151–156.

13. Rorschach, H. *Psychodiagnostics: A Diagnostic Test Based on Perception.* (Translated by Lemkau, P., and Kronenberg, B.) New York: Grune & Stratton, Inc.; 1951.

14. ——. and Oberholzer, E. "Zur Auswertung des Formdeuteversuchs für die Psychoanalyse," *Z. Ges. Neurol. und Psychiat.*, 1923, 82, 240–274. Also translated as "The Application of the Interpretation of Form to Psychoanalysis," *J. Nerv. Ment. Dis.*, 1924, 60, 225–248, 359–379.

15. Whipple, G. M. *Manual of Mental and Physical Tests.* Baltimore: Warwick and York; 1910.

Chapter Two

PERSONALITY APPRAISAL: THEORY AND METHOD

A BASIC assumption underlying the Rorschach technique is that there is a relationship between perception and personality. The way in which an individual organizes or "structures" the ink blots in forming his perceptions reflects fundamental aspects of his psychological functioning. Ink blots are suitable as stimuli because they are relatively ambiguous or "unstructured," i.e., they do not elicit particular learned responses, but permit a variety of possible responses. The subject, then, when asked to tell what he "sees" in the blots, must react in a personal, unlearned fashion, since there are no "right" or "wrong" answers. His perceptions are selected and organized in terms of his "projected" needs, experiences, and habitual patterns of response as well as by the physical properties of the blots themselves.

In the light of the above assumptions it follows that an analysis by a trained clinician of an individual's responses to the Rorschach ink blots should reveal such things as: the nature of that individual's inner promptings, his motivations and drive impulses, his capacity to control his impulses, the way he attacks problems, and other aspects of his personality. This formulation has been clearly expressed by L. K. Frank [2] as follows:

> The Rorschach method offers a procedure through which the individual is induced to reveal his "private world" by telling what he "sees" in the several cards upon which he may project his meanings, significance, and feelings, just because they are not socially standardized objects or situations to which he must give culturally prescribed responses. The Rorschach method is essentially a procedure for revealing the personality of the individual as an individual, as contrasted with rating or assessing him in terms of his likeness or conformity to special norms of action and

speech. It is just because a subject is not aware of what he is telling and has no cultural norms behind which to hide himself, that the Rorschach and other projective methods are so revealing.

In life situations, a person may tend to avoid relating to people because they make him uneasy or uncomfortable. So, in the Rorschach situation a subject may avoid *seeing* people, or actually be unable to see people in the blots. He may instead see a piece of machinery, a botanical specimen, or a huge mountain with clouds. In everyday life, an individual may avoid getting into the heart of a problem by skirting around it. In the Rorschach, similarly, he may pay attention only to the periphery of the blot material, or to the little details surrounding some of the blots. The part of a blot a person selects to use for his response, what he sees there or what he fails to see, how he organizes the material, how much time he takes to see what he selects to see—all are believed to reveal some of his personality characteristics.

Direct behavioral parallels may not always exist, however, and may not be the most important information revealed. The behavior of an individual in the Rorschach situation differs in one very important respect from the same individual's reaction to any unfamiliar situation in life. In life situations, a person tends to behave in a more or less socially acceptable way. He has learned, if he is a "normal" individual, to control himself, to appear pleasant and kindly rather than aggressive and hostile; to show those traits of personality that are generally valued in the culture, and to conceal from public view those traits that are not prized. Thus, a person's outward, observable behavior may often *not* reveal his true feelings and attitudes. In the Rorschach situation, on the other hand, a person does not know the correct way, the best way, or the typical way to respond. He must react in his own particular fashion. In so responding, he unwittingly or unconsciously reveals himself, even that part of himself of which he is not entirely aware.

In this quality of the Rorschach material, there exist both an advantage and a disadvantage. Because the Rorschach reveals a person's unlearned way of feeling and behaving, there may be only slight correspondence between actual behavior and predictions of isolated behavior based on the Rorschach protocol, because actual behavior is partly determined by learned responses to external circumstances.

The paramount purpose of the Rorschach is not to predict behavior in an atomistic way, but to provide a *description* of the subject's personality that is clinically meaningful. It offers the clinician the information he needs to help an individual make a healthier adjustment. The Rorschach material provides clues for the understanding of observable behavior because it taps the more basic, underlying structure of the personality. In a school situation, for example, a Rorschach evaluation may help a teacher to understand why John cannot read, or why Mary is shy in the classroom and not on the playground, or why Paul is so aggressive. This understanding should then lead to changes in the handling of John, Mary, and Paul both in and out of the classroom.

Observed Behavior

In psychology, as in medicine, it is necessary to work with only a sample of behavior. This sample is assumed to be representative of a person's behavior in general. It is also assumed that the major characteristics of an individual's behavior do not vary materially from sample to sample unless something traumatic has intervened. We assume, in addition, that all behavior is meaningful. Without making this assumption, it would be impossible to work with people at the behavioral level.

The sample we are concerned with is the subject's behavior during the Rorschach examination. The clinician studies the entire behavior of the individual during this period. He observes the individual's attitude toward the Rorschach technique and toward the examiner, his ability to attend and the amount of effort he puts forth, the extent of his physical activity, and the like. The examiner also takes note of the subject's verbalizations, his hesitations, his questions, and his exclamations. In short, the clinician's first evidence comes from observing the subject's total behavior during the examination period.

The clinician's major evidence, however, comes from the subject's specific reactions to the test material: his actual responses and the time he takes to give them. These reactions are the foundation on which the personality description is built. The nature of the Rorschach responses and how they are scored and interpreted are discussed later in this book.

Personality Aspects Revealed by the Rorschach

It is important to point up more specifically the personality characteristics that the Rorschach actually purports to describe.

Some workers have stated that the Rorschach can, better than other devices, tap something called the "total personality" or the "whole person." Anything so complex as personality, however, cannot be studied as a whole. It is rather foolhardy to think that any one instrument can catch the whole personality in one measure. Neither the Rorschach nor the psychoanalyst, neither the clinical psychologist nor the experimentalist, can "get at" the entire person directly.

Personality consists of different facets—needs, drives, motives, traits, abilities, behavior systems, or libido organizations, depending on one's frame of reference. These facets form the pattern regarded as an individual's relatively enduring personality. These needs, drives, or traits, both innate and learned, may be classified in many different ways. Some ordering of personality qualities is essential, but as yet no one system of ordering has proved altogether satisfactory.

With this background in mind, we shall list those qualities that the Rorschach usually reveals. Let us emphasize that not all of the traits listed will be evidenced in any single individual, either at any single moment of his life, or perhaps in his entire lifetime. Neither is the Rorschach capable of uncovering all the facets of personality characteristics of all people. We shall see, for example, that the Thematic Apperception Test (TAT) * often gives information of a different nature than does the Rorschach, and that the two devices together provide more complete and more accurate information about a person than either one alone.

Rorschach findings are complemented by the results of structured objective tests as well as by findings of other projective techniques. For example, the Rorschach may be especially revealing when combined with an intelligence test. A person who works better when told exactly what to do would probably receive a higher rating of mental capacity on an intelligence test than the same person would receive on a Rorschach examination, where he is left more to his own devices. Some people do their best when they feel free in a situation, while others do their best in controlled situations. For this reason, a combination of an intelligence test and the Rorschach may give a more complete picture of the personality than an examiner could obtain if he relied upon either alone.

The listing below indicates some of the major personality aspects about which we may expect to get information from an interpretation

---

* The TAT serves as an illustrative example. Other diagnostic devices, such as figure drawing or sentence completion, could also be used to make the same point.

of a Rorschach record. No attempt will be made here to relate these personality aspects to specific Rorschach responses. The personality aspects are considered under three major headings, with subcategories under each heading: (1) Cognitive, or Intellectual, Aspects, (2) Affective, or Emotional, Aspects, and (3) Aspects of Ego Functioning.

Cognitive, or Intellectual, Aspects

1. *Intellectual Status and Functioning:* A person's intellectual ability may be estimated from a Rorschach protocol. In addition, it is possible to ascertain whether he is functioning efficiently in terms of his potential capacity. Some of the questions that may be answered are: What is the individual's intellectual level? Is he operating up to or below his capacity, as measured by an intelligence test? Is his intellectual functioning impaired by emotional stress? Is his performance uneven? What is the language ability and vocabulary level of the person?

2. *Manner of Approach:* Is the individual's approach to problems logical or loose? methodical or confused? Is his thinking more inductive or deductive? How well can he organize material? Is he able to get to the heart of a problem, or does he skirt anxiously around the edges?

3. *Power of Observation:* Is he able to observe the obvious? Does the subject see the commonplace things that other people see? Does he overlook the ordinary and attend to the minute? Can he see more complex constellations?

4. *Originality of Thinking:* Is the individual capable of original thinking? Does he show creative ability? Are his creations based on reality, or are they bizarre?

5. *Productivity:* Does the individual have an average or greater than average fund of ideas? What is the quality of his productions? Are his responses rich? Are they subtle? Do they come easily?

6. *Breadth of Interests:* How varied are the person's interests? Are they limited and shallow? Are they rich and diverse? Are they concentrated in depth in one area? Has he any special interests? In what way do they reflect the person's emotional biases?

Affective, or Emotional, Aspects

7. *General Emotional Tone:* What is the general tone of a person's emotionality? Is it spontaneous? depressed? constricted? Is he generally anxious? Is he passive and withdrawn? or self-assertive and

aggressive? Does he show drive? How does the person respond to *immediate* emotional challenges in contrast to *anticipated* emotional situations? Is he confident or pessimistic about securing the love and affection he wants? Is he realistic or unrealistic? Is he too demanding or not demanding enough? Is he self-sufficient or dependent?

8. *Feelings About Self:* What is the individual's response to inner promptings? Is he at ease with himself? Does he accept himself and his own impulses? Are feelings of inadequacy evident?

9. *Responsiveness to People:* What is the individual's ability to establish rapport with people? Does he enjoy social intercourse? Is he comfortable with people? Or is he rather afraid of people and generally hostile toward them? Does he try to avoid human contact? Does he feel more at ease in a world of inanimate objects?

10. *Reaction to Emotional Stress:* Under stressful situations, how does a person respond? Is he able to cope with situations or does he fall apart? Does he panic or is he controlled? Can he recover? What are his reactions to new situations? Are they handled with confidence or are they disturbing to him?

11. *Control of Emotional Impulses:* How well does an individual control his spontaneous tendencies? adequately? rigidly? Does he give way to uncontrolled impulsiveness? Do his emotions become rampant? Or is genuine spontaneity evident? Does he show tact? Is he cautious?

Aspects of Ego Functioning

12. *Ego Strength:* Is the individual's reality testing sound? Are his perceptions clear? What is his self-appraisal? Is he self-confident or self-defeating? Does he feel that he needs some kind of counseling or psychotherapy?

13. *Conflict Areas:* Is he sexually adjusted? Is there confusion as to sex role and identification? Is there conflict concerning: attitude toward authority? dependency needs? passivity? self-assertiveness?

14. *Defenses:* What kinds of defenses does the individual use? repression? denial? intellectualization? Are his defenses few and rigid? or varied and flexible?

A Sample Personality Description

We can now demonstrate how some of the personality characteristics outlined in the preceding section may be revealed in a Rorschach protocol. For this purpose, the record of a ten-year-old boy (here called Tony) who was referred to the Bureau of Child Guidance of the New York City Board of Education will be used.*

Naturally this sample description will only refer to a few of the personality aspects mentioned in the preceding section. The remaining aspects as well as those covered in the following section will be discussed in the chapter on Interpretation and in the case demonstrations in Chapter Seven.

The interpretation of the record is given in its entirety at this point so that reference may be made to it later. The actual responses and their scoring are given in the Appendix.

Each paragraph in the interpretation is followed by a comment to help the student relate its contents to the personality aspects outlined above. The numbers in parentheses refer to the numbers of the headings on pages 18–19. No changes were made in the interpretation as originally written. Since this interpretation did not follow the order of traits as given above, there is some unavoidable overlapping and duplication from paragraph to paragraph.

Findings from the Rorschach

Par. 1: The Rorschach reveals that Tony's intellectual status is probably above average, but because of rather severe emotional difficulties he cannot function up to his capacity. His observations are usually accurate, but he is not able to organize the material well. He may fail, should he become overstimulated. His vocabulary is meager, his ideas few, and there is no evidence of originality.

COMMENT: Better than average intellectual ability but not functioning well (1). He shows no ability to organize and no originality of thought [2, 4].

Par. 2: He is struggling with many problems and has been able to develop few stabilizing coping mechanisms. He is a very insecure child for whom a dominant force is anxiety expressed through many fears. He fears the loss of his own integrity, as is vividly communicated by the splitting rock and slipping animals of Card I. He further fears attack from others, and he fears his own impulses. In fact, there is no area of experience that is not frightening to him.

---

* The authors are grateful to Mrs. Vera Henriquez, Psychologist at the Bronx Unit of the Bureau of Child Guidance, who supplied the record and who did the interpretation. She also supplied the TAT material used later.

COMMENTS: Anxious boy (7), unable to cope adequately with problems (10). Fears people (9) and his own impulses (8).

Par. 3: There is little ability to separate himself from external stimulation. When anxious he becomes distracted by a rather protective involvement in minutiae. At the same time his inner impulses and fears color most of his reactivity and buffet him from another source. He shows impaired ability to screen or to exercise objective control over this reactivity although he attempts to do just this, as is highlighted by the high form-level quality of his responses. He has, however, some awareness of this problem and is able to consciously direct himself to deal better with reality. His actual contact with reality is not basically impaired.

COMMENT: Easily disturbed by outer stimuli and becomes distracted (7); is not able to control his excitability, but has not lost contact with reality (11, 12).

Par. 4: He is particularly thrown off balance by emotional situations. He becomes excited and distracted under such pressure, and is stimulated without being able to follow through by dealing effectively or directly with the source of the stimulation. He becomes critical and disparaging of others because of his anxiety, thereby hoping to achieve distance, but actually he is overwhelmed by it all. Under the impact of dealing with the outside world and with his emotions, several of his fears and defenses are elicited. There is oral aggression, and a need to retreat and isolate and to shy away from feelings. He flirts with an intellectual defense but is not sustained. This is a pattern of his defenses. They are not maintained nor do they provide relief for him.

COMMENT: Upset by emotional stimulation (10); shows much fear (7). Has some defenses but these do not provide adequate relief for his anxiety (14).

Par. 5: He is very confused about himself. While basically it is evident that he feels quite weak, he attempts a façade of strength. This never holds up for he fools not even himself with it. The nonhuman qualities of the "people" he perceives give further indications of the confusion he feels about himself as a person.

COMMENT: Feels very confused about himself as a person (8).

Par. 6: His problems in the social sphere and in self-identification are bound up in his unsatisfactory relationship with his parents. His parents inspire a kind of respect for their strength. They are removed from him, rather omnipotent and at the same time rather passively oppressive. In this respect it is interesting that both Card IV and VII, commonly considered the father and mother cards, respectively, elicit concepts of figures sitting on top of mountains. The involvement with his father is more freely expressed. His father is a strong and feared one, a "beast" with "claws," a "ghost," one with whom he is insecure, and toward whom he is hostile. He is not able to really identify with his father because the relationship has not been sufficiently positive. He handles this by adopting a judgmentally critical attitude toward authority figures, a characteristic reaction when under emotional stress. He also projects his hostility against authority figures so that he feels victimized and menaced by others. This boy also experiences difficulty with his mother. He is as uncomfortable with her as with his father. He is dependent in relation to her and expresses the need for closer contact with her through his projection of breasts and food on Card III. He feels danger in closer attachment to her, however, because she represents a dominating person who will not afford him protection from his infantile impulses, represented by the "death flames" that issue from the roast. Neither parent, then, offers a source of comfort or security; hence his expectation of danger from all people, and his protective withdrawal from contact with the outside, despite his susceptibility to such stimulation.

COMMENT: Relationships with people, especially with his parents (and other authority figures), are unsatisfactory (9, 13).

Par. 7:   Since he cannot relate to people and his own feelings are so threatening to him, he withdraws to an immature fantasy world that provides little refuge. Even his fantasy is a fearful one of aggression and fear of victimization. His lack of control, his uncertainty about himself, his unsuccessful defenses, all leave him an unhappy child who is operating under a surface denial, but who structures his world to be most threatening. The picture would cause us to believe that he acts out on this basis. Although he is immature and his personality is not well balanced, there is potential in terms of developing better relationships with himself and with others. Psychotherapy is indicated.

COMMENT: Because of unhappy relationships to people and to himself, he withdraws (7, 9). He is an unhappy, immature child with potential ego strength, who should benefit from psychotherapy (12, 13, 14).

Findings from the Thematic Apperception Test (TAT)

Other techniques may reveal different facets of the personality not seen in the Rorschach, or may supply evidence either confirming or contradicting the Rorschach findings. It was decided to use the TAT for this purpose. The TAT presumably uncovers the surface dynamics of the personality, while the Rorschach presumably reveals the more basic personality structure. The Rorschach record might, for example, suggest that the subject has many inner conflicts, while the TAT may in addition indicate that these conflicts have to do with certain feelings toward a parental figure, toward sex, toward ambition, or all three.

Tony was given 11 TAT cards.* The interpretation of his stories leads essentially to the same personality picture as was provided by the Rorschach—that of an unhappy, fantasy-ridden child, torn by his own impulses and unable to establish satisfying relationships. The TAT points out more dramatically than did the Rorschach Tony's struggle with his parents (he sees his father as an unforgiving, rejecting person; his mother as a dangerous person) and with the world at large.

The TAT also shows more clearly than the Rorschach that Tony feels guilty specifically about his aggressive and hostile impulses, which make him feel that he is a "bad" person. The TAT adds to the picture the fact that he is looking to outside authority to protect and restrain him—even though he views authority figures as particular sources of trouble. The TAT provides the further information that, for Tony, the one source of protection and acceptance is in the figure of an aunt (confirmed by the case history). He cannot entirely permit himself even this relief, however.

Both the TAT and the Rorschach reveal that Tony is a fearful, anxious boy, but the TAT adds the specific information that he is afraid of being placed in an institution. (The family history brought out that he has been threatened with such action as a disciplinary measure.) The TAT confirms the Rorschach picture of Tony as a child living in a fearful, fantasy world in which he is the culprit, rejected by all with perhaps the exception of his aunt.

---

* The stories to these cards are given in the Appendix.

Problems of Validation

Although it seems clear that the Rorschach yields valuable clinical information, the question of validity still remains. To what extent does the Rorschach give an accurate picture of the personality? Widespread use of the Rorschach has resulted in a clinical validity that is not always substantiated by statistical validity. The literature on validation highlights a few seemingly "positive" findings in a context of many apparently "negative" findings and contradictory results. Perhaps it is not necessary to be concerned with validity in the usual sense; or perhaps a new technique of validation is necessary. No attempt will be made here to give a comprehensive coverage of the complexity of validation problems.* Rather, some reasons why validation is a problem will be pointed out.

Projective techniques may be used as "tests" of personality and may manifest a number of similarities to other psychological tests; however, the differences are crucial. The typical psychological test attempts to place all tested individuals on a continuum with respect to one or more functions. Projective techniques such as the Rorschach attempt to *describe* (rather than to *measure*) the individual in terms of a dynamic pattern of interrelated functions or variables. This multiplicity of interrelated and interdependent variables presents one of the greatest problems of validation. Whereas most tests achieve their results by adding up the scores of the different components such as vocabulary, repetition of digits, and so on, such a summative procedure is impossible in the Rorschach method. For instance, in evaluating the different components contributing to the picture of a subject's "intelligence," the Rorschach practitioner is concerned not with the sum of components but with a *configuration,* or *Gestalt.*

The product of a Rorschach session is not standardized in the sense that the product of a "right-wrong" or "true-false" test is standardized. The permissive atmosphere, despite the use of standardized materials, evokes a tremendous variety of responses, in the same way as does a nondirective interview or an open-ended question. The Ror-

---

* For a more complete discussion, as well as an eight-page bibliography, see "Problems of Validation," by M. D. Ainsworth, in *Developments in the Rorschach Technique, Vol. I,* B. Klopfer, et al. Pages 405–500.

schach technique provides a communicable way of classifying and interpreting certain aspects of these responses. This, in part, explains why in this text the Rorschach is referred to as a method or technique, rather than as a test.

References

1. Ainsworth, M. D. "Problems of Validation," in *Developments in the Rorschach Technique, Vol. I,* Klopfer, B., et al. New York: Harcourt, Brace & World; 1954. Pages 405–500.

2. Frank, L. K. "Projective Methods for the Study of Personality," *J. Psychol.,* 1939, 8, 389–413.

Chapter Three

ADMINISTRATION

THE purpose of administering the Rorschach is to obtain for evaluation as much individualized response as possible from a relatively standardized situation. The ambiguous or "unstructured" nature of the ink-blot stimuli encourages individualized or "unlearned" responses. The specific rules of administration provide the relatively standardized situation. One job for the examiner is to help create the relaxed but controlled atmosphere particularly important for obtaining a useful Rorschach protocol.

Setting the Stage for the Examination

Several factors must be considered in preparing the subject for the Rorschach examination. They include: (1) the nature of the test atmosphere, (2) the seating arrangement of the subject and examiner, and the test equipment, and (3) the initial instructions to the subject.

The Examination Atmosphere

The kind of atmosphere created will depend on the subject, the examiner, and the situation. The subject must be made to feel at ease while at the same time he must be made to understand that certain tasks are required of him. The good clinician will be able to create a relaxed but controlled atmosphere by assessing the subject and the situation and acting accordingly. Of course, the ideal atmosphere is not always attainable. However, it is possible, and desirable, for the examiner to be aware of the kind of test atmosphere that *does* exist—whether the subject is tense or hostile toward the examiner, for example. These factors provide important clues for evaluating Rorschach responses. It is often astonishing how much information the

Rorschach yields even when the subject is self-conscious or reluctant, or when the situation is not the most favorable.

Seating and Equipment

It is advisable for the examiner as well as the subject to be able to see the cards during the administration of the test. A recommended arrangement, therefore, is for the examiner to sit next to but slightly behind the subject. However, any arrangement comfortable for both examiner and subject is permissible.

Illumination apparently is not too important a factor. Daylight or artificial illumination may be used, with no apparent difference in results. The reactions of even color-blind subjects may be interpreted in the same way as those of subjects with normal vision.

The materials essential for administering a Rorschach are the following:

1.   The ten Rorschach cards arranged in order facing downward on the table.

2.   A Location Chart—either as a separate sheet or as part of the *Individual Record Blank*. These charts are necessary for marking the areas used by the subject for his concepts.

3.   Ruled paper for recording the responses of the subject. Pen or pencil.

4.   An ordinary watch or clock with a second hand, or a noiseless stop watch.

Initial Instructions to the Subject

There is no standard formulation for introducing the Rorschach cards. The preparation of the subject for what is going to happen must naturally vary with the age, experience, and cultural background of the subject.

Experience with administration of the Rorschach indicates that it may be advisable, but not always necessary, to explain how the cards were originally produced, that they are therefore symmetrical or almost symmetrical, that people see all sorts of things in the blots, and that the subject is expected to tell what he sees. But this is better done after the performance proper. Rorschach remarks in *Psychodiagnostik* that distrustful subjects will occasionally require a demonstration of how the pictures are made, but on the whole, the experiment is usually accepted even by distrustful and inhibited mental patients [16, p. 16]. It seems inadvisable to use a trial blot or to actually produce a blot in

front of the subject's eyes because either of these procedures may interfere with the very important factor of sequence of stimuli. It is sufficient to say, "You know you can drop ink on a sheet of paper, fold it,
press it, and when you open it, find a picture." The examiner may ac-
company this explanation with appropriate gestures.

The introduction may then conclude with a statement that the blots
or figures on the ten cards, lying face down on the table, have been
made in the same way and that they will be presented one by one to
the subject. An acceptable formulation which may be repeated at this
point is, "People see all sorts of things in these ink-blot pictures; now
tell me what you see, what it might be for you, what it makes you
think of."

Some subjects may ask questions as to how many answers to give or
whether turning of the card is allowed. Such questions should be answered by a general statement, such as, "That is entirely up to you."
If the examiner thinks it is necessary, he can add a remark: "People
handle the cards in different ways. You may do whatever you like."
Sometimes subjects want to know whether there are right or wrong
answers. It is then necessary to reassure them that there are no right
or wrong answers; that the cards do not represent anything specific;
that people see all kinds of things in the pictures and you are interested in what he sees.

If a subject should give only one response to Card I, the examiner
might think it advisable to say at that point, "Some people see more
than one thing in the cards—if you do, just tell me." No further urg-
ing is permissible. If a subject tends to describe the blot or associate
to the blot, the examiner should stop the subject from doing this by
repeating the instructions that he is to tell what he sees in the blots;
what the blot might be for him.

Sometimes subjects are very anxious to know the purpose of the
Rorschach. If refused an explanation, they are likely to develop an un-
favorable attitude. In such cases it seems advisable to explain that
these ten cards were selected from thousands of trial blots because
they give each individual an opportunity to say what they might be,
in his own way, and that it is this personal way of handling the task in
which the examiner is interested. Should subjects consider the method
a test of imagination or fantasy, it seems unnecessary to disillusion
them.

It is very important that the instructions simply set the task and leave the choice of procedure entirely to the subject. Therefore, the examiner should *avoid* formulations such as, "Look at each card as long as you like; only be sure to tell me everything that you see on the card as you look at it," or even casual remarks such as, "What else?" after having received a response to a card. Such comments seem to emphasize the quantity of responses, and this emphasis involves a restriction of the conditions.

The Examination Period

There is one inescapable limitation to creating the most favorable examination atmosphere. The administrator must obtain an exact picture of the way the subject forms his concepts in response to the cards, if he is to get from the Rorschach material all that it can yield. This requirement can be fulfilled only if all the necessary questions are asked. Such questions, even when asked as tactfully as possible, are sometimes disturbing and tend to keep the subject from relaxing as much as he otherwise might. It is necessary, therefore, to ask the questions *after* the projective material has been produced. This situation gives rise to a division of the administrative procedure into phases, incorporating one phase to obtain the subject's responses, and three phases to use different inquiry techniques in clarifying the responses for scoring purposes. The use of all three inquiry phases is not always necessary. The four phases may be considered as follows:

1. PERFORMANCE PROPER: During this phase, there is as little interference as possible with the subject's spontaneous reactions to the cards. The examiner does not pressure or guide the subject, but acts chiefly as a recorder.

2. INQUIRY: This second phase is designed to reveal how the subject arrived at his responses, in order to facilitate scoring. Judicious questions are asked by the examiner to clarify, but not to influence, the subject's responses.

3. ANALOGY, OR FOLLOW-UP, PERIOD: This optional phase uses all available clues produced during the two previous phases to help fill in the existing gaps in the reactions of the subject. The examiner asks whether a determinant, admittedly employed in connection with one response, is applicable to others. He asks analogy questions such as, "If color (or shading) helped you to see that, how was it here and here?"

4. TESTING-THE-LIMITS PHASE: This part of the examination is un-

dertaken only when the subject shows no reactions to some of the significant stimuli in the blots. Concepts not formed by the subjects are deliberately introduced.

The phases of administration, defined above, extend from the one extreme of complete noninterference with the subject's reactions to the stimulus material to the other extreme of considerable probing and prodding about his responses. The emphasis shifts from encouraging the subject to verbalize freely about his responses to prodding him for the equally important information that he is unwilling to volunteer spontaneously. The reasons for the subject's reluctance to give the desired information may be clarified during the prodding phases.

It is obvious that this shift in procedure changes the testing situation from a standardized experiment to one that is quite individualized. From the point of view of individual diagnosis or clinical clarification, this shift may be of little consequence. It becomes important, however, where statistical comparisons of Rorschach records are concerned. In such cases, the results obtained by prodding must not be scored.

The point of transition is usually reached between the analogy period and the testing-the-limits phase. The analogy period still represents a method to facilitate reactions that presumably have taken place in the performance proper but have not been verbalized. In the testing-the-limits phase, the examiner is deliberately probing for reactions that the subject was unwilling or unable to let take place in the performance proper.

The extent to which all phases of the administration have to be employed varies greatly in the clinical situation. The more spontaneously the subject reacts and verbalizes during the performance proper and the routine inquiry, the less work will remain to be accomplished in the other two phases; however, experience has shown that supplementary questioning can be helpful in almost every case.

The Performance Proper

In the performance proper, as we have seen, the subject is given the opportunity of producing his responses to the cards as spontaneously as possible without any pressure or guidance from the examiner.

Presentation of the Cards

The ten Rorschach cards should be placed on the examination table, face down, in their proper sequence, so that Card I is on top and

Card X is at the bottom. Each card has a number on the back indicating the succession; some printed material indicates the position of the blots on the card.

Each card must be presented to the subject in the upright position in sequence starting with Card I and ending with Card X. It is advisable to ask the subject to hold the card when it is given to him, and to indicate that he is to continue holding the card until he is through with it. The subject is further instructed to put the card face down on the table when he has finished, thus indicating that he is ready for the next card. This arrangement insures a more personal handling of the cards than if they were put on a table or leaned against a wall. It also insures that the distance between subject and cards is no greater than arm's length.

Items to Record During the Performance Proper

Responses: Responses are to be recorded word for word, if possible. It is easy to develop a personal shorthand system since certain expressions and certain words appear very frequently in Rorschach protocols. Use the left-hand column of paper which has been divided in half lengthwise for the responses given during the performance proper. The right-hand column is to be reserved for information obtained during the inquiry so that the inquiry information can be placed alongside the response to which it belongs. Ample space should be left between responses, for sometimes the inquiry will require more space than the performance proper. Also, new responses may be added during the inquiry and should be noted when they occur. (See sample record, p. 161.)

Number with arabic numbers the responses given to each card, beginning each card with number 1. In this way, the total number of responses to each card, as well as the total for all ten cards, is readily obtained. When it is difficult to decide whether a concept is a response or a remark—or whether the concept should be counted as one or two responses—the numbering should be delayed for that card until after the inquiry, at which time the necessary information may be elicited.

Sometimes subjects become rather apprehensive about the fact that the examiner is writing down everything they say. It is fairly easy to reassure them with the explanation that it would be impossible to keep all their responses in mind, and that since the examiner will want to consider these responses more carefully afterward, it seems better to eliminate the risk of forgetting by writing them down at once. At the same time, the subject must not see whatever descriptive remarks the examiner may put down about his behavior, and the record of exclamations and asides must be made as inconspicuously as possible.

Time Factors: Three kinds of time notations are usually made:

1.   *Reaction time*—The time between the presentation of the card and the subject's *first* response to it.

2.   *Total response time*—The length of time taken to complete the performance proper. The examiner should note the time when the examination begins and again when the performance proper is over.

3.   *Total response time per card*—This time measure is not essential, but becomes significant only when there are unusual delays, such as long intervals between responses. These intervals should be indicated by recording the approximate number of minutes elapsing. "Time out" might also be noted, if the subject engages in conversation between responses. The total response time for each card may be divided by the total number of responses to that card, giving the average time for each response.

These time notations do not have to be exact to the second but are satisfactory to the nearest five or ten seconds. A silent stop watch, or a standard watch with a second hand, may be used. Some examiners prefer to record the number of seconds by counting to themselves, saying, for example, "101" to account for one second. It is helpful that the examiner need not record anything else while he is noting such things as reaction time, or the time for longer silent intervals.

Position of the Cards: The position in which the card is held by the subject when he gives his response must be noted. Widely used is the method suggested by Loosli-Usteri [13]: The following four symbols ∧ > ∨ < are recorded to show the position of the cards, the apex always representing the top of the card in its original position. Even rarely chosen intermediate positions, such as ⌐, can be accurately recorded in this way. If the cards are turned around completely, once or several times, the symbol ɔ may be used. Every single turn need not be noted, but if a subject tends repeatedly to turn the card from the upright to the upside down position and then to the side, this is important information to record and would be shown in this manner ∧ ∨ > . If he then gives his response when the card is in the upside down position, the final recording would look like this: ∧ ∨ > ∨ . It is particularly important to record the *final* position in which the card is held.

The Inquiry

In this second phase of the administration, the examiner attempts to determine how the subject arrived at his spontaneous responses. This initial inquiry period provides a further opportunity for the subject to enrich his spontaneous productions, should he desire.

Purposes of the Inquiry

The main function of the inquiry is to elicit information from the subject regarding the way in which he sees each concept. This information is essential for scoring accurately. A satisfactory inquiry, therefore, is impossible without a thorough acquaintance with the scoring system and its interpretative values. (Scoring will be discussed in Chapter Four.) Responses that are clear and scorable do not require any inquiry. The second function of the inquiry is to give the subject a chance to supplement and complete spontaneously the responses given in the performance proper. This function makes the inquiry particularly useful with subjects of high intellectual level who may be hampered in expressing themselves adequately during the first encounter with the cards. In some cases only the combination of the responses given in the performance proper and the spontaneous additions in the inquiry produces an adequate picture of the subject's personality.

Sometimes the subject blocks so severely during the first encounter with the cards that he cannot produce more than a few responses to all ten cards. In the case of psychotic subjects it may be impossible to change the situation even after the performance proper is over. Many neurotics can overcome this blocking after the ten cards have lost their mystery, and can produce a fairly adequate record in the second encounter. Occasionally, the examiner is confronted by a situation in which the first encounter yields fewer than five responses and the second encounter produces ten or more. In such a case it seems more practical to consider this second encounter a retest rather than an inquiry to the original performance, and to score the responses of the retest by themselves.

To summarize, the inquiry should clarify the various aspects of each response, when needed for scoring: location on the blot, determinant used, and content. The inquiry should also give the subject the opportunity to add spontaneous elaborations to his old responses, or to add any new ideas he might want to express.

Conducting the Inquiry

There are two important considerations to keep in mind in conducting the inquiry: (1) The subject must not be made to feel that his ideas are being challenged. (2) The subject must not become aware of the type of information the examiner is seeking through his questioning.

The first consideration imposes upon the examiner the responsibility of asking questions in such a way as to make the subject feel at ease. This process is facilitated by conducting the inquiry in two parts—the initial inquiry and the follow-up, or analogy, period. Each part provides for different procedures that are described in the following discussion.

Start the inquiry by putting the cards face up on the table and handing them to the subject, while saying something like this: "Now you have seen all the cards and given your answers. Let us go over your answers together, because I want to be sure I see them the way you do." A remark of this nature emphasizes the cooperative nature of the inquiry. If the subject needs further assurance, say something like, "Your answers are very interesting, and I'd like to know what in the blot suggested them." With subjects who reject or give only one response to each card, it might be desirable to remind them that now they have the opportunity, if they should see something else, to tell the examiner what they see.

The great majority of Rorschach examiners will have no difficulty in developing a genuine interest in the reactions of their subjects. The more the examiner develops a facility for understanding the significance of the various reaction patterns, the more he will find each administration a new and enjoyable experience. He is eager to know how the subject will react to the next card, what he will do about the color, and so on. Regardless of whether the subject is feeble-minded or intelligent, well-adjusted, neurotic, or psychotic, the examiner should find a way of expressing this genuine interest. He should convey to the subject the impression that he really wants to know more about specific responses and that he wants to see them as clearly as the subject does.

The subject will not be surprised or upset by being asked *where* all the interesting creatures and objects are, or by a question such as,

"What was it in this particular card that made you think of this rather than something else?" All questioning in the inquiry should thus be related to the cards and their particular features. The examiner should not make the subject entirely responsible for the concept choice by asking, "*Why* did you see . . . ?"

In handling the *second general consideration* for conducting the inquiry, again, the advice to the examiner is to be as *simple* and as *concrete* as possible in his questions. Every concept chosen by a subject offers some very obvious intrinsic and essential features, and it is a great sin of omission to fail to ask about these features *before* asking about some relatively farfetched elements. It seems best to consider what a small child would like to know about a concept, when hearing about it for the first time. Then relate the most concrete and essential features of the concept to the blot or blot areas used by the subject, before inquiring about nuances and accessories. If, for instance, "two dogs kissing" is a response for Card II, the examiner must first know what portion of the card has been used, how much of the dog is seen (the whole dog or only his head and neck), and whether the ears and eyes are visible, *before* concerning himself with the possible use of shading for the surface appearances, or with the particular implications of the kissing (for example, whether it is a more human- or a more animal-like action).

If the examiner always starts with the *most essential, concrete,* and *obvious features,* he will soon find out whether it is necessary to go beyond, and how far to pursue the questioning. Usually the inquiry about the cruder features leads automatically to finer nuances, if and when the subject is responsive to them. In this way the examiner can avoid many senseless and irritating questions that yield no results and interfere with a relaxed and cooperative atmosphere. The specific techniques of questioning for the aspects of location, determinant, and content are elaborated below.

Inquiry for Location

As a rule, the inquiry will first be directed to the location of each response, that is, to determine what part of the blot area was used for the concept. A general question like, "Where on the card did you see the . . . ?" or "Show me the . . ." may yield the required information. If this does not result in a clear delineation of the area used, or if the examiner has difficulty in seeing exactly where the subject located his concept, other methods may be used: (1) The examiner may ask the subject to use his finger or the unsharpened end of a pencil to outline the area directly on the blot. (2) The subject may be asked to outline the area with a pencil on the Location Chart. (3) The subject may be asked to place a sheet of tracing paper over the card and outline the area. (4) The subject may be asked to draw a freehand picture of his concept. The last three methods are rarely necessary.

Inquiry for Determinants

Inquiry about determinants depends to a great extent on a familiarity with scoring categories and their interpretative values. (Chapter Four discusses scoring; Chapter Six, interpretation.) The qualities of greatest concern are: *form, movement, color,* and *shading.*

Information concerning the determinant or determinants used by a subject in forming his concept is somewhat more difficult to obtain than information concerning location. The principal danger lies in asking unnecessary questions or leading questions. For instance, the examiner in his questions should never use the words *color* or *action* or the concept of color or action, unless they are first mentioned by the subject. The kind of questioning to be employed will therefore depend upon what the *subject* says and what is implied in his response.

If the examiner does not already know about the determinants used, from the performance proper, a good first general question is: "Tell me more about the way you see . . ." or "What is it in the card that makes you think of . . . ?" or "Describe . . . in detail." However, if the subject has given some clue that he used color, for example, this should be followed up. If, for example, the subject says that the butterfly in Card III is "pretty" or that the bat in Card V "looks dirty," the examiner should ask immediately "What about the blot made it seem pretty to you? (or dirty to you?) "

Here is another example of how an examiner may use clues given by a subject: To Card VII the subject says, "These are Scottie dogs." The examiner might say, "What about this makes it seem like a Scottie dog in particular?" Usually such questions will yield enough information to enable the examiner to assign a determinant score for the response. Where this is not the case, the examiner must decide whether to continue with further questioning at this time, or to postpone the questioning until the analogy, or follow-up, period of the inquiry. The procedure followed will depend on the personality of the subject and the character of the responses. A general rule may be indicated, however. If the examiner feels the response can be clarified with a further simple question that is not suggestive, and that will not disturb the subject, it seems wise to continue. If the question might suggest to the subject that he *should* have used color, or shading, or action, then the question must be postponed.

Some suggestions for inquiring about each determinant are outlined below. Special follow-up procedures, the analogy and testing-the-limits periods, are described on pages 41–44.

Form: In the case of concepts with definite form, the major point to clear up is that of quality. Therefore, questions relating to part or parts of the concept usually bring forth answers that indicate how well the subject has actually perceived his concept. For example, consider the response "bat" to Card V. The subject has indicated that he has used the entire blot. A suitable question would then be, "Can you describe the bat to me?" or, better still, "Where is the head of the bat?" As an answer to this last question, the subject points out the head and may spontaneously point out the wings, the legs, and the body. This is quite sufficient for scoring purposes. Some subjects, however, might volunteer further information about the particularly long ears of the bat, the feet hanging down, the position of the wings, and so forth. The added information given *spontaneously* may be used for form-level scoring. Such information should not be forced from the subject, however.

Here is another example: Take the response to Card VII, "two women here." A question like, "Where are the head and hands?" might not only provide the necessary information for scoring form quality but also, as in the case of the previous example, stimulate the subject to give information about the legs, headdress, and the way he sees the women.

Movement: If the subject sees any figure, human or animal, or any mechanical object (such as a spinning top or a gyroscope), movement may be implied, even though it is not explicitly indicated. Particular caution must be exercised by the examiner in attempting to find out whether or not the concept was truly seen in movement. It may be advisable to ask just one question—for example, "How do you see the men?" (Card III) or "the butterfly" (Card V) or "How do you see the legs or arms?" in instances where the subject has included legs or arms in his response. Usually answers to questions about the main parts of the human or animal figures seen, and their positions, give indications as to the perception of movement.

Another indirect way of acquiring information about movement is through questions about adjacent parts and their relationships to the figures mentioned; for instance, questions about the black and gray lower center portions in Card III, as related to the two figures (if the figures have been mentioned only as "two figures"), usually produce an answer such as; "These are bags or hats they are holding." Direct questions, such as, "What are they doing?" or "Are they clapping hands?" are *never* allowed. If no action is elicited after the provocative but not leading questions suggested above, then the examiner must postpone the decision until the analogy period.

It has been the experience of Rorschach workers that when human beings are seen, they are usually seen in action. This is not necessarily true of animals, with the exception of the popular animal action responses of Card VIII. Therefore, if action is not indicated for the animals in Card VIII, it is advisable to make certain in the inquiry period whether this is or is not so by asking a question similar to the one suggested above, "Where do you see the legs?" or "Tell me how you see these animals." In the case of other animal concepts, it seems advisable to accept what the subject says spontaneously without further prodding for an action determinant.

Inanimate objects, such as an airplane or rocket, are usually seen in action, and the action factor comes out quite directly. If not, just one question such as, "How do you see it?" will elicit action if it is there at all. If action is not brought out in response to this question, the concept is not scored for movement.

Color: The use of color must be clearly indicated in the concept seen if it is to be scored. Responses like "flowers," "landscapes," "fire," and "blood" given to the brightly colored areas of the blots are usually scored for color without further inquiry unless there is strong indication to the contrary. However, if the examiner wants to make certain, he might ask a general question: "What about this part made you think of . . . ?" or, if necessary, "Was it just the shape that made you think of . . . ?" It is a better procedure to use some clue offered by the subject in the response. For instance, the subject might respond, to one of the yellow areas in Card X, "This is a pretty flower." The word "pretty" suggests that perhaps color was used. The examiner might then say something like this: "You said this part was 'a pretty flower' (pointing to the area) ; what made you think it looked pretty?" The examiner must be warned again that direct questions such as, "Is this colored?" are not allowed.

Sometimes the concept "butterfly" or "bow" given to the red areas in Card II or III, or "tree" to some area in Card VIII or IX, may not involve the use of color, even though given to brightly colored areas. It is necessary then to determine whether the score should be *F*, for form, or *FC*, for form plus color. At least one question might be asked, such as, "Was it just the shape that made you think of a butterfly?"

One of the difficult questions to settle during the inquiry is whether to score such responses as "flower," "sunset," "rainbow," or "fried eggs" *FC* or *CF*. Since both the interpretative significance of *FC* and *CF* and the relationship between *FC* and *CF* are extremely important, it is essential to determine as accurately as possible what the score should be. It is not the color we are concerned about now, since the use of color has been definitely established, but rather the clarity and definiteness of the form seen. Questions like, "What kind of flower is it?" or "Tell me more about how you see the rainbow," have been found helpful. Where the subject replies with a definite form concept (for example, "daffodil" or "the yolk of the egg is here surrounded by the white part") , these are clearly *FC* responses. On the other hand, if he says "Oh, it could be any kind of flower," or "It just looks like a scrambled egg," the responses are scored *CF*.

Shading: As in the case of color, the use of the shading qualities of the blot must be clearly indicated if shading is to be scored as a determinant. Shading responses usually require careful and subtle inquiry, since shading is often merely implied in the response and not directly expressed. When the concept implies the use of the shading qualities of the card (as in the responses "bear rug" to Cards IV or VI, "totem poles" to the upper detail of Card VI, or "the female genitals" to lower small detail of VII) , the examiner should ask at least one question to try to determine whether or not shading played a part. Questions similar to those suggested above for color or for form or for movement may be helpful.

The subject must indicate that it was differences in the light or dark qualities of the card (of the chromatic or the achromatic cards) that determined the concept for him before a shading score is permissible. Concepts not as common as the ones mentioned above (such as "marble statue" or "armchair" on Card VII, or "wooded scene" on Card IV held sideways) must likewise be described by the subject before a shading score can be assigned. Subjects who use shading as a determinant usually have no difficulty in describing their concepts to the examiner.

Certain scoring problems can be solved in the inquiry for shading. Special care must be taken to distinguish *Fc* from *cF*. The relative importance of the form and shading qualities in determining the concept must be weighed. Sometimes it may be difficult to decide whether a concept should be scored *Fc* or *FK*. Consider, for example, this response to all of Card IV: "A curled-up leaf; the dark shadow here makes it look like it is curled over." The examiner needs to ask a question such as, "Can you tell me more about the leaf?" The reply to this question may stress the markings of the leaf or the effect of distance. If the markings are emphasized, the score would be *Fc;* if difference in shading indicates differences in distance from the eye of the observer, or if one part of the leaf is seen as throwing a shadow on the other, the score would be *FK*.

Inquiry for Content

Inquiry for content is usually unnecessary, since the content category of what is seen is quite obvious. There is one exception, however: When a subject says he sees "figures" on Card III or on any other card, the examiner should determine whether they are human or animal, and if they are human, whether they are men or women. The question may be direct, such as, "Do these people look like men or women to you?"

Items to Record During the Inquiry

The record of the inquiry should include both the questions of the examiner and the answers of the subject. These should be written on the right-hand half of the page, next to the response to which they pertain. If the examiner needs to ask a question beyond the usual initial one for location, determinant, or content, such questioning should be indicated by the notation (Q.), as in the sample record on pages 224–27 (Appendix). The beginning student may want to record everything he says for future criticism.

The actual words of the subject should be recorded, as far as possible, and written next to the response about which he is talking. Any significant remarks might also be noted.

New responses given during the inquiry should be recorded when they occur and in the order in which they are given. These are additional responses, and are to be tallied as additional scores. If there are many such new responses during the inquiry, the examiner might designate their sequence by the small letters a, b, c, etc., starting each card with the letter a.

Most Rorschach examiners use the Location Chart during the inquiry period for recording the area used for each response. There is more time now than during the performance proper; moreover, it is permissible for the examiner to let the subject see what he is doing. In fact, as we have seen, when the location is not too clear, the subject may be asked to outline the area himself on the Location Chart.

After outlining the area used on the Location Chart, the examiner should number the outline to correspond with the number of the response. If it is an additional response, the outlined area should be lettered with the letter of the response. Sometimes it is desirable, especially when the concept is original or complex, to note on the Location Chart some of the details of the concept seen—a head, ears, eyes of an animal, petals of a flower, and the like. This kind of information will help in assigning form-level credits.

The Analogy Period

In many instances, the clues and spontaneous elaborations obtained in the inquiry make an accurate scoring possible. However, in almost every record there will be a few responses, and in some records, a considerable number of responses, that will not be scorable on the basis of the initial inquiry alone. It is therefore necessary to follow up the initial inquiry with further prodding questions. The examiner should still avoid asking questions that might suggest that certain kinds of answers are expected of the subject.

In most cases, the appropriate procedure for this follow-up inquiry to clarify responses is the use of analogy questions. Let us assume that the use of color or action in some of the responses needs clarification. Usually, there is one Rorschach response in which the subject has referred to the color of the area or to action. The examiner should point out this response to the subject and say, "In this case, you said the color made you think of . . . ; how was it here?" Or "Here you called it a beautiful butterfly because it was colored. Now try to select those responses in which color helped." If the subject says, "Yes, the color helped here," the examiner must not be satisfied; he must find out *how* it helped. Color can be scored only if the examiner is convinced that the subject used the color in his original concept. Another form of the question would be: "You said here that you saw the two men bowing; what about the people here?" The examiner must be especially careful not to give the subject the impression that using color or action or shading is preferable to not using these determinants.

When the procedure outlined above is not possible, because the subject had *no* responses mentioning movement, color, or shading, the analogy period resembles the procedure for the testing-the-limits period.

The main value of the analogy period is that many times it greatly simplifies the initial inquiry phase. The sometimes awkward task of finding out about the use of determinants can be accomplished in a single step, and other responses where the same determinant may have been used need not be separately queried. At the same time, it is much easier for the subject to reveal his attitude to these determinants when he is confronted with a whole group of responses in which they may have been used. He does not have to guess what the examiner is after with his annoying questions about each individual response.

One final word of warning about both the analogy and inquiry procedures. It is better to ask *too little* than *too much*. Pressing for determinants not actually used by a subject will distort a Rorschach record to a greater extent than will the overlooking of a determinant in one or two responses.

Testing the Limits

The aim of the testing-the-limits procedure is to find out whether or not a subject is *capable* of: (1) seeing specific kinds of concepts, or (2) using specific locations or determinants that he has not used in his spontaneous responses. This procedure is most useful to clinicians concerned with individual assessment, especially in cases where the total production of the subject is impoverished.

The information obtained from testing the limits cannot, as a rule, be used for scoring. One reason is that the fundamental test situation is changed; for example, direct suggestions are made to the subject so that he is no longer freely expressing himself. On the other hand, information obtained by this procedure may add immensely to the clarification of the personality picture. It demonstrates not only whether the subject *can* use a determinant he has not used previously, but also at what point he can change his attitudes and mode of attack. If he cannot change his concepts, or be persuaded to take the examiner's suggestions, the examiner should find out why. (He may do so by questions such as, "What do you think is wrong if somebody else sees that?")

When to Use the Testing-the-Limits Procedure

The testing-the-limits procedure can be extremely valuable with: (1) inarticulate subjects who may have been anxious during the examination period, (2) individuals who were confused about what was expected of them, or (3) subjects who produced very meager records for whatever reason.

Testing the limits may be necessary only when there is insufficient evidence in the subject's responses with regard to his ability to:

1. see W's or D's.
2. see human content and to project movement into it.
3. integrate form and color (FC responses).
4. use shading at least in the popular animal skin concept in Card VI or the near popular response in Card IV.
5. perceive and think along conventional lines (P, or popular responses).
6. perceive animals in action, especially the animals in Card VIII.

How to Conduct the Testing-the-Limits Procedure

After an over-all view of the subject's responses obtained during the performance proper, the initial inquiry, and the analogy period, the examiner decides what he wants to find out and how he is going to proceed. It is almost impossible for the beginner to handle this phase of the administration adequately, since it presupposes that the examiner is fully aware of conspicuous omissions in the performance proper and inquiry responses. The more experienced the Rorschach administrator becomes, the more nuances he will get in testing the limits.

Generally, questions raised during this part of the examination should proceed from the *general* to the *specific*. For example, if a subject has used W's (whole blots) only, the examiner might start out by saying: "Sometimes people use just a part of the blot in order to see something, and not all of the blot. Can you do that?" If this produces no results, he could go on to point out specific areas that are commonly used as D's (large details). This failing, he could suggest to the subject specific concepts that are popularly seen in parts of the blot, such as the "animals" in Card VIII, the "crabs" in Card X, or the "butterfly" in Card III. If the subject persists in saying he cannot see the D's pointed out, the examiner might want to ask, "What is wrong if people see it this way?" The response to such a question might show whether it is perceptual inability that hinders the subject, or just an unwillingness to see such a concept for one reason or another. If a subject says that he can see one of the D's pointed out, then the examiner should ask for a description of it.

Let us consider the case of a subject who saw a "bear rug" in Card VI and indicated during the initial phase of the inquiry that it was the shape that made him think of a bear rug. He pointed out the legs, the tail, and the fact that it had no head. There were no other responses in his record to indicate that he used shading. It would be worthwhile during the testing-the-limits phase to determine what problem this subject faces with regard to the use of the shading qualities of the blot. As a means of finding the problem, the examiner might suggest that a majority of people see the bear rug as having a furry skin because the shading in the blot makes it look that way. How does our subject react to this suggestion? Does he accept the suggestion, and if so, what does he do with it? Does he deny the possibility, and if so, why? Or is he indifferent? Each of these contradictions may be more decisive for the total personality organization than any other information derived from the Rorschach record, and this kind of information can be elicited only in the testing-the-limits period. The same kind of information, of course, can be obtained for determinants other than shading, and is equally meaningful.

Special Administration Situations

Special Subjects

What has been said thus far regarding administration is applicable to subjects within a normal range as to age and mental condition. It has been claimed that the procedure would have to be varied with young children, with old people, or with the mentally disturbed. The authors have found, however, that for the young and the old only the wording of the instructions has to be changed, not the principle of the method.

Disturbed subjects require different kinds of handling, depending upon the nature of the disturbance. The purpose of the examination may need to be explained. The examiner may have to be more directive; he will certainly have to be more flexible in his approach with the mentally sick.

The details of procedure for these special cases will not be discussed here. The interested reader may consult the pertinent references [1, 2, 3, 4, 6, 10, 11].

Long Protocols

Subjects who give over 50 responses are infrequently encountered. When one meets such an individual, the question of limiting him or allowing him to continue arises. The answer to this question depends on the subject, the examiner, and the situation. If time is of importance and the subject is amenable, the examiner may suggest that it is not necessary to give so many responses, that a large number of responses does not in and of itself make a better record, and so on. If the subject does not take the hint, the examiner may either allow him to go on or tell him that he will have to stop after giving four or five responses. The examiner may then recover the card and present the next one. It has been demonstrated that the first three responses to each card, or the first 50 per cent of the responses to each card of a long record, provide almost the same information as the entire record [17].

Special Procedures

Several special procedures, suggested by various investigators, may be useful in particular situations. These procedures include:

The *free association procedure,* suggested by Janis and Janis [9]. This consists of asking people to give free associations to certain Rorschach responses. It is possible to modify the procedure and ask for free associations only to certain contents within a protocol which seem to have a special personal significance to the subject.

The *concept formation technique,* a variation of which was suggested by Hutt [8]. It consists of asking the subject to put the cards into various piles on the basis of some principle of his own device. He may do this on the basis of content, affective attitudes, color or form differences, and the like.

The *graphic procedure,* originally proposed by Levine and Grassi [12]. This is a more elaborate device than either of the two previous techniques mentioned and has been more extensively developed [15]. The subject is asked to draw the object he has seen in the blot for the purpose of making the scoring and interpretation more conclusive. The drawing responses may also be classified along a scale from those that are "blot-dominated" to those that are "concept-dominated," thus providing further clues to personality dynamics.

The *like-dislike procedure*. The subject is asked to pick out the card he likes the best and the one he likes the least, and to give his reasons for these choices. Information can sometimes be obtained which will enhance the interpretative significance of the responses previously given to the cards.

Group Administration

The individual use of the Rorschach permits maximum benefits to be derived from the unstructured aspects of the test material and of the testing situation. Nevertheless, group administration of the Rorschach, by means of showing slides of the cards or of showing the cards themselves to groups, has been used for research purposes. This practice, however, should not be employed for clinical purposes. For an explanation and critical evaluation of the group method of administration the reader should consult the references [5, 7, 14].

References

1. Ames, L. B.; Learned, J.; Métraux, R. W.; and Walker, R. N. *Child Rorschach Responses*. New York: Paul B. Hoeber, Inc.; 1952.

2. Ford, M. *The Application of the Rorschach Test to Young Children*. University of Minnesota Institute of Child Welfare Monograph Series, No. 23, 1946.

3. Hallowell, A. I. "The Rorschach Technique in Personality and Culture Studies," in *Developments in the Rorschach Technique, Vol. II*, Klopfer, B., et al. New York: Harcourt, Brace & World; 1956. Pages 458–544.

4. Halpern, F. *A Clinical Approach to Children's Rorschachs*. New York: Grune & Stratton, Inc.; 1953.

5. Harrower, M. R., and Steiner, M. E. *Large Scale Rorschach Techniques*. Springfield, Illinois: Charles C. Thomas; 1944.

6. Hertz, M. R. "The Method of Administration of the Rorschach Ink-Blot Test," *Child Develop.*, 1936, 7, 237–254.

7. Hire, A. W. "A Group Administration of the Rorschach: Method and Results," *J. Consult. Psychol.*, 1950, 14, 496–499.

8. Hutt, M. L., and Shor, J. "Rationale for Routine Rorschach 'Testing-the-Limits,'" *Rorschach Res. Exch.*, 1946, 10, 70–76.

9. Janis, M. G., and Janis, I. L. "A Supplementary Test Based on Free Associations to Rorschach Responses," *Rorschach Res. Exch.*, 1946, 10, 1–19.

10. Klopfer, B.; Fox, J.; and Troup, E. "Problems in the Use of the Rorschach Technique with Children," in *Developments in the Rorschach Technique, Vol. II*, Klopfer, B., et al.

New York: Harcourt, Brace & World; 1956. Pages 3–21.

11. Klopfer, W. G. "The Application of the Rorschach Technique to Geriatrics," in *Developments in the Rorschach Technique, Vol. II*, Klopfer, B., et al. New York: Harcourt, Brace & World; 1956. Pages 195–212.

12. Levine, K. N., and Grassi, J. R. "The Relation Between Blot and Concept in Graphic Rorschach Responses," *Rorschach Res. Exch.*, 1942, 6, 71–73.

13. Loosli-Usteri, M. "Le Test de Rorschach Appliqué à Différents Groupes d'Enfants de 10–13 Ans" (The Rorschach Test Applied to Groups of 10–13 Year Old Children), *Arch. Psychol., Genève*, 1929, 22, 51–106.

14. Munroe, R. L. "The Use of Projective Methods in Group Testing," *J. Consult. Psychol.*, 1948, 12, 8–15.

15. Rochlin, G. N., and Levine, K. N. "The Graphic Rorschach Test I," *Arch. Neurol. Psychiat.*, 1942, 47, 438–448.

16. Rorschach, H. *Psychodiagnostics.* New York: Grune & Stratton, Inc.; 1951.

17. ——. "Three Rorschach Interpretations," *J. Proj. Tech.*, 1954, 18, 482–495.

Chapter Four

SCORING
THE RORSCHACH PROTOCOL

THE Rorschach record is scored for the purpose of providing a short-hand description of how a subject has reacted to the ten ink blots. Scoring a Rorschach protocol is a process of classifying the subject's verbal responses to the different aspects of the blot material. Each aspect is assigned a scoring symbol. Responses that are similar with respect to some significant characteristic are classified in the same scoring category. Quantification enters in only when a frequency count is made of the responses in each scoring category, and when these frequencies are compared in terms of absolute number, percentage, or ratio.

In the application of any system of classifying qualitative material, differences of opinion are likely to arise when responses fall on the borderline between one class and another. It is desirable to make the system as reliable as possible, so that different examiners will arrive at essentially similar classifications of the same set of responses. One way to achieve this reliability is to make the rules of classification as explicit as possible so that all examiners classify on exactly the same basis. That is the purpose of this chapter.

The Five Major Scoring Categories

Each Rorschach response is scored in terms of five characteristics:

1. LOCATION: Where on the card was the concept seen?
2. DETERMINANT: How was the concept seen? What qualities of the blot determined it?
3. CONTENT: What was the subject matter of the concept seen?
4. POPULARITY-ORIGINALITY, P-O: How commonly is the concept

seen by other subjects? A response is classified as *popular* if it tallies with the list of ten responses (given on pages 91 ff.) that have been found to be most frequent. An *original* classification is for responses that occur as rarely as once in 100 records in the experience of the individual examiner. Many responses are neither popular nor original according to these definitions.

5. FORM LEVEL: How accurately is the concept seen? How closely does the concept fit the blot area used? Also, what is the degree of elaboration of the concept?

The aspects or qualities of location, determinant, content, popularity-originality, and form level are scored because they, singly and in combination, give clues to important facets of the personality, according to established working hypotheses. Chapter Six will consider the interpretative significance of these scoring categories.

What Is a Response?

The subject tells what he sees in the ink blots. These verbalizations of percepts, or concepts, are his responses. Since the response is the basic unit of the Rorschach protocol, it becomes important to know how a response is defined. *A response is an independent, discrete idea given to a clearly specified portion, or to the whole, of the ink blot. It is scorable with respect to its use of certain qualities of the blot material.* If a response is given during the performance proper, it is a *main response;* if it is elicited during the inquiry, it is considered an *additional response.*

Subjects do not always respond to the blots in a clear-cut fashion, however, so that problems may arise as to what exactly constitutes a response. Some kinds of questions that arise are:

1. When is a reaction a true *response,* and when is it merely a *remark?* For instance, a subject may say to Card II, "This is different, there is some color here; oh! it looks like two clowns playing pattycake." Is the first part of this statement a response to the blot material, or is it a remark about it? Since remarks are not scored, it is necessary to decide whether the subject intended it to be a remark or a response.

2. When should a reaction be scored as more than one response? For example, a subject might say to Card V, "This is a bat and it could also be a butterfly." On what basis should the examiner decide whether this verbalization is one or two responses?

3. What part of a reaction should be scored as an independent, or

semi-independent, idea, and what part should be considered an elaboration or specification? For example, a response to Card IX might be, "A beautiful reflection of mountains in a lake and here is the lake of deep blue water and over here it looks just like a sunset because of the orange color." Clearly the description of the lake and sunset are elaborations of the scene perceived, but they are also part of the main idea. What should be done about the elaborations?

4.   What happens when a subject verbalizes a concept and then rejects it?

Most of the questions just raised are resolved by the provision of two major scoring divisions: *main* scores and *additional* scores. Each main response receives only *one main* location score, *one main* determinant score, *one main* content score, *one main* popularity-originality score, when called for, and *one main* form-level score. However, a main response may receive additional scores to account for the elaborations or specifications given either during the performance proper or during the inquiry. Other situations in which *additional scores* are called for follow:

1.   When a response is rejected during the inquiry. In such cases, the response receives all five scores in the additional division only.

2.   When scores are needed beyond the main score to describe completely a response given during the performance proper. These additional scores are usually necessary for organized, elaborated concepts. These additional scores may be for location, determinant, content, and P–O main scores.

3.   When scores are needed to describe new elaborations or new associations elicited during the inquiry to responses already given during the performance proper. These additional scores may be for location, determinant, content, and P–O main scores. In addition, these new elaborations and specifications may change the form level of the concept, usually raising it; sometimes, if the elaboration spoils the concept, the new elaboration will lower the form-level rating.

4.   When scores are needed to show that the subject uses qualities of the blot material rather reluctantly or indirectly. Usually this reluctance is manifested with regard to the determinant scores.

Scoring for Location

Scoring for location of responses consists of classifying each response according to the area of the blot used. There are five main categories of location scores: whole, large usual detail, small usual detail, unusual detail, and white space (with subcategories for the whole and unusual detail categories). The symbols used for scoring location are given below together with examples of typical responses. The response given during the performance proper plus any additional information obtained during the inquiry are indicated. The types of questions asked during the inquiry to obtain the necessary information for scoring were discussed in Chapter Three.

Whole Responses: *W*, *W̶*, and *DW*

1.   *W,* or *whole,* is scored when the subject employs the entire blot for his concept, or when the subject clearly intends to use the entire blot but inadvertently omits a small part. Examples follow: *

CARD I
It could be a bat. (Inq.) The whole thing. Head, wings.

> COMMENT: Clearly the whole blot area is used although the subject has identified only two specific features of the bat.

CARD II
Two women bowing to each other as they dance. They are laughing. Their hats are red, and they have red paint on their boots.

> COMMENT: The whole response is so tightly organized that it would be an abuse of the subject's intention to break it down into separate responses for the hats and boots.

CARD V
This is a butterfly (whole). (Inq.) Here are the feelers, the wings, the legs.

2.   *W̶,* or *cut-off whole,* is scored when the subject designates almost all of the blot (at least two-thirds), with the intention of using as much of the blot as possible. Three examples follow:

CARD I
A woman's pelvis. (Inq.) I used it all except for these (side earlike projections) which didn't fit.

CARD III
Here are a couple of men at a party whirling around. They might be having a tug of war over a punch bowl.

---

* In the examples given, the subject's words are recorded directly; the examiner's words are indicated in parentheses, including his questions (Q. . . .). If the nature of the question is obvious from the content, the notation (Q.) is made. The location of the response is shown, when necessary, in this manner: (*Location:* . . .). The abbreviation (Inq.) indicates the beginning of the inquiry. Where this break is indicated by a question (Q.) the notation (Inq.) is omitted as unnecessary.

COMMENT: The red areas have been omitted, but the response includes most of the blot area.

CARD VI

An animal skin, perhaps of a bear. (Inq.) It was the whole thing, only I sort of ignored this part up here. The general impression was of an animal skin.

COMMENT: The intention to use the whole blot is clear from the spontaneous formulation in the inquiry. The lower part of the blot is considered the main part of the card, and the upper detail is excluded by being "ignored."

3.   *DW,* or *confabulatory whole,* is scored when a subject interprets a detail and then assigns the same interpretation to the entire blot without justification, and without any consciously felt need to reconcile the qualities of the remaining blot material with the qualities of the concept. A *DW* response is always, therefore, a poor form response; that is, the concept is a poor match for the blot.

CARD I

Like a spider. (Inq.) Front part of it has the stickers (demonstrates) and two little parts look like eyes (upper middle bumps). The rest is the body.

CARD II

A fish. (Q. Where is the fish?) (Subject points to the whole in careless manner.) (Q. What about the blot made it look like a fish?) (Subject points to the top center small detail.) Here is its long pointed face and mouth. (Q. What about this part and this part?) That's the whole fish, the rest of it is its body.

COMMENT: Here the subject overgeneralizes from one area which resembles part of a fish to the whole blot, which cannot be reconciled with the shape of a fish.

Large Usual Detail Responses: *D*

D, or *large usual detail,* is scored when a subject employs a comparatively large area for his concept, easily marked off by space, shading, or color from the rest of the blot.

Small Usual Detail Responses: *d*

d, or *small usual detail,* is scored when a subject employs for his concept a relatively small area, but one that is easily marked off by space, shading, or color from the rest of the blot.

Since these large and small usual details represent the obvious subdivisions of the blots, they are the ones most frequently used by subjects. A list of these areas for each card plus the areas outlined on achromatic reproductions of the blots is given on pages 54–63. Note that the number of each area in the list is the same number used on the blot in which the area is delineated. These numbers will henceforth be used when referring to the particular large or small usual details. In scoring, some latitude in the delineation of these areas is permissible.

Unusual Detail Responses: *dd, de, di,* and *dr*

Unusual detail (symbolized by the letters *Dd* *) is used to describe responses that are not whole responses, not listed among the usual details, and not space responses. The unusual detail response differs primarily from the usual detail response in terms of frequency of occurrence. They are less frequently used than the usual details and, except for the *dr* response, are also smaller in area. There are four subdivisions to the *Dd* response; each is described below with its scoring symbol. See also the Location Chart, page 64.

1. *dd,* or *tiny detail,* is used to describe areas that, like *d,* are marked off from the rest of the blot by space, shading, or color. Three examples follow:

CARD I
Another part is a turtle's head. (Inq.) (Tiny projection on left side, often seen as the nose of a man.) (Q. Can you describe it?) Just the head. Just the shape.

CARD II
Icicles. (Inq.) (Tiny light projections in lower center portion.)
COMMENT: These projections are clearly marked off areas of the blot.

CARD VII
I think it is a paw or a foot held out. It has claws, but not very large claws. (Inq.) (Outermost side projections.)

2. *de,* or *edge detail,* is employed for locations using only the edge of the blot. For example:

CARD V
This could be a face, same on the other side. (Inq.) (Upper edge of wings.)

---

* Note that *Dd* itself is not used as a scoring symbol for individual responses, but only as a summarizing symbol for *all* unusual detail responses.

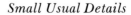

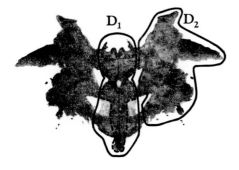

Card I

Large Usual Details

D_1 Entire center with or without lighter gray in lower portion.

D_2 Entire side.

D_3 Bottom center without lighter gray.

D_4 Entire lower center.

D_5 Upper side.

D_6 Upper center.

Small Usual Details

d_1 Upper outer projection.

d_2 Lower side.

d_3 Upper, inner, clawlike extension.

d_4 Uppermost projection.

d_5 Upper innermost projection.

d_6 Bottom projection.

d_7 Small knoblike extension at lower side.

Popular Response

W or W: Any creature with the body in the center D and wings at the sides.

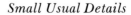

Card II

Large Usual Details

D_1 Lower red with or without black-red mixture.

D_2 Upper red.

D_3 Entire side black.

D_4 Upper side black.

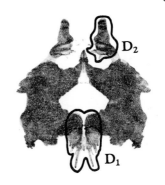

Small Usual Details

d_1 Upper center with or without outer gray.

d_2 Bottom outer projection.

d_3 Bottom projection adjacent to d_2.

d_4 Upper side projection.

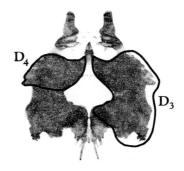

Popular Response

Black area, either as an organized W with or without upper center d, or as a D: Any animal or part of an animal of the dog, bear, rabbit, bull, or rhinoceros variety.

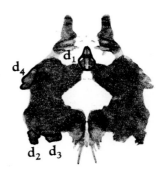

56

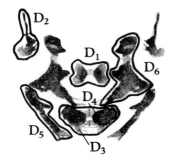

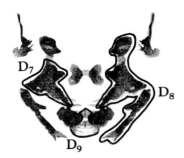

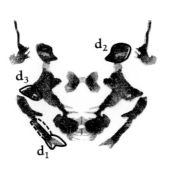

Card III

Large Usual Details

D_1 Inner red.

D_2 Outer red with or without tail-like tension.

D_3 Entire lower center.

D_4 Lower center black.

D_5 Lower side black.

D_6 Upper side black (head and upper part of body of usual figure).

D_7 Middle side black.

D_8 Entire side black.

D_9 Lower center light gray.

Small Usual Details

d_1 Bottom side black, sometimes with lower part of "leg."

d_2 Top side black.

d_3 Middle side black lateral protrusion, usually upside down.

Popular Responses

1. Entire black area: Two human figures in a bending position. Legs must be seen in lower side D and figures in action. Includes dressed up animals. If legs are seen where arms usually are, or nondressed up animals with two pairs of legs, at most the score is an additional P.

2. Inner red D: "Bow tie," "hair ribbon," or "butterfly." The shape alone or shape combined with color.

Card IV

Large Usual Details

D_1 Lower center.

D_2 Lower side black and gray, sometimes with upper side portion.

D_3 Lower side light gray.

D_4 Vertical dark center, sometimes with d_2.

D_5 Lower side black.

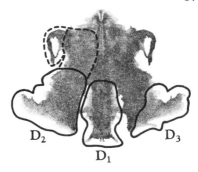

Small Usual Details

d_1 Upper side extension with or without small adjacent portion.

d_2 Uppermost portion, sometimes with adjacent shaded portion.

d_3 Outermost lower side extension.

d_4 Lowermost center portion.

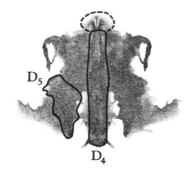

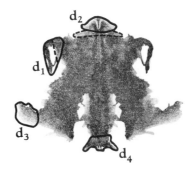

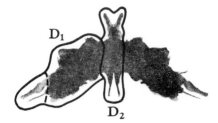

Card V

Large Usual Details

D_1 Side with or without light gray extensions.

D_2 Entire vertical center.

Small Usual Details

d_1 Bottom center.

d_2 Side extension, sometimes with adjacent thin extension.

d_3 Top center with or without uppermost protrusions.

d_4 Upper side projection.

Popular Response

W or W: Any winged creature with the body in the center *D* and the wings at the sides. Same concept with card upside down.

Card VI

Large Usual Details

D_1 Entire lower portion or half of lower portion.

D_2 Entire upper portion, sometimes with light gray uppermost portion of lower detail.

D_3 Upper black portion only of center column, sometimes without lightly shaded outer portion.

D_4 Entire dark vertical center.

D_5 Lighter part only of upper portion.

Small Usual Details

d_1 Uppermost portion with or without "whiskers."

d_2 Lower lateral extension.

d_3 Two inner light gray ovals.

d_4 Bottom inner projections.

Popular Response

With or without the top *D:* The skin of an animal. The use of shading for furriness or markings on the inside of the skin is essential.

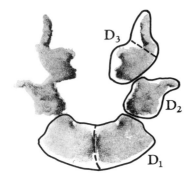

Card VII

Large Usual Details

D_1 Entire bottom or half of bottom.

D_2 Middle.

D_3 Top with or without uppermost projection.

D_4 Upper two-thirds.

Small Usual Details

d_1 Dark center bottom.

d_2 Top projection.

d_3 Light gray projection on upper inner corner of top.

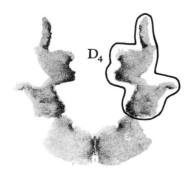

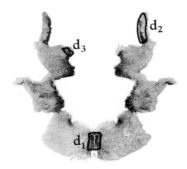

Card VIII

Large Usual Details

D_1 Side pink.

D_2 Bottom pink and orange.

D_3 Top gray with or without center line, sometimes with riblike figure and/or blue portion.

D_4 Middle blue.

D_5 Riblike figure in upper center.

D_6 Bottom pink.

D_7 Bottom orange.

Small Usual Details

d_1 Lateral extension of bottom orange.

Popular Response

Side *D:* Any kind of four-legged animal in any kind of motion. If not seen in action or if inaccurately called bird or fish, only a tendency toward *P* can be scored. If color is used, an additional original score is given.

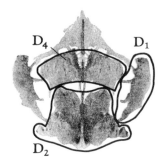

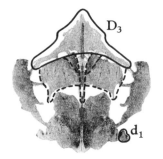

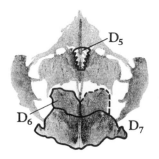

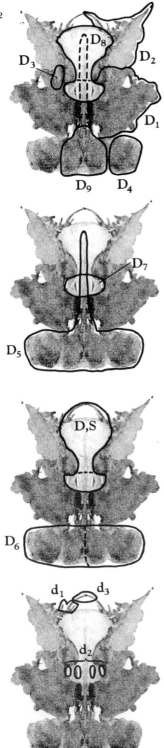

Card IX

Large Usual Details

D_1 Green.

D_2 Orange.

D_3 Small inner portion at junction of green and orange (sometimes seen as moose's head).

D_4 Lateral pink.

D_5 Entire pink plus vertical center area.

D_6 Entire pink or either half.

D_7 Center portion between lateral greens.

D_8 Center gray with or without D_7.

D_9 Inner pink, sometimes with vertical center area.

D,S Center gray and white space with or without D_7.

Small Usual Details

d_1 All or most of upper inner orange projections.

d_2 Eyelike portion in middle including green and white slits.

d_3 Archlike light orange at top center.

Card X

Large Usual Details

D_1 Outer blue, sometimes with upper green.

D_2 Dark lower green, sometimes with light bottom portion.

D_3 Entire top gray.

D_4 Gray "animal" at top without inner gray column.

D_5 Entire lower green.

D_6 Outer gray-brown figure.

D_7 Light upper green of D_5.

D_8 Inner blue.

D_9 Pink.

D_{10} Inner yellow.

D_{11} Outer orange.

D_{12} Inner orange.

D_{13} Upper green.

D_{14} Gray column at top without gray "animals" beside it.

D_{15} Outer yellow.

D_{16} Pink with entire top gray, card inverted.

D_{17} Pink with inner blue.

Popular Responses

1. Outer blue D: Any many-legged animal, such as a spider, crab, or octopus. Use of color gives an additional original score.

2. Dark lower green D (D_2): Any elongated greenish animal, such as a caterpillar, garden snake, or tobacco worm. Color must be used; otherwise, only additional P is scored.

3. Light green D (D_7): The head of an animal with long ears or horns, such as a rabbit, donkey, or goat. Any addition (e.g., D_2 or S) adds an original element scored as an additional O.

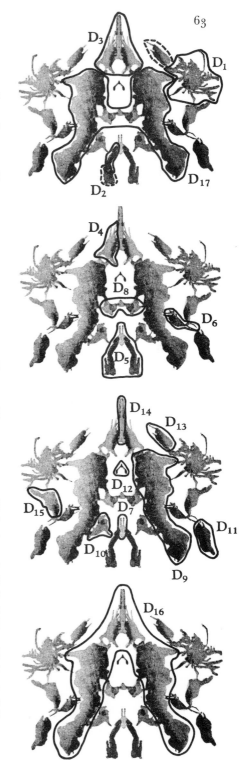

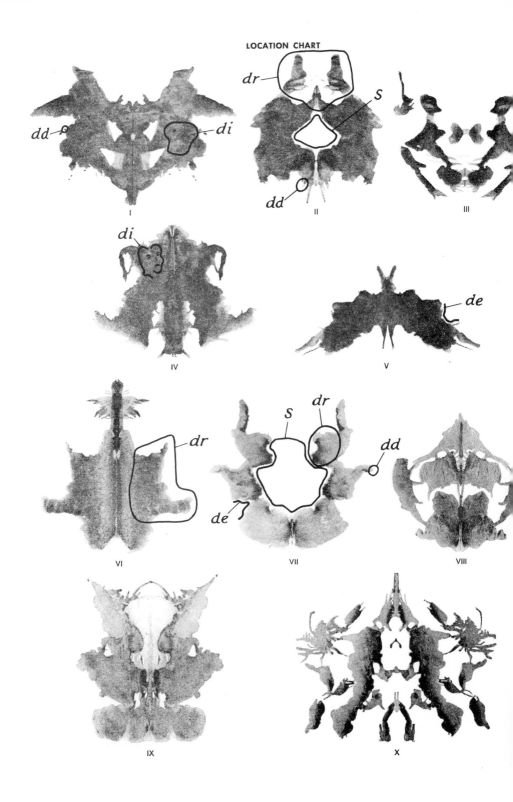

LOCATION CHART

CARD VII

Here is—they are partly disguised things you might see in clouds. This is the female, this is the male, and he is kissing her on the forehead—strange shapes. (Inq.) (Only the edge between middle and bottom thirds was used.)

3. *di,* or *inside detail,* is used for locations which are not easily separated from the rest of the blot by space, color, or shading. These locations are inside the blot. For example:

CARD I

A pair of breasts, with nipples and part of the rest of the torso. (Inq.) (Shaded section in right, lower side portion) The breasts are beautifully modeled and firm.

> COMMENT: Although the "nipples" are clearly enough marked off to be *dd* themselves, the best scoring for the whole location used is *di.*

CARD IV

This is a Cavalier from the time of Charles I. (Inq.) (Upper shaded section in left side) Here are his eyes; eyebrows; long, curling hair; nose; mustache; beard; and the suggestion of a ruff here.

> COMMENT: This is scored *di,* because the location is carved out of the inner part of the blot in the shaded area.

4. *dr,* or *rare detail,* is used to score responses using unusual blot locations. These locations cannot be classified as *dd, de,* or *di,* and are sufficiently differentiated from a *D, d,* or *W* that they cannot be scored as such. The rare detail may be *large* or *small* in size. Examples follow:

CARD II

This part could be two women talking over a fence or something. They have terrific hats or hairdos or something. (Inq.) (*Location:* upper red portions for the women and upper gray center *d* for fence) (Q.) They are facing each other and their hands are up.

> COMMENT. A *dr* is score for the combination of two *D*'s and one *d.*

CARD VI

Here is a woman. Here is her fancy hair curls. She is blonde, looking at her foot stretched out here (lower side projection is head, upper side is foot). Looks like a sponge in her lap. Maybe she is going to take a bath.

> COMMENT: This response cuts across the usual delineations of this blot and is sufficiently larger than the *d* which it includes and smaller than the *D* of which it is a part to warrant a score of *dr.*

CARD VII

This looks like a face. (*Location:* part of top third)

    COMMENT: This concept does not include the entire *D* area, but it does include more than the edge detail; therefore, it is scored *dr.*

White Space Responses: S

S, or *white space*, is scored when there is complete reversal of figure and ground, and the white space is the location for the concept itself. If the whole blot or part of the blot material is used in addition and in an accessory manner, the blot or parts are scored as additional locations. For example:

CARD II

Well, the center could be a ceiling light, like the white globes you see.

    COMMENT: Only the white space outlined by the blot area has been used for these responses.

CARD VII

Looks somewhat like a type of vase of the early American period. (*Location:* center space)

Multiple Location Scores

There are four chief conditions for combining location scores. These conditions apply also to scores for determinants, content, and *P–O.*

Condition 1: When a concept involves a number of independent or semi-independent ideas that are given during the performance proper or during the inquiry, but that are loosely combined to form a response. The several ideas receive main scores or additional scores in each category, depending on whether the response is given during the performance proper or during the inquiry. The organizational element is shown by the use of braces, as in the following examples:

CARD III

Here are two African natives—rather skinny females—and here is a crab (D_3). (Inq.) This part looks like a crab—all the legs. They seem to be fighting over the crab.

    COMMENT: The crab was first seen separately from the natives, and then was organized into the larger concept. Therefore, two main responses are scored, the organization being shown by a

brace, thus: $\left.\begin{matrix} W \\ D \end{matrix}\right\}$

CARD IV

A huge insect. It seems to be crawling out from behind a split leaf. (Inq.) The insect is here. (*Location:* D_1 and D_2) It has two antennae. It reminds me of a bee. The thick part is the thorax. This part is the leaf, the curled wide sides.

> COMMENT: This seems loosely enough organized to justify two main responses being scored, their relationship being shown by
>
> the brace: $\left.\begin{matrix} D \\ W \end{matrix}\right\}$

Condition 2: When a main idea involves the use of *two* location areas—for example, a *W* or *D* combined with white space, or white space combined with a usual detail or a whole. Examples follow:

CARD I

It could be a wolf, like a wolf's face, with features. (Inq.) The whole thing. Here are the eyes, nose, mouth, ears, chin.

> COMMENT: Because the white space is used specifically for the eyes and mouth, it should be scored in addition to the *W* for the whole blot area: *W,S.* (Note the use of the comma [,] to describe this kind of response. See below, page 69, for explanation.)

CARD VIII

Something like shells in the center. Can't make it out quite. Very fine shells. (Inq.) (*Location:* upper center riblike portion) The white part. The shape and the shading coming in. White shells.

> COMMENT: Since the subject placed so much emphasis on the white space, the main score is *S,* with an additional *D* for the large usual detail; thus, the scoring is: *S,D.*

CARD X

A wolf's head. (Inq.) (*Location:* upper, inner part of outer blue) Here are the nose, ears, eye. (Q. Was it the shape?) Yes, and the white for the eye.

> COMMENT: Score is *dr,S.*

Condition 3: When, in addition to the area selected for the main concept, the subject tends to employ another area reluctantly or indirectly to complete the main idea. For example:

CARD II

This little part (upper *d*) is the tall building and all the rest (black only) are trees and walks leading to it.

    COMMENTS   The score is *d*→*W̶* because a small area was used and almost the rest of the blot was used to form a logical *W̶* concept. (Note the use of the arrow [→] to describe this type of response. See below, page 69, for explanation.)

CARD VIII

Two animals climbing up something. (Inq.) These are the animals, (*Location:* *D*) and they're climbing up this mountain. (Q. Mountain?) It all looks sort of rocky.

    COMMENT: The mountain was not mentioned until the inquiry, and only as an afterthought; therefore, the score is *D*→*W*.

Condition 4:   When a concept involves two or more semi-independent ideas that are loosely combined and in this combination employs another area. For example:

CARD VIII

Well, these look like two bears climbing up or something. And these look like flags. The whole thing gives the impression of an emblem or crest. (Inq.) The bears are this pink part. Here are the two flags, they're crossed (middle blue portion). The shape of the whole thing is sort of like a crest, and it seems to make sense that way.

    COMMENT: The need to combine the two separate main detail responses into a more organized response has resulted in a concept that fits the blot area and that is loose enough to encompass both ideas. The location score is therefore: $\left.\begin{array}{c}D\\D\end{array}\right\}W$ (Note the use of the brace [}] to describe this type of response. See below, page 69, for explanation.)

CARD X

These two look like crabs (outer blue, D_1), and this could be coral, like a coral reef (D_9). These top ones also look like some sort of crabs (D_4). And this could be seaweed (D_9, D_{13}). The thing reminds me of a marine scene, the colors and the shapes and all.

    COMMENT:There are four separate concepts which are brought together into a whole concept. The score is therefore: $\left.\begin{array}{c}D\\D\\D\\D\end{array}\right\}W$

Special Symbols

All scores after a comma, an arrow, or a brace are counted as additional scores. These symbols are used not only in connection with location scores, but also with the determinant, content, and *P–O* scoring categories. The purpose for each of these minor scoring symbols is as follows:

Comma (,) to indicate that the subject uses more than one location area, more than one determinant, more than one content, or more than one *P–O*.

Arrow (→) to indicate that the subject tends to employ in his response, or uses secondarily or reluctantly, an additional location, determinant, content, or *P–O*. Use (←) to indicate that a response given during the performance proper was rejected.

Brace (}) to indicate that two or more semi-independent concepts are combined into a larger main concept, or that one response contains two or more concepts, each deserving a separate score.

Scoring for Determinants

Scoring for determinants consists of classifying each response according to the quality of the blot material that determined the response. The question, "What about the blot gave you the impression of a . . . ?" will usually suggest the determinant or determinants to be scored. Was it just the shape? Or was it primarily some other aspect of the blot material such as color or shading? Or was it not so much the shape and character of the blot material itself that determined the response as something the subject read into the material, a subjective contribution to the percept?

There are four main categories for the determinant scores: form, movement, shading, and color (with subclasses for the movement, shading, and color categories). The symbols used for scoring determinants are given below together with examples of typical responses.*

Form Responses: *F*

F, or *form*, is used to score responses in which the shape or contour of the blot determines the concept, and where there is no other main

---

* Additional examples for each category are given on pages 105–19.

determinant (such as movement, shading, or color). *F* is scored even for responses where the form is vague, indefinite, or abstract. Four examples follow:

CARD III

This looks like a butterfly. (*Location:* center red *D*) (Q. What makes it like a butterfly?) It's got the shape of one, that's all.

CARD V

Looks a little bit like a bat, I guess (whole). (Q. What about it makes it seem like a bat?) The shape. (Q. How do you see it?) Stretched out. Just the shape.

CARD VII

This is far-fetched, but it looks something like Spain (*Location:* middle area) or some other country jutting out and surrounded by water.

CARD IX

I can't get anything out of the thing as a whole except an abstract pattern. It is symmetrical, with this balancing that.

> COMMENT: The last two concepts are vague, but only the shape was used. Therefore, they are scored *F*.

Movement Responses: *M*, *FM*, and *m*

Movement responses include concepts in which the subject has read into the static ink blots some kind of action, expression, posture, or life. Movement responses also include the projection onto the blot of abstract forces, or movements, and natural and mechanical forces. Three main classes of movement responses are: human movement, animal movement, and inanimate movement.

1. *M*, or human movement, is used to score concepts involving any kind of humanlike action, posture, or expression, regardless of whether this action is attributed to whole human figures, to a portion of a human figure, to caricatures, to statues, or to animals. Note that form, *F*, is subsumed in the *M* score and therefore need not be written. There is always a form element in the *M* score even though the form quality may be vague or poor. Five examples follow:

CARD I

It might be two witches doing a devil's dance. (*Location:* side figures)

> COMMENT: The humanlike concept "witches" and the fact that they are dancing warrant scoring this response *M*.

CARD II

A couple of clowns clapping hands. (Inq.) They are having a good time being clownish.

CARD III

Looks like a funny-book page. (Inq.) Looks like the Gumps, talking maybe, but like something added for a little color.

    COMMENT: Although "the Gumps" are a drawing, they are scored as human figures seen in action.

CARD V

Two women asleep. Long black hair which covers their backs. (*Location:* side *D*'s) Here is the face, eyelash, hair, arms folded. Here are the legs.

    COMMENT: This is an *M* by reason of the live posture, despite the fact that there is no active movement.

CARD VIII

Like these two hands are reaching out to take hold of the mice (usual animals) on either side. (*Location:* lateral extremities of top gray portion)

    COMMENT: This is human movement ascribed to part of a living human being, and so is scored *M*.

2. *FM,* or *animal movement,* is used to score concepts that attribute animal-like action to animals or parts of living animals, even if qualified as caricatures, drawings, or ornaments. Score *FM* also for animals trained to perform like humans (for instance, trained bears dancing, or trained seals juggling).

Note that the *FM* symbol was adopted to differentiate animal action from human action; the form factor is always present, as in *M,* even though it may be vague or poor. Examples follow:

CARD I

Bat (whole). (Inq.) Bat in flight, wings are spread out.

    COMMENT: This is a typical animal-like movement attributed to an animal.

CARD VI

The top part looks like a bird sitting on something.

    COMMENT: Since the posture is clearly animal-like, this response is scored *FM* although the word "sitting" was used to describe it.

CARD VIII

A bullfrog croaking. (*Location:* lower pink *D*) (Inq.) His head is up in the air. He is croaking. Here is his mouth. Just the upper part of the body.

COMMENT: This is still scored as animal movement though only part of the animal is seen.

3. *m,* or *inanimate movement*—including *Fm, mF,* and *m*—is used to score concepts that employ ideas of mechanical force or that are abstract in nature. The *Fm* score implies perception of inanimate movement in a concept that has a definite and recognizable shape, such as "flags waving in the breeze." The *mF* score is used for objects with semidefinite shape, such as "flames leaping in the air." The *m* score is used for concepts involving abstract force where form is completely indefinite—as, for example, "this reminds me of confusion and turmoil." The differentiation among *Fm, mF,* and *m* follows the general scoring principle of indicating the fusion of a determinant with definite, semidefinite or indefinite form. In order to keep the traditional scoring symbol for human action and to distinguish human action, *M,* from animal action, *FM,* this general scoring principle was not applied to the human action and animal action categories. Examples of inanimate movement responses follow:

CARD II
A beautiful spinning top. (Inq.) The white part. It stands upright, therefore it is spinning. It's just a drawing of one. These little lines indicate the movement.

COMMENT: A "top" has definite form, therefore the movement is scored *Fm.* The fact that it is qualified as a "drawing" does not detract from the movement score.

CARD VII
All I get here is a feeling of disintegration, of things falling apart. (Inq.) It's just a feeling this card gives me. (Q. Can you tell me more about the things that are falling apart?) It could be *anything.*

COMMENT: Here is an example of inanimate movement where form seems to be quite indefinite. Score is *m.*

CARD IX
There is a billowing of red clouds at the top and the darker clouds underneath (whole card, upside down).

COMMENT: Here an *mF* is scored for moving clouds of semidefinite shape.

CARD X
Leaves falling down to earth (whole). (Inq.) Slowly sifting down, just the shape of different kinds of leaves, maybe distorted by the wind as they are falling.

COMMENT: As the leaves are of varied shape, rather than of one particular kind, this concept must be scored *mF*.

Shading Responses: *c*, *K*, and *k*

Shading responses include those in which the subject uses the darker and lighter shading of the achromatic or chromatic areas to suggest one of three major effects: (1) surface or texture qualities—*Fc, cF, c;* (2) three dimensions or depth, either in the sense of vista, *FK,* or of diffusion, *KF,* or *K;* and (3) three-dimensional expanse projected on a two-dimensional plane, *Fk, kF,* and *k.*

Cutting across this threefold classification is the distinction between differentiated and undifferentiated shading responses. In *differentiated* shading responses—*Fc, FK,* and *Fk*—the three effects of shading are combined with *definite* outline form, or the surface qualities themselves are finely observed and represent a definite inner-form structure.* The *undifferentiated* shading responses include all others, especially those combining the three major effects of shading with vague or *indefinite* form—*cF, KF,* and *kF*—or entirely disregarding the form element—*c, K,* and *k.*

Surface or Texture Responses: Fc, cF, and c

1. *Fc,* or *differentiated surface or texture,* is the score assigned to two major types of responses: (a) those in which an object with definite form is seen as having surface qualities, such as smoothness, roughness, softness, hardness, a carved effect, and the like, and where it is firmly established that these qualities resulted from the shading; (b) those in which an object with indefinite outline form is seen with finely differentiated texture effects, as in a piece of brocade where the differentiation applies to the texture effect itself, even though the outline form is vague or indefinite. *Fc* is also scored when fine differentiations in the shading are used to specify parts of definite objects. Seven examples illustrate these types of responses:

CARD I

A woman wearing a transparent skirt. She might be a dancer from the way her feet are placed. (Inq.) You can see her from the waist down, here in the center. You can see her hips and thighs through the skirt.

---

* *Fc* and *FK* responses are characterized by the use of both definite outline form and finely observed surface or vista qualities. Definite outline form is also used in *Fk* responses, but in these responses the shading is used in an unspecific way.

COMMENT: This response indicates a transparency effect with no suggestion of distance between surfaces, and it is therefore scored *Fc*. This can serve as the main score, since the other determinant, *M*, is much less emphasized.

CARD IV

A bearskin rug spread out in front of the fireplace, and here are the forefeet and hind feet. (Q. What made it seem like a bearskin?) It looks thick, like thick fur. It has a pile—a feeling that it would change form under your hand.

COMMENT: Here the animal skin with feet specified is an object of definite shape; the texture is also differentiated; hence the score is *Fc*.

CARD VI

This looks like a brass post. (*Location:* part of D_3) (Inq.) It looks as though it is so highly polished that light is reflected off it.

COMMENT: The highlight on a highly polished surface or a smooth glossy impression is scored *Fc*.

CARD VI

Red, yellow, and purple butterfly. (*Location:* D_5) (Inq.) The different shades look like the different colors.

COMMENT: The shading has been interpreted as representing bright colors used in a differentiated way. The score is *Fc*.

CARD VI

This might seem funny, but you know what it suggests to me? A watermelon (lower center section) cut in two and here are the seeds.

COMMENT: The fine differentiations in shading have been used to specify the parts of the object. The score is *Fc*.

CARD VIII

It looks like little snakeskins. (*Location:* D_4). This is the design on the back. (Inq.) It was the design in the shading and the frayed edge that made me think of a snakeskin. Not the color. It is opened out, flat, ready for use.

COMMENT: Emphasis on differentiated texture is scored *Fc* even though the object has a vague shape.

CARD X

Organ pipe roughly speaking. (Inq.) It's round—has shading and light in the front. (*Location:* D_{14})

COMMENT: The emphasis is on the rounded effect given by the shading, hence the score *Fc*.

2. *cF and c*, or *undifferentiated surface or texture scores,* are assigned under these circumstances: *cF* is used to score responses in which the object seen has semidefinite form and in which the surface effect itself is not highly differentiated. It must be established that the shading contributed to the surface emphasis. A *c* score is used for responses in which there is complete disregard for outline, and shading is used in an undifferentiated way. The use of shading in this way is rare. Examples of *cF* and *c* responses follow:

CARD IV
I just respond to it in terms of a touching quality. I know I should try to make something of it (whole). (Inq.) Would like to touch it, it's soft and maybe spongy.

> COMMENT: This is an example of an undifferentiated shading response, with no regard for form. It is scored *c*.

CARD VI
The whole formation reminds me of rocks. (Inq.) It was the way it was shaded. (Q. How did the shading make it seem like rock?) It made it look rough.

> COMMENT: Here the object is of semidefinite form and the shading contributed to a surface or texture effect, which is not itself differentiated. The score is *cF*.

CARD VIII
In a way it looks like snow over a bank, soft and fluffy. (*Location:* D_7)

> COMMENT: The score is *cF* because some form is implied.

Vista, Depth, and Diffusion Responses: FK, KF, and K

1. *FK*, or *differentiated vista or depth,* is the score for all vistas. Score *FK* when the shading is used to suggest distance between two or more objects. The lighter and darker shades of gray indicate different distances from the eye of the observer. Depending on the imagined illumination, either the lighter or the darker shades may seem farther away. Examples of *FK* responses follow:

CARD I
This little hole in the middle looks like a knothole that you look through in a fence to see the construction going on. (Inq.) I can about make out the foundation of a building in the wide open space beyond it.

> COMMENT: *FK* is scored for a vista seen through holes or archways, or seen through an entrance to a cave, with a three-dimensional effect that can be attributed to shading.

CARD II

A circular staircase. (*Location:* top red portion) (Inq.) It is a balustrade on a staircase winding upwards. The shading gives the impression of winding.

> COMMENT: Shading is mentioned as the basis for the architectural vista, occurring in an area that has sufficient differentiation of shading to make this plausible, even though it is a chromatic area. The effect of distance is quite clearly due to the shading.

CARD V

As if I'm up in the air I see a landscape down below; and this (white around figure) would be water, and land there and water around, having docks coming out; I can visualize that. (Inq.) You see sand bars under water on both sides.

> COMMENT: This differentiated aerial view is scored *FK*.

CARD IX

It could be an animal here, the head here is just perfect, and he is on the edge of the pond—and he is looking into the water. It looks blurry here, as though reflected. (*Location:* D_3)

> COMMENT: This is a reflected vista where the water is not merely a device to explain the symmetry of the blot.

2. *KF and K*, or *undifferentiated depth or diffusion scores: KF* and *K* are used to score diffusion responses, *KF* for concepts with semidefinite form, and *K* for responses with indefinite form. The criterion of diffusion is that "one could put a knife through it without separating it." This kind of response implies the use of the shading qualities of the blot to describe unorganized, space-filling diffuse substances, such as fog, mist, or smoke. Examples follow:

CARD II

Thick smoke, sort of in a spiral—might have been a heavy oil fire (whole). (Inq.) The smoke looks thick.

> COMMENT: The "spiral" gives enough form to the concept to make the score *KF* rather than *K*.

CARD V

I get the suggestion of darkness, a dark room. (Inq.) It's sort of a three-dimensional effect.

> COMMENT: The space-filling "darkness" is scored *K*.

CARD VI

Here we have a summer's night with northern lights flickering in the sky. And low-lying land on the horizon. The whole thing is reflected.

(Q. What about the card gave the impression of northern lights?) The dark sky here, and this irregular band of lighter shading.

    COMMENT: The differentiation of the landscape warrants a main *FK* score, but the space-filling quality of the "northern lights" should receive an additional *K*.

CARD VII

Clouds in the sky (whole). (Q. What about it made them seem like clouds?) The outline is not distinct. There is depth and thickness and light.

    COMMENT: Although these clouds are vaguely shaped there is some form involved, and the response is scored *KF*.

CARD IX

A mist. (*Location:* central portion of card, a *dr* location) (Inq.) A mist, probably a fine morning mist like you see in the country. It may be clearing.

    COMMENT: The shading has been used for a diffusion response with no form, and is therefore scored *K*.

Three-Dimensional Effect Projected on Two-Dimensional Plane: Fk, kF, and k

Fk, kF, and *k* are scores assigned to two chief kinds of responses: X-ray pictures and topographical maps. Score *Fk* when the form is definite, *kF* when the form is semidefinite, and *k* when the form is disregarded. The shading is used in a vague or unspecific way in the *Fk, kF,* and *k* responses. Samples follow:

CARD I

Some parts look like it might be part of a map. (Inq.) Ocean here, kind you see in geography books. Perhaps they resemble the topographical maps.

    COMMENT: Since no particular country or area was mentioned, this topographical map is scored *kF*.

CARD I

This is faintly reminiscent of an X ray. Dark seen through a lighter surface. (*Location:* lower center portion) (Inq.) The bones are showing through.

    COMMENT: This response is scored *kF* because there is no specific area mentioned.

CARD IV

Looks like the state of Maine with mountains and terrain. (Inq.) It is like a map of Maine showing mountains and valley. I'm not sure of the name, it has a special name.

> COMMENT: A topographical map of a specific area is scored *Fk*.

CARD IV

Spots on lungs, chest area. (Inq.) Looks like X ray showing spots in the lungs. There is a lack of clarity. (*Location:* inner portion between *D*, and d_1 below d_2)

> COMMENT: Since the X ray is of a specific part of the anatomy with definite shape, the score is *Fk*.

CARD IV

Just looks like an X ray because of the difference in shading here *(di)*.

> COMMENT: Since no particular form is mentioned, the score is *k*.

Color Responses: *C* and *C'*

Color responses include concepts in which the subject uses the color of the blot material. There are two main classes of color responses: *chromatic,* or *C,* in which colors, such as red, brown, green and yellow are used, and *achromatic,* or *C',* in which elements of the blot—black, gray, and white—are used as colors.

Chromatic Color Responses: FC, CF, and C

FC is scored when a concept combines color with definite form. *CF* is scored when the concept combines color with semidefinite form. *C* is scored when the form is disregarded entirely. Each of these scores has three variations which are significant because of different interpretative hypotheses attached to each. The variations will be discussed below under each scoring category.

FC Responses (including its variations: F↔C, F / C, and FC$_{sym}$): *FC,* or *form-color score,* is used to score responses in which the color employed is that of the object in its natural state. Three criteria must be met before *FC* can be scored: (1) The object (or person, animal, plant, article of clothing, etc.), must be of definite form. (2) The color must be "used" in the concept. (3) The color used must be the natural color of the creature or object (that is, an object of that kind could be found in that color in its natural or usual state). Three examples of *FC* responses follow:

CARD IX

Beautiful green ball dress. (Inq.) Lovely green evening dress lying ready to be worn, skirt spread so it won't get crushed.

> COMMENT: An evening dress has a definite shape and can, of course, be green.

CARD IX

The green blots give me a feeling of horses, china ones. (Inq.) They are jade green china. Here is the eye and here are the ears and the nose (included "moose's head") . Here is the rest of the body.

> COMMENT: Since the horses are not real but china horses, they could very well be green, and so are scored *FC*.

CARD X

I can see several flowers. The yellow ones look like gladiolas. (*Location:* D_{15})

> COMMENT: The specification of "gladiolas," which have a definite shape, warrants an *FC* score.

$F \leftrightarrow C$, or *forced FC*, is the score used for responses in which the object is of definite form and the color is used in a forced way. The specific color on the blot is not the natural or usual color of the object; the subject "forces" the use of color, as in the following responses:

CARD II

Two red seals. (*Location:* D_2) (Q. Did you mean them as red seals or did you just mean that you were using the red part of the blot?) I meant red seals. They are artificially colored. They are red and they are seals.

> COMMENT: Because the subject apparently feels constrained to use the color, he is forced to explain the redness of the seals.

CARD VIII

A red rat on each side. (Inq.) It has a head like a rat. No tail or whiskers but the shape of the body and legs. Ears and pointed noses like rats. (Q. When you said they were red rats did you mean just that, or did you mean that you were using the red areas for the rats?) They are rats and they are red. It's like the purple cow. You never hope to see one.

F/C, or *arbitrary FC,* is scored when the color is used merely to mark off subdivisions in an object of definite form. The particular color is immaterial; any color would serve equally well. There are two chief concepts in which arbitrary use of color enters: (1) colored maps, and (2) medical charts. F/C is not a common scoring classification, since it is unusual to find this arbitrary use of color for an object of definite form; C/F is more common. (See page 8.) Examples of F/C responses follow:

CARD VIII

Looks like the frame of the body—the chest, the stomach, the ribs and the tubes running into the lungs. (*Location:* whole blot with the exception of D_1) (Inq.) Body not actually constructed that way. The color—very often in anatomy books.

> COMMENT: Since specific organs of the body were specified, this response is scored F/C.

CARD X

This in the center looks like the perfect map drawing of two shore lines of two countries with what looks like a bridge between them. (*Location:* D_{17}) (Inq.) Looks like the west shore of South America. Here is Peru and Chile. (Q. What about the blot gave you this impression?) The color. It is the color they put on maps for contrast.

> COMMENT: The mention of definite countries and the bridge makes this of definite form. This arbitrary use of color is scored F/C.

FC_{sym}, or *symbolic color*, is used to score responses in which the color is used symbolically for an object with definite form. For example:

CARD II

Looks like two disagreeable people sticking their tongues out at each other. (Q. Disagreeable?) The tongues, and the red signified disagreeableness or anger.

> COMMENTS: The score is a main M, with an additional FC_{sym}.

CARD III

This red part (center) symbolizes heartbreak. (Inq. How does the red symbolize heartbreak?) Each side has a little red heart and there is a bond between them, symbolizing that they are united in both being rejected.

> COMMENT: Red hearts alone would have been FC, but to use the colored objects of definite form in the symbolic way illustrated makes the scoring FC_{sym}.

CARD X

It looks like two women in pink nightgowns. (*Location:* D_9). (Inq.) Pink sort of symbolizes a woman.

> COMMENT: The score is FC_{sym}.

CF Responses (*including its variations:* $C{\leftrightarrow}F$, C/F, *and* C_{sym}) : **CF** or *color-form score,* $C{\leftrightarrow}F$, or *forced color-form score,* C/F, or *arbitrary color-form score,* CF_{sym} or *symbolic color-form score,* are scored in exactly the same way as are the several forms of the *FC* score, except that the *CF* score and its variations apply to objects of semidefinite form. Examples of *CF* responses follow:

CARD VIII
Some beautiful strawberry ice cream, with orange water ice and apricot down below that. (Inq.) The pink is the strawberry. The center orange is the water ice, and the rest of the orange is apricot ice cream.

> COMMENT: The subject differentiated finely with respect to the shades and matched them carefully to the concept; but since the shape is indefinite the response is scored *CF*.

CARD X
Could be a meadow (whole). (Inq.) Because it has many colors.

> COMMENT: Since no specific plant was identified, the scoring is *CF*.

CARD X
A design in pastels. (Inq.) Fresh and gay. The sort of thing you find in chintz made to freshen up a room.

> COMMENT: Design implies form semantically; but in fact the form is indefinite, and *CF* is scored.

$C{\leftrightarrow}F$ example follows:

CARD VIII
Colored rock. (*Location:* D_2) it is hard, smooth, slightly bumpy. (Q. What about it made it seem like rock?) The shape, nice smooth rocks. (Q. What did you mean when you said colored rocks?) They are pink rocks. They are colored pink on the card. They are rocks and they are colored pink. Not that rocks are ever like that.

> COMMENT: The criterion for forced use of color seems to be met. It does not matter that rocks can actually be pinkish, because this subject thinks it is artificial to have them so.

C/F responses follow:

CARD VIII
Looks like inside of your body (whole). (Inq.) I saw colored pictures like that—like a stomach or your insides.

> COMMENT: The anatomical parts are vaguely specified, the response being prompted primarily by the color.

CARD IX

I think it would be more a map if I'd take it in three colors. (Inq.) The whole thing, because of the colors, and also there are inlets and shapes.

> COMMENT: No particular countries are mentioned, and the "inlets and shapes" are almost an afterthought.

CF_{sym} example follows:

CARD IX

Fire, hell, brimstone and fire. The red underneath is the fire of hell. It suggests something threatening. (Inq.) It was the whole thing.

> COMMENT: Fire is of semidefinite shape and would be scored CF, but the symbolic tone of the entire response ("the fire of hell"), is more adequately indicated by a score of CF_{sym} for the entire concept.

C Responses (including C_n, C_{des}, and C_{sym} variations): Pure color responses, C, C_n, C_{des}, and C_{sym}, have in common an emphasis on color without any implication of form; the form aspect is left indefinite. Four divisions need to be distinguished because there are different interpretative hypotheses attached to each.

C, or *crude color,* is scored when the natural color of an object (such as red for blood, or blue for sky,) is used in a stereotyped fashion. The criteria for scoring *C* are that the association between color and concept is (1) repetitive, (2) totally without form, and (3) without relationship to other concepts on the card. Note this example:

CARD II

This red part on top is blood.

CARD III

Here's more blood, here, and here and here (red D's).

> COMMENT: The stereotyped, repeated association of red with blood to both cards, together with the omission of other responses to these cards, fulfills the requirements of a C score.

C_n, or *color naming,* is the score used when the response to color is to name the various colors or hues in the card. Three criteria should be met before color naming is scored C_n: (1) There must be evidence that the subject feels that color naming is an adequate way of handling the material. (2) He must say that it is a response and not merely a remark. (3) He must fail to follow the color naming with an adequate response. An example of C_n follows:

CARD VIII
There are a lot of bright colors here, red, blue, pink, and orange. (Inq.) Here's red, pink, blue, orange. (Q. Is this what you see in the card?) Yes, I see just the colors, nothing else.

CARD X
What a lot of colors, pink and blue and yellow and green. That's all. (Inq.) Pink, green, blue, yellow, gold, brown, gray, just about every color I can think of.

COMMENT: This subject obviously shows a tendency to name the colors.

C_{des}, or *color description,* is scored when the subject describes the colors appearing in the card, usually specifying the artistic quality of the colors. Do not score C_{des} unless it is established that the subject means it as a response, not a remark, and that this response is not an elaboration to a response already scored *FC* or *CF*. An example follows:

CARD IX
Green in the center runs into the orange on top and blends with the pink below. A water color exercise, perhaps. (Inq.) They all blend and fuse in the center but spread out and are thinned with the white.

COMMENT: The color description is emphasized by the elaboration in the inquiry.

C_{sym}, or *color symbolism,* is the score assigned when the subject uses the color to represent an abstract idea such as evil, youth, gaiety. These ideas must completely disregard form, as in these examples:

CARD X
What a happy picture. The colors of springtime and rebirth. (Inq.) Starting with the gray remains of last year, everything becomes alive again and there is the rosy tint of renewed hope.

COMMENT: This is clearly formless, the colors being used in a symbolic manner.

CARD X
—And there's green on the bottom, sort of signifies envy.

COMMENT: The color has been used to symbolize an emotion.

Achromatic Color Responses: FC', C'F, and C'

The *achromatic* color responses are those in which the subject uses the achromatic elements—the gray, black, or white of the cards—as color in the formation of his concepts. Three divisions of achromatic responses are made, according to the now familiar principle of degree of definiteness of form in the concept: (1) *FC'* when an object of definite form is designated as black, white, or gray; (2) *C'F* when an object of semidefinite or vague form is designated as black, white, or gray; (3) *C'* something with no form is designated as gray, white, or black. Examples follow:

FC' Examples

CARD I
A black and white butterfly (whole). (Inq.) It's black and white, the way you see sometimes. The head's about here.

COMMENT: Since achromatic color was stressed both in the response and the inquiry, the score is *FC'*.

CARD VII
Gray toy terriers. (Inq.) They're the color of terriers and the faces are shaped like some I've seen.

COMMENT: Achromatic color is here the sole determinant, integrated with definite form. The score is *FC'*.

C'F Examples

CARD I
I'll call it a thundercloud. (Inq.) It's so black, like thunder.

COMMENT: An object of vague form which is designated as black (or white, or gray) is scored *C'F*.

C' Examples

CARD IV
Cloudlike, a storm. (Inq.) Just the general effect of a storm because of the black and dark gray.

COMMENT: There is no form, the achromatic quality of the blot being the basis for the response.

Rules of Precedence for Assigning of Determinant Scores

It has already been stated that a response given during the performance proper can be assigned only *one main* location score, *one main* determinant score, *one main* content score, and *one main P–O* score. In many instances, however, more than one determinant contributes to the production of the concept—-as, for example, in this response to Card IX: "Two witches dressed in orange costumes preparing a brew." It then becomes necessary to decide which determinant should be assigned the main score.* The following rules apply:

1.   Score as the main determinant that which is clearly given most emphasis by the subject in his description and in his elaboration of the response.

2.   A determinant mentioned or clearly implied in the performance proper is considered more important than a determinant that does not emerge until the inquiry; and therefore, the main score should be given to the determinant mentioned in the performance proper.

3.   If two or more determinants are mentioned in the performance proper, and both or all seem of equal importance, the following rules of precedence serve in selecting the main determinant score:

   a.   Precedence is given to human movement (M) unless it is very reluctant, repressed, or minor, in which case it would in any event be given an additional rather than a main determinant score.

   b.   Precedence is given to color responses $(FC, CF,$ or $C)$ over every determinant except human movement (M).

   c.   Precedence is given to differentiated texture responses (e.g., Fc) over every determinant except human movement and color.

Scoring for Content

There are so many possible classifications for the content of responses to Rorschach blots that scoring for content could be a very complex matter. Despite the importance of content for interpretation, the quantitative aspects of content analysis have not been developed to such a point that a more detailed scoring system seems warranted.

The more usual scoring categories for content are listed below, together with examples. A quantitative evaluation of these usual scoring categories serves as a yardstick for the narrowness or spread of the subject's interests as expressed in his content choices. Concepts that do not fall within these categories are recorded by adding such categories as the content itself dictates, "death," "explosion," "fire," and the like.

---

* Examples of responses scored with multiple determinants are in the section "Scoring Examples," pages 105–19. See responses numbered 1, 5, 9, 10, 14, 35, 47, 48, and 50.

H, human figures, whole or almost whole.

CARD I
This is a woman standing with hands raised and feet together. (Inq.) Seen from the back, can't see her head, hands up.

CARD V
Lady at a costume ball dressed as some insect (whole). (Inq.) Burdened, a Carmen Miranda sort of thing, velvety fluff, arms out.

(H), human figures portrayed as drawings, sculpture, caricatures, and the like, or mythological figures such as ghosts, monsters, witches. The symbol *(H)* is used to indicate that the human figure is remote from reality in some manner.

CARD II
Could be a statue depicting a toast. (Inq.) Putting thin glasses up together.

CARD III
Two little puppets on strings. (Inq.) String, tongue sticking out already, feet suspended from strings, not real human quality.

CARD IX
Witches engaged in some kind of potent activity.

Hd, parts of human figures which can be thought of as belonging to a living body (that is, not anatomical).

CARD IV
A foot upraised. (Inq.) A dance movement.

CARD V
Man's head.

(Hd), parts of human figures portrayed in drawings, caricatures, sculpture, and the like, or parts of mythological human figures.

CARD I
Here is the finger of scorn. (*Location:* top portion of side detail)

CARD II
These two pieces (*Location:* outside halves of the gray portions) are like ship's figureheads seen sideways. A thrust out look of the chest and chin.

AH, figures that are part human and part animal, such as "Pan— half-goat, half-man."

CARD III

Two people bending over ground or something. Really looks like half people and half animal. (Inq.) Well, the top part looks like a person, but the bottom looks more like an animal's hoof.

H_{obj}, objects that are closely associated with the human, such as false teeth.

CARD X

Tooth in center. (*Location:* D_7) . (Inq.) I've had two teeth pulled recently.

At, parts of the human body, or concepts dealing with the human body in the anatomical sense (except sex organs) .

CARD VII

Looks like a dissection; parts of intestines. (Inq.) A lot of organs vaguely connected with bits of bone and nerve in the middle.

CARD VIII

Ribs. (*Location:* D_5) Looks like an X ray of human ribs.

Sex, sexual organs or sexual activity, or anatomical concepts (such as pelvis) with reference to their sexual function.

CARD I

A penis. (Inq.) Whole central area, no, maybe just this. (*Location:* D_3)

CARD I

The female pelvic area. (Inq.) I used it all except for these (side ear-like projections) . It is three-dimensional. It seemed like something in a medical book, or an X ray. Vertebrae and bones around the pelvis.

CARD IV

Like breasts. Here is the nipple. (*Location:* shaded area in upper part of D_2)

A, animal figures, whole or almost whole.

CARD II

Double bear. (Inq.) Kinky black bear with no head, shaggy bear.

CARD VII

Scottie dogs sniffing head of larger dog, noses touching (whole) . (Inq.) Looks like Scottie, square face, short tail, and legs.

(*A*) , mythological animals; monsters with animal characteristics; caricatures, drawings, or the like of animal figures. The symbol (*A*) is generally used when the animal figure is either remote from reality or is humanized.

CARD I
Some kind of mythical animal with animal shape and wings. (Inq.) Head down, maybe grazing; head, wings, haunches of some kind of bull.

CARD X
Green worms with high aspirations considering idealistic matters. (Inq.) Looking high up and reading.

Ad, parts of animals, usually a head or paw.

CARD VI
Cat's whiskers but no cat, just whiskers.

CARD VIII
Head of a lamb.

(Ad), parts of animals deprived of reality, or humanized.

CARD IV
Head of an animal, dragon or something, a strange dragon with a crown. (Inq.) Dragon with eyes, eyelashes, ears, whiskers, nostrils, snout, crowned king.

A_{obj}, objects derived from, or connected with, the body of an animal. These objects serve some decorative or practical function, or are in a stage of preparation to do so.

CARD VI
Skin of a creature that's been nailed up on a wall, like skin of a raccoon; fur markings and striped fur (whole). (Inq.)

CARD X
A gold turkey wishbone. (Inq.) It was the shape. (*Location:* D_{12})

A.At, animal anatomy concepts, including dissections: X ray of an animal, biological charts, and so on.

CARD I
Looks like the bone from an animal (whole, space). (Inq.) Like a bone you would see in a biology book. Like a skeleton.

Food, animal parts, fruits, or vegetables prepared for eating (classified as food, rather than as animal objects, A_{obj}, or as plants, Pl).

CARD VI
A piece of moldy bread. (Inq.) Shading—mold forming on bread mass.

CARD IX
Sea food—can see in restaurants, with claws. (Inq.) Lobsters—claws and color—may not have nails like that.

N, nature concepts, including landscapes, aerial views, sunsets, rivers, and lakes when they are part of scenery.

CARD VI
A crevasse in the ice. A deep crevasse with water at the bottom.

CARD X
This looks like a garden scene, and off there in the distance is something that looks like a tower.

Geo, geographical concepts, including maps of all kinds, and such concepts as islands, gulfs, lakes, and rivers, not seen in vista or as part of a landscape.

CARD VIII
This top portion looks like a mountain peak. (Inq.) The shape looks like it. Looks like a topological drawing.

Pl, plants of all kinds and parts of plants.

CARD X
This part looks like an autumn leaf. (*Location:* D_{10}) (Inq.) Oh, because of the way it looks and the color.

Bot, plants or parts of plants seen as botanical specimens—for instance, as a botanical display or as a botanical chart.

CARD X
This could also be a colored chart of some kind—of botany, probably.

Obj, all manmade objects; distinguished from statues, which are scored (*H*) if of humans, or (*A*) if of animals or animal-shaped ornaments.

CARD IV
Seven-league boots—old-fashioned boots.

CARD IX
Some sort of sundial that you might see in a garden.

Arch, architectural concepts.

CARD I
Looks like fantastic gargoyles on a fifteenth-century building.

CARD X
This thing on top could be the Eiffel Tower.

Art, concepts such as designs, or drawings, or paintings, in which the drawing or painting has no specific content. A drawing of a human figure would be scored (H), a painting of a landscape would be scored N, and so on.

CARD IX
This is a water-color exercise, perhaps.

Abs, abstract concepts in which there is no other specific content. A specific content symbolizing something abstract would be scored for content and the subscript *sym* would be added to it.

CARD VII
All I get here is a feeling of disintegration, of things falling apart.

CARD VIII
Actively enclosing and protecting quality about the top. (Inq.) Comes down over other structures, coming down over.

Scoring for Popular and Original Responses

Requirements for popular and original scores are given below. It should be noted that many responses are assigned neither a P nor an O score, being neither common enough to be "popular" nor unusual enough to be scored "original."

Popular Responses: *P*

P, or *popular responses,* are those responses given frequently to a particular blot area. In this scoring system only *ten* responses are scored as popular. These have proved to have universal popularity in different cultures and age groups. In addition, the degree of popularity of any response that is popular only in a specific group of subjects can be ascertained through simple statistics. The ten universally popular responses are listed below, together with examples. (Note that Cards IV, VII, and IX have no universally popular responses.)

1. *Card I* (whole, *W*, or cut-off whole, *W̶*) : Any creature with the body in center *D* and wings at the side. The creature may be seen stationary or in action. Two examples follow:

A butterfly. (Inq.) It looks as if it's flying. Here are the wings (side *D*'s), the body (center *D*), and these could be the antenna, I guess (top *d*'s).
    Score: W   FM   A   P

A big bat, maybe. (Inq.) Well, without these and these (d_3, d_4, d_7) it could be a bat. The wings here, and here's the head, and here's the body.
    Score: W   F   A   P

2. *Card II* (black area, either as a *W* or a *D*) : Any whole animal or part of an animal of the dog, bear, rabbit, or bull variety seen in the black area, with or without center *d*. Sometimes the texture quality of the skin is used, as in the first of the two examples cited here.

Two little bears with noses together. (Inq.) Little paws, noses up, texture of fur.
    Score: W̶   FM,Fc   A   P

Looks like the heads of two Scottie dogs. (Inq.) Just the head—here's the nose, the ears.
    Score: D   F   Ad   P

3. *Card III* (entire black area) : Two human beings, or animals dressed as humans, with legs seen in side bottom area. The figures must be seen in action. For example:

Looks like two men holding a package and putting it down.
    Score: W̶   M   H   P

Two kangaroos dressed as butlers carrying trays.
    Score: W̶   M   (A)   P

4. *Card III* (center red area, D_1) : Bow tie, hair ribbon, or butterfly. The color may or may not be used.

Butterfly in center, wings, and body. (Inq.) Just the shape, that's all.
    Score: D   F   A   P

This looks like a big red bow or a bow tie in the middle. (Inq.) The shape and the color.

    Score: *D*   *FC*   *Obj*   *P*

5. *Card V* (whole area) : Any winged creature with body in center *D* and wings at the side. The card may be held right-side up or upside down. The creature may be seen in action or stationary. Note these examples:

A bat. (Inq.) Wings outstretched, ears, can't tell which side it's facing.

    Score: *W*   *F*   *A*   *P*

Insect with antenna flying with back to us. It's got long legs. (Inq.) Wings out, flying.

    Score: *W*   *FM*   *A*   *P*

This could be a butterfly and it's flying. (Inq.) Without these (side extensions) it's the shape of one.

    Score: *W*   *$\overline{FM}$*   *A*   *P*

6. *Card VI* (entire card, or entire card without top area, D_2, or lower area) : A skin of an animal where the shading is used to give the impression of furriness or skin markings. If shading is denied, only a tendency to *P* may be scored ($\rightarrow P$). Two responses scored *P* follow:

A piece of fur, a fur rug maybe. (Inq.) It's just this part (D_1). The way it's shaded, it gives the feeling of fur. (Q. . . . Shape?) It doesn't have any particular shape.

    Score: *D*   *cF*   *A_{obj}*   *P*

Skin of a creature that's been nailed up on a wall, like skin of a raccoon; fur markings and striped fur (whole) . (Inq.) The head's on top and it's got the kind of markings.

    Score: *W*   *Fc*   *A_{obj}*   *P*

7. *Card VIII* (outer pink area, D_1) : Any kind of four-legged animal in any kind of motion. A fish or bird to this area is scored as a tendency to *P* ($\rightarrow P$). Three illustrations follow:

These two look like beavers. (Inq.) The way they're shaped, here's the head, and they're climbing.

    Score: *D*   *FM*   *A*   *P*

Here are two animals, they're part of a coat of arms (the usual animals).
     Score: D→W   F   A→P

A fish—the long body and fins.
     Score: D   F   A→P

  8.   *Card* X (outer blue, D_1) : Any many-legged animal, such as a spider, an octopus, or a crab (as in the following response) :

Crabs. (Inq.) The shape and the appendages.
     Score: D   F   A   P

  9.   *Card* X (center green, D_2, with or without the light green area, D_7) : Any elongated greenish animal, such as a caterpillar or garden snake. The color must be used. For example:

These could be tobacco worms in here. (Inq.) Both the shape and the color make it look like that (D_2).
     Score: D   FC   A   P

Down here it looks like a couple of caterpillars on a leaf. (Inq.) Well, these are the color of caterpillars, and the shape too. They could be eating the leaf (D_2 and D_7).
     Score: D   FC,FM   A   P

  10.   *Card* X (light green area, D_7) : The head of an animal with long ears or horns. (Any addition, such as the darker green D's seen as something coming out of the eyes, or the white space as the body, forms an original element to be scored as an additional original.) An example of a *P* response to this card follows:

This part in here is a rabbit's head. (Inq.) Just this light green part— here are the ears and the nose.
     Score: D   F   Ad   P

Original Responses: *O* and *O*−

  O, or *original responses,* are those responses given by not more than one subject out of 100 to a particular blot area. If an original concept is not a good fit, but is so distorted as to produce bizarreness, it is scored by the symbol *O*−. The recognition of original responses is a matter of experience which may be obtained by using the Rorschach with a wide variety of subjects, or by extensive reading of published protocols. Beginners are not equipped to score properly original responses. Three examples of O responses and three examples of $O-$ responses will be cited here.*

O Responses

CARD II

Monkeys in the zoo. (Inq.) Just their red behinds, ugly sort of thing (D_1).

Score: D   FC   Ad   O

CARD III

A bagpipe. (Inq.) Tube, windbag, shape (D_2).

Score: D   F   Obj   O

CARD V

Looks like Mephistopheles with horns and feet ensconced in a flowing cape (whole). (Inq.) Horns, back of his head, feet, arms holding out huge cape.

Score: W   M   (H)   O

O— Responses

CARD VI

A turtle with lots of heads (D_1). (Inq.) A dead turtle with lots of heads, shell may be folded over—no.

Score: D   F—   A   O—

CARD VIII

It might be a man (D_3) swimming under water and the frogs are shaking hands with him. (Frogs are D.) (Inq.) It looks like he's swimming in the water. I didn't notice any head.

Score: D   M   H   O—

CARD X

This down here is a princess, queen, has a crown on and long gown. She has four legs (one side of lower green D; four legs are four tiny projections at bottom).

Score: D   M   H   O—

---

* Most often, original contributions are not totally original responses; they are original elaborations or specifications of more or less usual concepts. In such cases, the responses are given additional O or $O-$ scores.

Scoring for Form Level

Most subjects respond to the ink blots by trying to fit the outline or form of a blot area to a concept they see. Some subjects do this better than others, and a few may even disregard the fit. People also vary in their capacity to elaborate or specify their concepts, and in their ability to organize the various parts of the blot into a meaningful larger concept. Since the differences in ability are significant interpretatively, they are scored by assigning a rating, called the form-level rating. The form-level rating is applied to all responses, main and additional, regardless of their location, their determinant, their content, or their *P−O* scores.

The form level of the individual responses serves as the backbone of the form-level rating but is significant in merely indicating a capacity for doing things in a certain way, which may or may not be reflected in the routine intellectual behavior of the subject. The average total form level comes closer to indicating what can be expected in actual behavior, whereas the weighted average form level is found to be closer to the subject's potential.

Form level is based on three considerations: *accuracy, specification,* and *organization.* Each response is rated on a scale from a low of −2.0 to a high of +5.0. The process involves (1) assigning a basal plus or a basal minus rating, determined primarily by the accuracy of the fit, and (2) *adding* to the basal rating in units of 0.5 for good elaborations or specifications and for good organization, or *subtracting* from the basal rating in units of 0.5 for poor or inaccurate specifications and for organization that weakens the concept.

Three significant levels of form quality are rated: (1) Concepts considered adequate or better are assigned plus ratings of 1.0 or higher. (2) Concepts considered indifferent are assigned 0.0 and 0.5 ratings. (3) Concepts considered poor or inaccurate are assigned the minus ratings of −0.5 to −2.0.

The meanings of accuracy, specification, and organization, and the criteria for assigning the basal ratings, are briefly discussed below.

Accuracy

Accuracy applies to the fit or match of concept to the blot area in terms of outline, shape, or form. There are three levels of accuracy:

1. *Accurate responses* provide concepts that fit the area, as "butterfly" to D_1 of Card III, or "witch" to D_2 of Card IX.

2. *Semidefinite or indefinite responses* refer to objects that are vague or variable in shape—for instance, "clouds" to Card VII, or "flower" to the whole of Card IX.

3. *Inaccurate responses* are those in which the concept is definite in form but refers to a blot area of dissimilar form, as "house" to the whole of Card VII, or "snake" to the whole of Card IV. Another example would be "sunset clouds" to D_1 of Card VIII. Although the subject uses an indefinite concept, he applies it to an area of such definite shape that the match must be considered inaccurate.

Specification

Specification applies to the way a subject elaborates or describes the concept seen. If the elaborations fit the structure of the blot area, they improve the concept; if they do not, they spoil the concept. There are three levels of specifications:

1. *Constructive specifications* are elaborations of the concept that match the particular structure of the blot area, for example, adding whiskers on a cat, or specifying detailed facial features, or specifying accurately certain qualities of the movement, shading, and color aspects of the blot. Three examples follow— (a) constructive movement specification, (b) constructive color specification, and (c) constructive shading specification.

CARD IV
A man riding a motorcycle. It's out of focus, as if you're looking up at him from in front of him and from below.

> COMMENT: To specify that the frequently seen man is "riding a motorcycle" improves the match of concept to blot. Therefore, two criteria for constructive movement specification are met: (1) that the movement must be within the context of definite form, and (2) that the elaboration be justified by the structural qualities of the blot.

CARD X
Two parakeets. (*Location:* D_{13}) (Inq.) Because they are green. Parrots aren't always green.

> COMMENT: The color is an essential component of the concept named and is more specific than a response such as "bird" would have been.

CARD VI

A polished walnut bedpost. Walnut because it is dark, polished because of the highlight. (*Location:* D_3)

    COMMENT: There are two constructive specifications, "polished" combining form and shading, and "walnut" combining form and achromatic color, both being essential to the total concept "polished walnut bedpost."

2. *Irrelevant specifications* are those verbalizations by the subject which neither add to nor detract from the accuracy of the match of concept to blot. For instance, seeing men bowing in Card III and then saying, "their backs are bent over," does not improve the concept.

3. *Destructive specifications* are those verbalizations that weaken or destroy the form level of the concept. For instance, seeing legs in both the lower and side extensions of the bat in Card V, or saying that the caterpillars of the lower green in Card X are coming out of the eyes of the rabbit, spoils the two otherwise popular concepts.

Organization

Organization applies to the procedure used by a subject to tie together the various parts of the blot into a meaningful larger concept. For example, in this response to Card I, "Two people dancing around a Maypole," the two large side areas are brought into a more meaningful relationship with the center area. Sometimes a subject tries to organize the blot material and in so doing *weakens* the form level, as in the $O-$ example previously mentioned in which the man swimming underwater shakes hands with frogs.

Assigning a Basal Rating

There are seven basal ratings: 1.5, 1.0, 0.5, 0.0, −1.00, −1.5, −2.0. Each may be raised or lowered in units of 0.5, depending upon whether the concept is elaborated and organized well or poorly.

Basal Rating of 1.0

A form-level rating of 1.0 is the key rating and therefore will be considered first. Concepts that are definite in shape and fit the blot area are assigned a basal rating of 1.0. These include the ten popular responses and all the near-popular responses—such as "butterfly" to the lower center detail (D_1) in Card II, or the two bugs in the upper gray area (D_3) in Card X. Here are examples of responses assigned a basal rating of 1.0.

Card I:	Hands (upper center projections d_3) .
Card II:	Butterfly (lower red D) .
Card III:	Crab, spider, or stomach (bottom center D) ; lungs (center red D) .
Card IV:	Animal's head (bottom center D) ; boots (lower, outer D's) .
Card V:	A woman's leg (side projection d_2) .
Card VI:	Butterfly (top D) .
Card IX:	Animal's head (shaded brown-green D_3) .
Card X:	Animal (lower outer gray D) ; two bugs (upper center gray D) .
Any Card:	Butterfly (any area with central narrow, smaller "body" and symmetrical "wings" on each side; the wings alone can fulfill the basic requirements for a definite concept) . Animal (any area with a reasonable shape for body, head, and legs) . Fish (any long, narrow area) . Tree (any area with a narrow projection for a trunk with a larger spread above for the rest of the tree) .

Basal Rating of 1.5

This rating is assigned to concepts in which there is more definiteness of form than in the 1.0 concepts. For example, seeing a human profile or a human figure, or a specific animal figure would receive a 1.5 basal rating. Examples of 1.5 ratings follow:

CARD I

In the middle, there's a woman standing with her arms raised. Her back is to us. (*Location:* D_1)

> *Score:* D   M   H   1.5

> COMMENT: A human figure implies a long, relatively narrow body, a head that is rounded, smaller, and above, legs appropriately placed, and possibly arms as well.

CARD II

Two Scotties looking at each other, nose, ears, paws.

> *Score:* W   FM   A   P   1.5

COMMENT: A specific animal name, such as "Scotties," implies a distinctive shape. Such increased specificity places more rigorous demands regarding basic accuracy and so warrants a higher basal rating.

CARD IX
A man's face, a profile. You can see the head, the brow, the nose, his eyes. (*Location:* D_1)

Score: D   F   Hd   1.5

COMMENT: At least four essential form characteristics are involved in the concept "profile." As a minimum, such a concept implies a nose projecting from a face which has a forehead, chin, and mouth.

Basal Rating of 0.5

The 0.5 rating is reserved for responses that are vague or semidefinite in form but in which the form is not completely neglected. Most CF, C'F, cF, KF, kF, mF and vague F responses are assigned a form-level rating of 0.5 by definition. Examples follow:

CARD II
Really conveys hardly anything at all. Slight thought of a woman's sex organ. A vague idea. (*Location:* D_1) (Q. What made it seem like a woman's sex organ?) It was suggested by the redness, indicating the breaking of the membrane. It was only a vague impression; something like you might see in medical books.

Score: D   CF   Sex   0.5

COMMENT: Although a specific organ was mentioned, it was used in a vague way; therefore, it is treated in the same way as other vague anatomical concepts, such as "internal organs."

CARD VIII
A piece of coral rock of different colors. You are looking straight down through the water at it.

Score: W   CF   N   0.5

COMMENT: Coral rock has only a semidefinite shape.

Basal Rating of 0.0

This rating is reserved for responses in which the concept is completely indefinite in form, and which are given to areas of the blot which themselves are not structured. All responses scored C, C_{des}, C_n, C_{sym}, C', c, K, k, and m are assigned the 0.0 form-level rating by definition. For example:

CARD II

Red and black blotches. What it looks like I can't describe (whole) .

Score: W C_n Abs   0.0

COMMENT: The basal rating is 0.0 by definition, since the scoring for this response would be C_n.

CARD VII

Black smoke. (Inq.) (whole) The differences in the coloring make it seem like smoke.

Score: W   K,C'   Smoke   0.0

COMMENT: The scoring for this response would be K for the smoke, the principal concept, with an additional C' for the "black." The basal rating is therefore 0.0.

Basal Ratings of −1.0, −1.5, and −2.0

These ratings are assigned as follows: *A basal rating of −1.0* is given to a concept in which the subject makes some effort to reconcile the concept with the shape of the blot area used, but fails to meet the minimum requirements of accuracy. *A basal rating of −1.5* is reserved for responses in which a concept that would fit just one detail of a blot is assigned to the total blot area without any regard for the discrepancies between the form qualities of the blot area and the concept. *A basal rating of −2.0* is given when the response implies a definite concept, the form qualities of which obviously do not fit the blot area chosen; this choice clearly implies bizarre thinking. In the examples that follow, note that whenever a minus form-level rating is assigned, a minus sign is also assigned with the determinant score.

CARD I

You could say the whole shape might be someone sitting down with his arms out. (Inq.) These side things are the arms. It is just an impression.

Score: W   M−   H   Add. O−   −1.0

COMMENT: There is basic inaccuracy in the match of concept to blot, in spite of the attempt to reconcile the fit by pointing out the arms.

CARD IV
A snake. (Inq.) (whole, vaguely) (Q. What about it made it seem like
a snake?) Here is the head and neck (left side projection). (Q. Did
you use this [pointing to main part of blot]?) That's the rest of the
snake.

Score: dW   F−   A   O−   −1.5

COMMENT: This is a typical confabulatory response: a generalization from one clearly seen detail to the whole blot. It therefore
receives a basal rating of −1.5 and an additional O− because of
the unusual organization.

CARD IV
The upper part is quite hard to describe—a combination of all nationalities—a pretty good representation of a clock that tells the time
of all lands—Berlin, Paris, Genoa. I don't know what that fourth is.

Score: dr   F−   Obj   O−   −2.0

COMMENT: This response is a contamination; the area is frequently seen as a face, but has apparently become associated with
the face of a clock, and irrationally leads to the generalization "a
combination of all nationalities." The form-level rating is therefore −2.0, and the concept is a bizarre original.

A Rating of −0.5

Note that −0.5 is not considered a basal rating. A −0.5 rating can result if a subject receives a basal rating of 1.5 or 1.0 for his concept and
then weakens it by inaccurate specification. A rating of −0.5 is con-
ventionally assigned to such spoiled concepts, because the ratings 0.0
and 0.5 are reserved for semidefinite and indefinite concepts. A −0.5
rating is also possible for indefinite concepts such as "blood" or "fire"
when they are given to areas of very definite shape, such as the center
red *D* in Card III, or the side pink areas in Card VIII. Examples of responses scored as −0.5 follow:

CARD VIII
A sunset. (Inq.) It was the color. The whole thing but especially these
pink clouds (outer and lower pink portions). (Q. What about the blot
made it seem like clouds?) The color. Sunset clouds, with the sun reflected on them.

Score: W   CF−   Clouds   −0.5

COMMENT: The side pink areas are so definite in structure that the indefinite concept "clouds" represents an abuse of the structure of the blot.

CARD IX
Up further, the skull of a cow, or deer; horns, nostrils at bottom, two sets of nostrils really. (*Location:* D_3)

> *Score:*   *D,S*   *F*−   *A.At*   −0.5

COMMENT: Although the concept "skull" is adequate enough for the blot area to receive a basal rating of 1.0, the concept is weakened by the "two sets of nostrils"; thus the form-level rating is reduced to −0.5.

Adding Credits

Each constructive specification or organization adds 0.5 credit to one of the basal plus ratings (usually 1.0 or 1.5) . Sometimes credit is added to a 0.0 or 0.5 rating. The upper limit of form-level rating is 5.0. Minus ratings *cannot* be improved by constructive specifications. Five examples of adding credits follow:

CARD I
An insect of some sort. (Inq.) The whole thing. A hard black type of insect. A winged beetle. It is a stag beetle, and here are the typical "stags" (clawlike projections) . (Q. What makes it seem hard?) It has the hard modeling effect of a beetle; that's part of why I called it a stag beetle. They are hard and black like this.

> *Score:*   *W*   *Fc,FC′*   *A*   2.5

COMMENT: The basal rating for "stag beetle" is 1.5. In addition, the color and the "hardness" are also credited. Had the concept been "winged beetle" with no further elaboration, the basal rating would have been 1.0 for a popular response.

CARD II
Two little dogs, sitting up begging. Their noses are practically touching. (Inq.) Here are their paws, noses, ears, foreheads. You can't see their hind feet, but they are sitting up begging. (Q. What kind of dogs could they be?) They are terrier pups. (Q. What makes them seem like terrier pups?) They have the shape of puppies' heads and the

roundness. The shape through the noses and puppylike thick necks. (Q. Was this part of it [center D]?) It could be a little tidbit that they are both begging for.

Score: W̸ FM *Ad* *P* 3.0

COMMENT: To the basal rating of 1.0 for the popular concept was added: 0.5 for the position of "begging" including the "paws"; 0.5 for "nose," which is a particularly good match; 0.5 for "terrier pups"; 0.5 for organization (seeing the dogs in relationship). Credit was not added for either the "tidbit," which resulted from a prodding question, or for "forehead," which cannot be considered independent of "nose," or for "ears," which is a part of the "terrier pups" specification.

CARD II

A big fat white rabbit, and here are its ears. (Inq.) (*Location:* center white space plus the light gray bit above) This line suggests a heavy fold at its neck because it is so plump. Here is the tail, although it isn't really like a rabbit's tail. It is sitting down, back to us, and the light gray is the ears.

Score: S,dd FC',FM *A* *O* 2.5

COMMENT: To the basal rating of 1.5 for "rabbit," a distinctive shape, the following credits are added: 0.5 for "white," an additional essential aspect of the concept "rabbit"; 0.5 for the "plump" specification justified by the "fold," making the match more precise. Neither the "ears" nor the "tail" receive additional credit, the "ears" having been included in the basal rating, and the tail not being a good match.

CARD IV

Looks like an incision being made in flesh in the middle. Poor-looking flesh. The knife is still pulling along. (Inq.) The flesh looks soft in comparison to the hard instrument. It looks light, as when you just make an incision. It is still going on.

Score: W̸ Fm,cF,Fe *Obj,At* 1.5

COMMENT: Through constructive specification an indefinite concept has been changed to a definite one, so that the main determinant *Fm* masks the fairly undifferentiated underlying concept. This concept, "flesh," receives a basal rating of 0.5, but additional credits for the "instrument" and the motion attributed to it raise the final form-level rating to 1.5.

CARD V

Two cobras just sizing each other up, or courting maybe. (*Location: d_1, card inverted*) The suspended motion that snakes have, swaying. (Q. What about them made them seem like cobras especially?) That is the way cobras behave.

> *Score:*   *d*   *FM*   *A*   2.0

COMMENT: The basal level is 1.0, "cobra" implying no more definite shape than "snake." The additional credits were given for each of the elements of movement and organization.

Subtracting Credits

Each specification that weakens a concept, or any strange organizational element, subtracts 0.5 from the basal plus rating of 1.5. A 1.5 form-level rating thus may be lowered to 1.0. Note, however, that a +1.0 rating automatically becomes a −0.5 if lowered by an inaccurate specification. Indefinite concepts receiving ratings of 0.5 or 0.0 usually cannot become inaccurate. Basal minus ratings *cannot* be lowered. The following response illustrates the lowering of a form-level rating:

CARD VIII

I see two animals. Not bears—muskrats. They're not the color of muskrats. They're pink. Makes me think of polar bears. They are slowlike anyway. (Inq.) It is the shape of a muskrat, but polar bears are pink. Just as icebergs are pink. Pink is a frigid color. I think of pink in the Arctic Circle. (Q. You mean that you think of polar bears as pink?) No, they are usually white, but pink is one degree off white. (Q. You said they are slowlike.) Yes, they are walking, lumbering across the ice. (Q. What makes it seem like ice?) Ice is a neutral color like this.

> *Score: D→W*   *F→C,FM,C'F*   *A*   *P→O*   1.0

COMMENT: In addition to the basal credit of 1.0 for the popular animals, 0.5 credit can be given for organization. However, the forced use of color is a weakening specification, and therefore reduces the form level to 1.0.

For further help in learning how to score responses, the student should study the scored samples in the section that follows.

Scoring Examples

This section presents 50 sample responses, each with its complete scoring, and with a comment explaining its score.

Each example is listed in terms of its sole or its main determinant. In instances where a response is scored for multiple determinants, it is listed under its main determinant.

Some of the responses use unusual location areas. These locations are shown by number on the Location Chart on page 106. Usual large *D*'s and usual small *d*'s are indicated in the standard fashion—D_1, D_2, d_1, d_2, and so on, and are not marked on the Location Chart.

Pure Form Responses

F as Sole Determinant

1. CARD I

This little part in here is a turtle's head. (*Location:* tiny projection on left side often seen as the nose of a man) (Q. Can you describe it?) Just the head. Just the shape.

Score: dd   F   Ad   O   1.5

COMMENT: Since more than the edge was used, the response was scored *dd*. Although no specifications were made, the concept is an excellent match to the area; the form-level rating is therefore 1.5.

2. CARD II

The head of a Scottie. (*Location:* d_2 turned sideways) (Q. What makes it look like a Scottie?) It is clear-cut and regular, just like a soap carving. (Q. Was it just the outline?) Yes.

Score: d   F   Ad   O   1.5

COMMENT: Although shading was implied, it was not used and therefore cannot be scored. The definite shape of a dog's head is improved because specified as a Scottie's head, raising the form level to 1.5. The response is scored *O,* because the concept is unusual for this area of the blot.

3. CARD V

This looks like a face—a man's face. (*Location:* D_1) (Inq.) It's a profile. Here's his forehead, the nose, mouth, and this looks like it may be a mustache. (Q.) It's just the shape.

Score: D   F   Hd   1.5

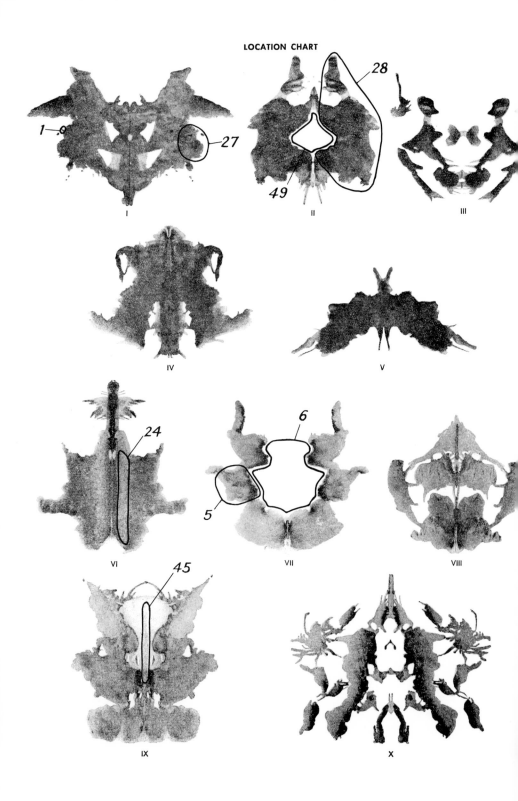

LOCATION CHART

COMMENT: Although the response was first prompted by the shape of the upper edge of the side *D,* the whole side area without the outer extension is usually used for the man's face; therefore, it is scored *D,* rather than *de.*

4. CARD VI
Nasty kids put pins in the wings of flies and spread them out. (Inq.) The whole thing. It is spread out flat.

Score: W   F   A   1.0

COMMENT: Since there is apparently no feeling of tension in the object contained in this response, the score is *F.* Where a "hanging" or "stretched" concept seems logical or positional, and does not contain a feeling of tension, the score is *F* rather than *m.* If the shading had been used for surface quality, then the score would have been *Fc.*

5. CARD VII
This part, you see right here, like this, looks like India surrounded partly by water. And this part doesn't belong. (*Location:* see Location Chart) (Inq.) It was the shape.

Score: dr   F   Geo   1.0

COMMENT: Because the area was carved out to improve the fit, the response is scored *dr.* The form level is raised from 0.5 for maps to 1.0 because a specific country was mentioned which matched the blot area.

6. CARD VII
This looks like the harbor at St. Thomas viewed from above. (*Location:* center white area. See Location Chart.) (Q. What made it seem "viewed from above?") Otherwise you couldn't see it like this. (Q. Could be outline map?) Yes.

Score: S   F   Geo   1.0

COMMENT: The inquiry makes it clear that the emphasis is on the form. The "viewed from above" was dictated by positional need, no shading being used for vista, or topographical map; thus, no *FK* or *Fk* score is involved.

7. CARD VIII
Skeletal structure of the rib area. (*Location:* D_5) (Inq.) It's got the same shape that the ribs do.

Score: D   F   At   1.0

COMMENT: Since there is no shading implied in this response, the score is *F*. Had this been designated on an X ray, the scoring would, of course, be *Fk*.

8. CARD IX

I can see the head of a moose and it's reflected in the water. (*Location: D_3*) (Inq.) I can see the eyes, and the long face and the horns. (Q. Impression of reflection?) It's exactly the same on both sides.

Score: D   F   Ad   2.0

COMMENT: The reflection is apparently a matter of symmetry, with no suggestion of shading for a three-dimensional effect; therefore, the score is *F,* not *FK*. The animal head is a popular-level response for this area, but this has one additional elaboration (the "horns") and an organizational detail (the reflection) which add one point credit to the popular form level of 1.0.

9. CARD X

Two dogs facing in opposite directions. (*Location: D_{11}*) (Inq.) It's just the heads, really. (Q. Facing?) Well, there's one on each side, but this head is placed this way but that head goes the other way.

Score: D   F   Ad   1.0

COMMENT: There seems to be no movement implied in the response; the term "facing" appears to have been used only to indicate position.

F— as Sole or as Main Determinant

10. CARD IV

Looks like a skate, a variety of fish belonging to shark family with sucker in front (whole) . (Inq.) Fish with big winglike structures.

Score: W   F—   A   —1.0

COMMENT: The whole blot area has been used, and an attempt made to reconcile a clear detail with the whole blot with some success. The result, however, is still inaccurate.

11. CARD V

That looks like a butterfly, too, the middle, and the butterfly has some beautiful jewels on top (usual antennae) , very attractive, rather pleasant. (Inq.) Just the center, and the head was very pretty. (Q.) The wings could be here, they are sort of dark. (Q. Jewels?) Sparkling; I don't know, just struck me like that, little sort of stones in the head.

Score: W   F,Fc,FC'   A,Jewels   P,O−   −0.5

COMMENT: Not a *DW* even though the subject emphasizes the large center *D*. The wings are finally seen as part of the butterfly. *Fc* for the shiny effect and *FC'* for the black color of the wings. It is a popular response spoiled by bizarre specifications (adding the stones to the head) ; hence the −0.5 rating.

Movement Responses

M as Sole or as Main Determinant

12. CARD II

This could be two people clapping hands. They are wearing black, long gowns, and their knees touch.

Score: W̶   M,FC'   H   3.0

COMMENT: The whole card except part of the lower red was used; therefore, a *W̶* score was assigned. The basal rating of 1.5 was increased by 0.5 for the organization, 0.5 for the black gown, and 0.5 for the specification of knees.

13. CARD V

Knock-kneed kid standing here holding up a furry set of wings. (*Location:* D_2) (Inq.) Holding up a lot of junk in either hand, not wings, like an old hide of some sort.

Score: D→W   M,Fc   H,A$_{obj}$ 2.5

COMMENT: The center figure is clear, as is the use of *Fc* as determinant for the rest of the blot area. This is clearly not a *DW* response, since the two concepts are reasonable but loosely organized. The most appropriate location score is therefore *D→W*. The form-level rating is arrived at as follows: 1.5 for the human figure; +0.5 for specification "knock-kneed kid"; and another +0.5 for the organizational element.

14. CARD VII

Two little boys looking very nasty. (*Location:* D_4) (Inq.) Just the upper half of them. There's a feather stuck in their hair. Here are the eyes, noses (D_4).

Score: D   M   Hd   2.0

COMMENT: The expressions are alive and are not threatening symbols of an abstract or evil force; therefore, the score is *M*. A basal form-level rating of 1.5, usually assigned to human figures, is raised to 2.0 because of the "nasty" specification, enhanced by the "feather stuck in their hair."

15. CARD IX

A little girl walking with her mother. The mother is holding the little girl's hand, and the little girl is pointing to something. (*Location: D_1*) (Inq.) Here's the mother, this large part, and this smaller part is the girl. Their hair looks as if it's being blown by the wind, and they are both wearing full dresses that stand out. The mother seems to be carrying a package, the end of it sticks out here. The little girl seems to be pointing, or maybe waving to somebody with this hand.

Score: D   M   H   O   4.5

COMMENT: A basal form-level rating of 1.5 was assigned for the human figures. To this was added 0.5 for the organization, walking together; 0.5 for the blown hair; 0.5 for their holding hands; 0.5 for the little girl pointing; 0.5 for the full dresses; and 0.5 for the package being carried. All the additional specifications increased the accuracy of the fit of the concept to the blot area.

16. CARD X

Two crickets sassing each other. (*Location: D_3*)

Score: D   M   (A)   1.5

COMMENT: "Sassing" is a humanlike activity and is therefore scored *M*. However, the content score is in parentheses to indicate that a human activity is performed by an animal.

17. CARD X

Dancers stretched out on floor in costume. (*Location: D_{10}*) (Inq.) Dancers, resting on arms, stretched out on floor.

Score: D   M   H   O   2.5

COMMENT: Where the movement of an object or the "force" is clearly the result of human or animal movement, the response is scored *M* or *FM*. Here, "stretched out" is the movement of the dancers. The basal form-level rating of 1.5 for a human figure was raised to 2.5 by the additional specification of "arms" and by the organization.

FM as Sole Determinant

18. CARD I

Bears sitting on their hind legs facing in opposite directions. (*Location:* D_2) (Inq.) Paws out like this, fur hanging down (just edges), head looks up in air, here the haunches, hind leg haunches.

> *Score:* D FM A 3.0
>
> COMMENT: This is a conceivable bearlike activity and is therefore scored *FM* rather than *M*. The form level of 3.0 results from: 1.5 for sitting bears; 0.5 for specification of "head looks up in air"; 0.5 for paws; 0.5 for fur hanging down.

19. CARD V

A purple and yellow butterfly. It's flying. (Inq.) Here are the wings, the antennae. (Q. Purple and yellow impression?) I just think of it as those colors. This isn't actually colored that way, of course.

> *Score:* W FM A P 1.0
>
> COMMENT: The color is apparently a purely capricious projection not related to the shadings on the card. This is not similar to the use of shading for photographic representation of color, which is scored *Fc*.

20. CARD VIII

These are two pink animals climbing up. (*Location:* D_1) (Q. Pink animals?) No, the animals aren't pink—I just meant that this pink part looked like two animals. They could be bears.

> *Score:* D FM A P 1.0
>
> COMMENT: Although the verbalization implied the use of color, the inquiry established that color was used only to designate the location and was not part of the concept.

21. CARD VIII

Two furry animals, they seem to be climbing up. (*Location:* D_1) (Inq.) They have long, slim bodies, four legs, an eye here, and short muzzles. They seem to be climbing up a mountainside. (Q. Furry?) You can see the irregularity of the edge. Little hairs standing up. It looks like fur.

> *Score:* D→W FM A P 2.5
>
> COMMENT: Although the intention was to include the whole blot, only the animals were clear; therefore, the response is scored

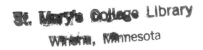

$D \rightarrow W$. Since only the outline, and not the shading, was used for the fur effect, texture is not scored. The basal form-level rating of 1.0 for a popular response was raised to 2.5 by three additional specifications ("long, slim bodies"; "eye"; "short muzzles") not absolutely necessary for the animal concept.

Fm or mF, as Sole or as Main Determinant

22. CARD I

Here is the finger of scorn. (*Location:* d_3) (Q. Did you think of it as belonging to anyone?) No, it is just a finger, kind of a symbol. The finger of scorn pointing at you.

> *Score:* d   Fm   (Hd)   1.0

> COMMENT: This is scored *Fm* rather than *M* because this human detail is thought of as an abstract symbol rather than part of a person in action.

23. CARD IV

A horrible-looking monster, something seen in a nightmare. Here are his huge feet, legs; head right here. I see his eyes, nose. These (upper sides) serve as arms for him, not really arms, but they grow out where arms would ordinarily be. (Q. Monster?) It has a fiendish look on its face, nothing human. It's more like you would imagine the devil looked like.

> *Score:* W   Fm   (H)   2.5

> COMMENT: The emphasis is on the fearful aspect of the concept and on the symbolic nature of the expression; hence the *Fm* determinant. The response contains at least two details to warrant raising the basic form-level rating of 1.5 to 2.5. The content score might be (H) or (A); but since the description seems to imply a humanlike figure from which "humanness" is removed, (H) is scored.

24. CARD VI

The light part here looks rather like the—wake of a boat which has just passed through. (*Location:* inner center detail. See Location Chart.) (Inq.) It seems as if the water is flowing back and erasing the path of the ship. (Q.) The shading makes it look foamy.

> *Score:* di   mF,FK   Water   0.5

> COMMENT: The *di* location score was assigned because the subject selected an area which is not clearly differentiated from the

surrounding area to fit the needs of his concept. An *mF* score was given since the subject emphasized the movement of the water with some definite form; the *FK* score accounts for the differentiated use of the shading qualities of the blot.

25. CARD IX

Two devils. They've got an evil look. (*Location:* D_2) (Inq.) Hands outstretched, tall hats, color of devils. (Q. Evil look?) Well, devils represent evil in a way. They're like a caricature.

Score: D *Fm,M,FC* *(H)* 2.0

COMMENT: The "evil look" receives an *Fm* score because the expression is symbolic of an abstract force and action is not involved. However, the outstretched hands receive an additional *M* score; color is appropriate for the concept and therefore scored *FC*.

Shading Responses

Fc or cF as Sole or as Main Determinant

26. CARD I

Some sort of bones. (Inq.) Looking at the whole thing as a mass, not flat. It's reminiscent of a pelvis; rounded and three-dimensional. The effect of difference in densities gives it a modeling effect. (Q. What part is closer to you?) This center part. It's rounded.

Score: W *Fc* *At* 1.0

COMMENT: The *Fc* score is given for "rounded and three-dimensional." No additional *FK* is scored, since separate surfaces are not seen. Had the subject specified either a male or female pelvis, the content would have been scored *Sex*.

27. CARD I

A rodent of some sort. Paw and eyes. (*Location:* shaded section in right middle portion of the blot, towards the edge) (Inq.) It is a mother mouse, peeking out of a hole. A little one is snuggled up next to her. Two little feet. It is soft and gray. Furry and mouse-colored.

Score: dr *Fc,FC',FM* *Ad* 3.0

COMMENT: Because the edge is definitely used to help delineate the concept, and the tiny peninsular portions are used for the "feet," this response is scored *dr* instead of *di* or *dd*.

28. CARD II

This is a man with a funny face. (*Location:* D_2 and D_3) (Q. Tell me about the man.) Here is his head, and here are his feet. (Q. What made his face seem funny?) It looks funny. All streaky because of the shadows here.

Score: dr   Fc   H   1.5

COMMENT: As the term "funny" seems to imply odd or peculiar, rather than an expression, no movement score is assigned.

29. CARD II

These look like those fluffy toy dogs you can buy—just this black part. (*Location:* D_3) (Inq.) It's the shape, of course, but more than that you get a feeling of softness and furriness, as if it would sort of give if you touched it.

Score: D   Fc   (A)   P   1.5

COMMENT: Even where the emphasis is primarily on the texture effect, when the object has a definite shape the score is *Fc*. The basic rating of 1.0 is raised to 1.5 because of the added specification of furriness. Note that no score for "black" was given, because this verbalization merely indicated the area.

30. CARD IV

It looks like a piece of snakeskin I once saw—the pattern of it (whole). (Q. Piece of snakeskin?) You know the sort of thing that's used for women's shoes, or bags, and such—it's all ready to be made into something. (Q. Pattern?) It's like the markings on a snakeskin—the different subtleties in tone, and it looks as if it has that smooth, brittle feel to it.

Score: W   Fc A_{obj} 1.0

COMMENT: Although the "piece of snakeskin" is of indefinite outline, this is a differentiated texture effect and is therefore scored *Fc*.

31. CARD VI

A scaly surface of some kind. (*Location:* D_1) (Inq.) It looks like it is a section of scales of some kind, the shading makes it look like that. Just scales. No special kind.

Score: D   cF A_{obj} 0.5

COMMENT: The object is of indefinite form and the shading contributed to a surface effect which is undifferentiated; therefore the score is *cF*. The basal form-level rating of 0.5 is reserved for such vague responses.

32. CARD VI
An Indian rug with all the different colors. (*Location:* W; D_2 omitted) (Inq.) You can see the variations from light to dark—from pale yellow, maybe, to green, red, dark blue.

Score: W̶   *Fc*   *Obj*   1.0

COMMENT: Here it is definitely the shading that is interpreted as a chromatic color effect; therefore, the scoring is *Fc*.

33. CARD VII
This could be a kind of map of a group of islands, maybe in the Caribbean—like a relief map. (whole) (Q. Relief map?) You know, sort of a small-scale model, made out of clay. The shading gives a feeling of high and low.

Score: W   *Fc*   *Geo*   1.0

COMMENT: This response is scored *Fc* for surface modeling. If this map had been seen in pictorial form with the shading used to show depth and height, it would have been scored *FK*. The differentiation and shape are definite enough to warrant a rating of 1.0.

34. CARD VIII
Square pieces of cellophane. (Inq.) (*Location:* D_4) Looks so shiny.

Score: D   *Fc*   *Obj*   O   1.0

COMMENT: The transparency without separate surfaces is scored *Fc* rather than *FK*.

FK or KF as Sole or as Main Determinant

35. CARD I
An airplane picture of an island on a foggy day. (*Location:* W, S) (Inq.) Lagoons and inlets on the edges. The spaces are lakes. And it rises like mountains on a topographical map—all this shading here.

Score: W,S   FK   *Geo*   1.0

COMMENT: The specification of lagoons, inlets, and lakes warrants an *FK* score because of the clear emphasis on detail ("it rises like mountains").

36. CARD IV

A beautiful scene, like you would see from an airplane (whole).
(Inq.) Mountains, dark trees, some vegetation, river down here.

Score: W   FK   N   1.0

COMMENT: The shading is used to create the effect of distance between objects; therefore, it is scored *FK,* not *Fk.*

37. CARD VI

A highway under construction. It's not finished—dug out of a hill
(whole). (Inq.) Down here is the finished road made into a valley—
shading makes it look like a road deep in a valley. You're above looking down. There's also a gleam of water down there.

Score: W   FK   N   2.0

COMMENT: The score is *FK* for a vista response. The "gleam of
water" adds merely another separate surface effect in the total
landscape; no additional texture score is given.

38. CARD VII

Looks like smoke rising from the center (whole, inverted). (Q. What
made it seem like smoke?) The outline is not distinct. There is depth
and thickness and light.

Score: W   KF,mF   Clouds   0.5

COMMENT: The vaguely shaped smoke is scored *KF;* only absolutely formless smoke would be scored *K.* The additional *mF* is
scored for the inanimate movement of "rising." The 0.5 basal
form-level rating is reserved for responses such as this that are
vague or semidefinite in form.

39. CARD X

This part reminds me of Paris—like when you see the Eiffel Tower
across the formal gardens which lead to it. (*Location:* D_{16}) (Inq.)
The color in these parts reminds me of the gardens, and you can see
the top structure of the tower at the end of the gardens.

Score: D   FK,CF   Arch,Pl   2.0

COMMENT: This is a clearly seen detail where vista is definitely
specified as the major determinant for the response. An additional
CF score was given for the color used in a concept with indefinite
form. To a basal rating of 1.5 was added 0.5 for the organizational
element.

Fk as Sole Determinant

40. CARD IV

Looks like an aerial view of Italy, the shadings show mountains and terrain. (*Location:* D_2) (Inq.) The map of Italy showing mountains and valleys. I don't know the name, it has a special name. (Q.) No, not really an aerial, more like one of those maps showing mountains.

> Score: D   Fk   Geo   1.0

> · COMMENT: The *Fk* seems to be a better score for this response than *FK*. The outline specification in making it a map of a specific country warrants scoring this response *Fk*.

Color Responses

Chromatic: FC, CF, or C as Sole or as Main Determinant

41. CARD II

That's a busted bleeding heart, really shattered. That's all. (*Location:* D_1) (Inq.) Yes, it looks like a bleeding heart, a very good picture.

> Score: D   CF   At   0.5

> COMMENT: This response is vague and determined primarily by the color, although the form is not neglected. Since the heart is seen as shattered, the appropriate score is *CF*.

42. CARD II

These would be little—I don't know what except the color implies blood. (*Location:* D_2) (Inq.) Just blood because the red color symbolized blood.

> Score: D C_{sym} Blood   0.0

> COMMENT: The response emphasizes the symbolic meaning of the color with no emphasis on form.

43. CARD VIII

This reminds me of the kind of chart they would have in a medical book—chest area, lungs, and down here the internal organs, the intestines (whole). (Inq.) It's just an impression. The color is for the different parts, the way it would be in such a chart.

> Score: W   F/C   At   1.0

> COMMENT: The colors have been used arbitrarily to mark off subdivisions which have definite form. If specific anatomical areas

had not been mentioned, the scoring would have been *C/F* rather than *F/C*.

44. CARD IX

Clouds sometimes look like this when the sun is setting. (*Location: D_6*) (Inq.) It's the rosy color, and the shape could be like a cloud.

Score: D   CF   Clouds   0.5

COMMENT: In this case the response seems to be determined primarily by the color and the vague outline, with no indication that shading contributed to the concept. Since there is no diffuse effect, the scoring is *CF*, not *KF*.

45. CARD IX

Here is a candle with the wax dripping. (*Location:* elongated area above D_9) (Q. Wax dripping?) It was the irregular outline that looked like a candle with the wax on the sides. You know how they look when you have burned them for a while. It's sort of a green candle.

Score: dr   FC   Obj   1.0

COMMENT: Although the language of the performance implied movement, no movement seems to be seen. The response combines form and color adequately and is therefore scored *FC*.

46. CARD IX

This up here is a pumpkin. (*Location: D_2*) (Inq.) It makes me think of Hallowe'en because of the orange pumpkin. (Q. Pumpkin?) All this is the pumpkin, and it's the right color.

Score: D   FC−   Pl   −1.0

COMMENT: The object is of definite form, and the color has been used, but the concept does not match the blot area; therefore, the score is *FC−*, the minus for an inaccurate idea.

47. CARD X

A mouse. (*Location: D_6*) (Inq.) The shape and color. (Q. What color?) Brown.

Score: D   FC   A   1.5

COMMENT: Had the subject said "gray," *FC'* would have been scored; for "brown" the scoring is *FC*. In general, where the subject sees chromatic color of low saturation, such as brown, green, or blue, in an area seen by many as gray, the score is *FC* or *CF* rather than *FC'* or *C'F*.

48. CARD X

A map of England and Scotland. (*Location:* D_9) (Inq.) The shape and the color, both. (Q. Color?) It's always shown in red on a map.

Score: *D* *FC* *Geo* 1.0

COMMENT: Since maps do usually show this geographical area in red, this response is scored *FC*, not *F/C*.

Achromatic: FC' as Sole Determinant

49. CARD II

This looks like a lighted globe. (*Location:* white space. See Location Chart.) It's so white. (Inq.) Only the white space here, nothing else. (Q. Why lighted?) Because it's so white.

Score: *S* *FC'* *Obj* 1.0

COMMENT: The lighted effect is due entirely to the whiteness; therefore, there is no shading score.

50. CARD IV

Here this dark part reminds me of a grand piano set at sort of an angle to me. (*Location:* D_5) (Inq.) It is the curving line of this dark part that reminds me of a grand piano, and the dark color of course. (Q. Angle?) With the curved line of that shape it would have to be at an angle. It's the perspective of the thing.

Score: *D* *FC'* *Obj* *O* 2.0

COMMENT: The implied depth effect is purely a matter of linear perspective, and the shading is not used to differentiate the surface of the piano from other surfaces, except to delineate its form; therefore, the score is *FC'* rather than *FK*. This response receives a basal rating of 1.5, to which 0.5 is added for the color.

Chapter Five

TABULATION OF THE SCORES: USE OF THE INDIVIDUAL RECORD BLANK

TABULATION of the Rorschach responses facilitates the analysis of a record by providing a summarization of the scores, the sequence of scores to each card, and the entire record. The tabulation includes the listing and summation of all main and additional scores, the recording of the form-level rating assigned to each response, the calculation of a number of percentages and ratios, and a graphic representation of the determinant scores. Reaction time, response time, and position of the card when a response is given are also recorded.

The tabulation process is facilitated by the use of the *Individual Record Blank*,* illustrated on pages 172–74 and 206–09 for the two case records in Chapter Seven, and in the Appendix. This Record Blank consists of four pages as follows: (1) The first page includes spaces for recording pertinent identifying information, such as name, address, and age of the subject and name of the examiner. The lower portion of this page provides space for the examiner's remarks and notations. (2) The second page is the Tabulation and Scoring Sheet, used for recording the scores and tabulating the results. (3) The third page is used for preparing the bar graph (that is, psychogram) of the determinant scores as well as for recording certain basic and supplementary relationships among the Rorschach scores. (4) The fourth page contains the Location Chart, on which the ten Rorschach ink blots are reduced and reproduced in black and white.

---

* By B. Klopfer and H. Davidson, published by Harcourt, Brace & World, Inc.

Preparation of the Tabulation and Scoring Sheet

Even though the examiner may score a record while administering it, a separate scoring list is desirable. The second page of the *Individual Record Blank* provides space for this listing of scores. There are a number of columns for recording all the information required for each response.

The first column is for recording the card number, the response number, and the position of the card when the response was given. Roman numerals should be used for the cards, arabic numerals for the main responses, and letters for any additional responses. Reaction time in seconds is shown in the second column.

The next four columns are used for recording the main and additional location scores. The main location scores are divided into three categories to facilitate tabulation and summation of the whole responses $(W, W\!\!\!\prime)$; of the usual details (D, d); and of the unusual areas $(Dd$ and $S)$. The additional location scores are not so differentiated; any additional location score is listed in the fourth location column. If there is a combination of location scores, such as $D{\rightarrow}W$, the D score is placed in the appropriate column with an arrow $(D{\rightarrow})$, and the W score is put in the additional column. The combination $\left.\begin{array}{c}D\\D\end{array}\right\}W$ may be similarly handled: the $\left.\begin{array}{c}D\\D\end{array}\right\}$ goes into the D, d column, occupying two spaces since these are two main responses; the W is recorded in the additional column. In this manner relationships between scores are clearly represented.

There are six columns for listing the determinant scores: one column each for the five major determinant scoring categories, and one column for any additional determinant score or scores. All movement scores $(M, FM, Fm, mF,$ and $m)$ are written in the Movement column; all vista and depth scores $(Fk, kF, k, FK, KF,$ and $K)$ are listed in the Vista or Depth column; only the form score (F) is placed in the Form column; the texture and achromatic color responses (Fc, c, FC') and the bright color scores (FC, CF, C) are written in their respective columns.

Any combination of determinant scores, such as *M,FC*, is shown as follows: the first score, in this case *M*, is listed in the Main Response column, and the second score, in this case *FC*, is listed in the Additional (Add.) column. If there is more than one additional determinant score, as, for example, *M,FC,Fc,* the two additional determinants are listed one under the other in the Additional (Add.) column. Only one determinant per response should be listed in the Main Response column.

There are two columns for listing the content scores: Main and Additional (Add.). The content scores are not subdivided because of the large number of possible categories. However, there are spaces at the bottoms of the columns for totaling these frequently used content categories: *H, Hd, A,* and *Ad.*

The popular and original scores *(P* and *O)* are recorded in their own columns, separated into main and additional scores.

The last column is used to record the form-level rating (FLR) for each main and each additional response.

When all the scores are listed in columns, all the main and all the additional scores are totaled for each of the scoring categories. At the bottom on page 2 of the Record Blank, spaces are provided for indicating the sums of all the main and the additional scores, and for indicating the sum (Sum FLR) and average (Average FLR) form-level ratings.

The sum of all the main location scores should equal the total number of main responses *(R)*, and, likewise, the sum of all the main determinant scores should equal the total number of main responses. The content scores are totaled only for the number of responses scored as *H, Hd, A,* and *Ad.* Spaces for recording main and additional content scores are included in these four categories.

The Sum and Average FLR entries are handled as follows: First, the sum of the form-level ratings is calculated by adding the main responses only in each location and determinant category; the average is simply determined by dividing the sum by the total number of main responses in the category. Then, in the unlabeled boxes at the extreme lower right-hand corner of the Scoring Sheet, the Sum FLR and Average FLR for the entire record are entered, this time including main and additional responses. When form-level ratings were introduced, main and additional ratings were always treated separately. Experience has indicated that it is best to combine both ratings to obtain the Sum and Average FLR for an over-all estimate of the subject's perceptual accuracy. In general, spontaneous additional responses are not too frequent. However, even when frequent, they make little difference in the final calculations. When there is a considerable number of spontaneous additional responses, the form level of these responses should not be overlooked in the total form-level picture.

Preparation of the Psychogram and the Quantitative Relationships

The Psychogram

The psychogram is a bar graph representing the distribution of the main and additional determinant scores. A form for entering these values is given on page 3 of the Individual Record Blank. On the horizontal axis, spaces for the major determinant scoring categories are provided; on the vertical axis, spaces are provided for indicating the number of responses. Units of 1 are usually applicable for the number of responses; for long records, however, it may be necessary to use units of 2 or 3 responses for each bar space. A solid line is drawn to show the number of main responses for each determinant, and a dotted line, extended upward, to show the number of additional scores in the category. The frequencies may be noted by placing the number within the bar. The psychogram may also be used to record other aspects of the responses, such as content which is particularly significant, or types of color responses.

It should be observed that, in drawing the psychogram, some of the scores are grouped together (as mentioned previously) because there are usually too few scores in these categories and also because a clearer picture is obtained with this grouping. These groupings are as follows:

Under m, include Fm, mF, and m.
Under k, include Fk, kF, and k.
Under K, include KF and K.
Under c, include cF and c.
Under C', include FC', $C'F$, and C'.
Under C, include C_{des}, C_n, C_{sym}, and C.

Basic Relationships

A number of important quantitative relationships are calculated and recorded on the third page of the Record Blank. *In computing the basic relationships only main scores are used.* The intent is to keep these relationships comparable with the traditional Rorschach literature, in which additional scores are not usually used statistically. Methods for calculating the basic relationships follow:

Total responses, or R

Total the number of responses given.

Total time, or T

Total the time for the entire performance proper; express in minutes and seconds.

Average time per response, or T/R

Divide T by the total number of responses; express answer in seconds.

Average reaction time to achromatic cards

Total the reaction times to the five achromatic cards (I, IV, V, VI, and VII), and divide by five. Express answer in seconds. Do not count rejections in calculation.

Average reaction time for chromatic cards

As above, for the five chromatic cards (II, III, VIII, IX, and X).

$F\%$

Total all pure F responses, divide by R, and multiply by 100.

$$\frac{FK + F + Fc}{R}\%$$

Self-explanatory.

$A\%$

Total the A and Ad scores, divide by R, and multiply by 100.

$(H + A):(Hd + Ad)$

Self-explanatory.

Popular responses

Total the number of main and additional populars. Separate the two numbers by a comma or by parentheses.

Original responses

Total the number of main and additional originals. Indicate the number of original minus scores.

Sum C

Use this formula: $\dfrac{FC + 2CF + 3C}{2}$

M:Sum C

Self-explanatory.

$(FM + m):(Fc + c + C')$

Self-explanatory.

$(VIII + IX + X)\%$

Total the number of responses to the last three cards, divide by R, and multiply by 100. Make a note when more than 20% of the responses are given to Card X.

$W:M$

Self-explanatory.

Supplementary Relationships

Certain supplementary relationships have come to have significance in the interpretative process. For the calculation of these relationships *both main and additional scores are used, the additional scores being given a weighting of one-half.* The six supplementary relationships are as follows:

$M:FM$	Self-explanatory.
$M:(FM + m)$	As above.
$(FK + Fc):F$	Self-explanatory.
Achromatic:Chromatic	Compute the Achromatic side of the ratio by totaling the Fc, cF, c, FC', $C'F$, and C' scores. Compute the Chromatic side of the ratio by totaling the FC, CF, and C scores. (Note that the Chromatic side of the ratio is not the same as Sum C.)
Differentiated:Undifferentiated shading	Total the differentiated shading responses—FK, Fk, and Fc. Compare with the sum of the undifferentiated shading responses—K, KF, k, kF, c, and cF.
$FC:(CF + C)$	Self-explanatory. Give equal weight to FC, CF, and C scores.

Manner of Approach

The interpretative hypotheses connected with the percentages of the various locations are related to the intellectual manner of approach. The location scores in each category are considered in terms of their percentage of the total number of responses. For example, the $W\%$ is equal to the total number of W's divided by R and multiplied by 100. The $D\%$, $d\%$, and $Dd + S\%$ are similarly computed. This procedure is necessary, since the actual number of location scores varies with the subject's tendency to give few or many responses.

The location percentages are used to analyze the relationships among the several location scoring categories as well as to compare the obtained percentages with the expected percentages. A table of location percentages with their symbolic representations (parentheses and underlinings) follows:

W%		D%		d%		Dd + S%	
< 10%	((W))	< 30%	((D))				
10–19%	(W)	30–44%	(D)	< 5%	(d)		
20–30%	W	45–55%	D	5–15%	d	< 10%	Dd + S
31–45%	W	56–65%	D	16–25%	d	10–19%	Dd + S
46–60%	W	66–80%	D	26–35%	d	20–29%	Dd + S
> 60%	W	> 80%	D	36–45%	d	30–40%	Dd + S
				> 45%	d	> 40%	Dd + S

Note that underemphasis of any location score is indicated in the table by single and double parentheses (depending on the extent); overemphasis is shown by single, double, triple, and quadruple underlinings. The normal expectancy is shown within the two solid lines. That is, most people give 20–30% W's, 45–55% D's, 5–15% d's, and less than 10% Dd + S scores.

The form on the third page of the *Individual Record Blank* provides spaces for entering the number of each type of location response, the percentage of each type of location response, and the number of additional scores for each location category. The expected normal percentages are listed for ease of comparison.

Estimate of Intellectual Level

The examiner must evaluate the intellectual level of the subject in terms of both capacity and efficiency, for too often there is a discrepancy between the two. Both estimates are based primarily on the following factors: (1) number and quality of W responses; (2) number and quality of M responses; (3) number and quality of O responses; (4) level of form accuracy and organization (FLR); (5) variety of content; (6) orderliness of succession.

Succession

Succession refers to the order in which location categories are used. On the Record Blank, four evaluations are listed to characterize the degree of order: *Rigid, Orderly, Loose,* and *Confused.*

The most usual succession is to respond to the blot as a whole first, then to give one or two large usual detail responses, and then perhaps to give a small usual detail, a rare detail, or a space response. This succession of $W-D-d-Dd$(or S) is termed a systematic succession. The succession of Dd(or S)$-d-D-W$ is also designated as systematic. Not all four types of location need be used. An unsystematic succession is any violation of the systematic sequence. For some cards succession cannot be termed either systematic or unsystematic—for example, for Card X when several D responses are given and no other locations are used, or for any card when only one W response is given and no detail responses are given at all. The number of systematic successions is counted, and then the number of unsystematic successions. If any cards have no succession, they are counted either as systematic or unsystematic, whichever classification is the more frequent.

The four categories for rating succession are defined as follows: *Rigid Succession*—ten systematic successions; *Orderly Succession*—seven to nine systematic successions: *Loose Succession*—three to six systematic successions; *Confused Succession*—fewer than three systematic successions.

Form-Level Summary

Space is provided on the Record Blank for recording: (1) the average unweighted form-level rating for the main plus additional responses (Average Unweighted FLR), and (2) the average weighted form-level rating for the main plus additional responses (Average Weighted FLR). The average *unweighted* form-level rating is the sum of all the ratings divided by the number of responses. The average *weighted* form-level rating is the sum of all the ratings 2.5 and higher multiplied by 2 plus the sum of all the ratings below 2.5, divided by the total number of responses.

The Location Chart

The need to establish accurately the exact area of the blot used by the subject for his response has already been indicated. On the fourth page of the Record Blank is a Location Chart, showing the ten blots in miniature and in black and white. On these reproductions the examiner can outline the area of the blot used, as well as note any of the details pointed out by the subject. The assignment of location scores and the evaluation of the quality of the responses will be greatly facilitated by the use of such a chart.

Chapter Six

INTERPRETATION

THE interpretation of a Rorschach record is a complex process. It requires a wealth of knowledge concerning personality dynamics generally, as well as considerable experience with the Rorschach method specifically. Proficiency as a Rorschach *administrator* can be gained within a few months. However, even those who are able and qualified to become Rorschach *interpreters* usually remain in a "learning stage" for a number of years.

This chapter presents the basic hypotheses on which the interpretative process is built. They should serve to introduce the beginning Rorschach worker to some of the intricacies of interpretation.

General Considerations

The interpretative meaning of the various scores must be considered merely as working hypotheses. In most cases, the significance of the scores has not been put to an experimental test. Their interpretative meanings, however, have proved to be extremely useful in clinical situations for understanding personality dynamics. The meanings attached to the scores, therefore, possess *clinical* rather than *experimental* validity.

An important point to be remembered by interpreters is the interrelated nature of Rorschach scores. A single factor in the Rorschach record (such as the number of *FC* responses, or the number of *W* responses) has a certain general meaning in itself, but may mean something much more specific when seen in the light of another factor (such as *CF* responses, or form level). It may have still another, more individual, meaning in the context of the entire record. The card to which a response is given is another factor to be considered in interpreting a score. Also, the interpretation of scores will vary according to the age, sex, and cultural background of the subject.

Another factor that reflects the same interwovenness between a scoring category and the total structural setting is the *quality* of the responses within the scoring categories. The *W* category may serve as an example: One subject may use the whole card for each response because of a complete inability to organize the given material into meaningful subdivisions. The result of this incapacity for organization may be either completely noncommittal *W*'s (such as the perseveration of the response "insides of a human body" through all ten cards), or fairly accurate crude outline responses (such as "butterflies," "birds," or "leaves"). Another subject may produce a series of ten *W* responses because he greatly enjoys using his immense and almost unlimited organizational abilities. He may form a concept in each one of the ten cards that incorporates and uses every single one of the clearly perceived and organized natural subdivisions of the blot.

To a certain extent the scoring system can indicate such qualitative differences so long as they are based on measurable qualities. This can be done, for instance, through the addition of plus and minus signs, or the combination of *F* with other scoring symbols to express the definiteness of a concept in regard to its form qualities. However, although these qualitative differences can be quantified, they are made scorable only to a limited extent.

Another item of limited quantifiability is the relationship between *main* and *additional* scores. The Rorschach reactions given additional scores represent a sort of potential—elements in the subject's personality that are less ready to function than those represented by the main scores. These additional scores should never be entirely neglected; on the other hand, neither should they be given equal weight with the main scores. They may serve as modifying factors where the number of main scores indicates the lack of a certain capacity, or as a tendency to overflowing where the number of main scores indicates strength in a given capacity.

The interpreter must work in the context of a total configuration or pattern. He should be aware of and make use of all the information obtained from the Rorschach, both quantitative and qualitative. The list that follows outlines the kinds of information obtained and the kinds of analytic procedures that are suitable:

1. *The quantitative results of the tabulation,* representing the crude totals for the major scoring categories.

2. *The configurational results of the tabulation,* showing some important interrelationships among the various scoring categories.

3. *The distribution of the quantitative scoring results for* all ten cards, as seen on the Tabulation Sheet.

4. *The sequence analysis of the scores* in terms of the succession of various location and determinant scores within each card and from card to card.

5. *The qualitative analysis of all individual responses* in terms of organization, form accuracy, and integration of various determinants.

6. *Analysis of the general symbolic characteristics of the* content, especially in movement, color, and original responses.

7. *The use of conspicuous behavior* exhibited during the Rorschach administration: characteristic features in the verbal formulations, asides, remarks, and other unscorable elements.

The interpretative process is presented in this chapter starting from the meaning of the single elements, or scoring categories, through the simple score relationships to the more complex ones. Then follows the section on sequence analysis and content analysis of responses.

Interpretative Meanings of the Scoring Categories

The individual scoring categories are discussed below in the same order in which they were presented in the chapter on scoring: (1) Location Scores; (2) Determinant Scores; (3) Content Scores; (4) Popular-Original Scores; and (5) Form-Level Rating.

Location Scores

Location scores in general relate to the intellectual manner of approach, reflecting the way in which the subject customarily handles any set of data: deductive or inductive, sweeping or meticulous, with or without regard for the obvious. If an individual uses locations within the average range of expectation (that is, 20–30% W, 45–55% D, 5–15% d, and less than 10% Dd and S), it is assumed that he shows a balanced intellectual approach.

The location scores are considered in terms of percentages of the total responses because, as noted earlier, they are a function of the total number of responses. The absolute number of W's in a record, for example, would not tell us whether the subject saw a high or low proportion of W's.

It is important to remember that different hypotheses can be attached to a given location percentage. A $W\%$ will have one meaning, for example, if the record contains about the expected number of D responses and the form level is high, but a quite different meaning if there are no D responses and the form level is low.

Hypotheses Related to Whole Scores—$W\%$

The use of W, in general, is considered to reflect the ability to organize material, to relate details, to be concerned with the abstract and theoretical. All this is true only when the W's are more than approximately 30% of the responses and are good W's, that is, are combined with high form level. If combined with mediocre form level, an emphasis on W might indicate an ambitiousness that is not substantiated by ability. Little emphasis on W may result from lack of interest in seeking relationships among the separate facts of experience. The use of the cut-off whole, W^x may be indicative of a criticalness that prompts the subject to omit what he thinks does not fit; on the other hand, it may indicate an overcriticalness that tends to interfere with functioning. The use of DW (confabulatory whole) shows a weakness in the perception of reality, a tendency to overgeneralize without paying adequate attention to obvious details. All tendencies to W ($\rightarrow W$) show an interest in theoretical thinking, but less success in organizing experience than is shown by a well-integrated W.

Hypotheses Related to Detail Scores—$D\%$ and $d\%$

$D\%$ and $d\%$ indicate, in general, an interest in the specific, in details, in the concrete. This may be interpreted as a practical, everyday, common-sense application of intelligence.

An overemphasis on D and d responses combined with adequate or better form level may mean that the individual feels somewhat insecure and feels safest when he sticks close to the obvious. Over 15% d is often associated with pedantry, a need to be accurate, correct, and exact.

If D is underemphasized, there is in most cases a corresponding overemphasis on W. If such a situation occurs with subjects whose W's are vague and unorganized, it may result from poor intellectual ability or some emotional disturbance. Schizophrenics, for instance, characteristically underemphasize D and emphasize W or Dd or both. An underemphasis on or even total lack of d (less than 5%) is not particularly significant and merely indicates little interest in the minutiae of experience.

Hypotheses Related to Unusual Detail and White Space Scores— Dd% and S%

Dd and *S* responses generally indicate the ability of an individual to perceive unusual details. They may show a rich responsiveness to the environment, or they may indicate keen concern with the unusual, provided the form level of these *Dd*'s is high. There is no significance to the lack of *Dd* and *S* in a record, since this is an expected finding.

The following interpretative hypotheses are offered for the various kinds of location represented by the *Dd%* and *S%*:

1. *dd* (very small but clearly defined area) may represent obsessional, meticulous, or pedantic trends, if emphasized.

2. *de* (edge only of blot area) if stressed may indicate a fear of becoming involved if one goes into anything too deeply. This tendency may be found in anxiety states.

3. *di* (inside area carved out of shaded mass) if associated with a good form-level response indicates an anxious preoccupation with interpersonal relationships. If not associated with good form, the *di* response may be pathological in a paranoid direction.

4. *dr* (rarely delineated area) if associated with good form, and if not numerous, may reveal great perceptiveness and flexibility of approach. If *dr* is associated with poor form, it represents a conspicuous lack of common sense or a negativistic attitude toward the obvious.

5. *S* (reversal of figure and ground) is related to an oppositional tendency in the intellectual sphere, the degree of negativism or stubbornness being related to the manner in which the white space is used. A complete reversal of figure and ground is associated with a greater degree of intellectual opposition than, for instance, the use of the white space for the mouth and eyes of the cat's face in Card I. In some instances, a moderate amount of *S* might indicate ego strength, or a desirable amount of self-assertiveness.

Determinant Scores

In general, the determinant scores relate to the emotional aspects of the personality. The interpretative hypotheses attached to each determinant category are discussed below.

Hypotheses Related to the Form Score—F% and Form Quality

The F score, given to responses determined exclusively by shape, generally refers to the degree of intellectual control available to the individual. Form responses may also be interpreted as evidence of ego strength.

Because the F score as such can have a variety of meanings, two of its most significant aspects—$F\%$ and form quality—are considered jointly below.

$F\%$ (the total number of F scores, divided by the total number of responses, multiplied by 100) with adequate form level relates to an individual's degree of control, his ability to handle situations without becoming emotionally involved. The higher the $F\%$, the more is the person able to be impersonal and matter-of-fact. The normal range for $F\%$ is between 20 and 50%. The hypothesis is, of course, subject to modification in the light of the entire record. For example, a high $F\%$ (50–80%) in a record without much movement, shading, or color indicates rigidity and constriction. On the other hand, a high $F\%$ in a record with a reasonable number of movement, shading, and color scores indicates a rich personality that can be matter-of-fact when necessary. A low $F\%$ (under 20%) has the opposite interpretation. A person who underemphasizes F, but who gives M's, Fc's, and FC's, in reasonable numbers, places little emphasis on maintaining impersonal relationships but *may* be spontaneous, creative, and sensitive to others. If other control factors are poorly represented, a low $F\%$ would indicate inadequate control, a too highly personalized reaction.

An $F\%$ over 80% is pathological. If combined with adequate form level, it means a high degree of constriction or lack of spontaneity, as found in highly compulsive or depressed states. If combined with mediocre or poor form level, it indicates a person who is intellectually and emotionally so poorly differentiated that he is unable to respond to anything outside the barest outlines of reality. This hypothesis will need modification in view of the form quality of the responses.

Form quality * relates to the accuracy of perception, that is, the extent to which an individual fits his concept to the blot material. Three levels of form accuracy may be distinguished: $F+$, forms better than the popular or near popular responses; F, forms of the popular or near

---

* Form quality, or accuracy, is only one aspect of the form-level rating (see pages 139, 148). Only this aspect is under discussion here.

popular variety, and $F-$, inaccurate forms. The higher the form accuracy, the more the individual is concerned with exactness and with the reality situation. Such an individual may be very intelligent, very compulsive, or both.

Individuals whose form responses are at the average level (F) or at the poor level $(F-)$ are generally not as intelligent or as controlled emotionally as those individuals who give higher form accuracy $(F+)$ responses.

Hypotheses Related to Movement Scores

The movement scores (M for human movement; FM, for animal movement; m, for inanimate movement) generally relate to an individual's attitude and feelings about the inner reality of his experiences: his self concept, his tensions and conflicts surrounding the acceptance of his self, his fantasies and impulses.

M Scores: M is perhaps the most significant and yet, interpretatively, the most complex single determinant. Numerous hypotheses are attached to M responses based upon three main features of M-perception: (1) By projecting movement into a static ink blot, M-perception involves a process of imagination that the individual feels free to use. (2) M-perception entails a human concept, or one entailing human attributes, that implies an ability to empathize with other people. (3) M responses involve perception of a highly differentiated kind.

The individual who possesses all these characteristics has a relatively high level of ego functioning. He is one who can accept himself, his impulses, his fantasies and, at the same time, can maintain good object relations. Other things being equal, he is probably an intelligent, well-integrated individual, capable of creative experiences.

The total number of M responses must also be considered in interpretation. It is felt that the well-adjusted intelligent adult should be able to give at least three M concepts.

M responses combined with minus form-level ratings are considered a sign of defective ego organization.

FM Scores: FM, in contrast to M, represents the less mature, the less conscious, and sometimes the less acceptable part of a person's basic impulses. It reflects the strength of these urges as well as their acceptability to the individual. These are the impulses that demand immediate gratification and that consequently need to be controlled. Therefore, the *FM* responses need to be interpreted in the light of the *M* responses in particular, and, as always, in the context of the entire record. When a subject fails to give *FM* responses, or when they are given reluctantly and therefore scored as additionals, the interpretation is that the individual tends to repress his more primitive impulses, probably because they are unacceptable to him. The impulses represented by *FM* are often difficult to identify; and analysis of the content of the *FM* responses may be helpful in this regard.

m Scores: *m* responses, in general, seem to indicate tension and conflict, if there are more than one or two of them. *m* responses may represent inner or outer forces that the individual cannot control and that therefore threaten his ego. Since *m* is believed to indicate that the individual is aware of hostile forces or threats to the personality, an absence of *m* in a subject with conflicts may be a danger signal. The presence of *m* has repeatedly been found to indicate higher adjustment ability.

Hypotheses Related to Shading Scores

The shading scores, in general, indicate the way in which an individual manages his needs for affection, for belonging, and for obtaining satisfying contacts. All people possess these elemental needs. The anticipation of satisfaction of these needs, and the extent of a person's difficulty in handling them, is reflected in the nature of the shading scores. The separate hypotheses attached to each of the shading categories are given below:

Fc, cF, and c Scores: *Fc, cF,* and *c* scores relate to a person's awareness of his needs for affection and dependency. An individual reveals, through the presence or absence of texture responses and by the relationships among the *Fc, cF,* and *c* scores, that he is sensitive to the finer nuances in his subjective and objective environment and that he is concerned about how much affection and attention he can expect to receive from the world. The variations in these feelings may be observed in the way the individual uses the three kinds of texture responses, that range from a crude expression—*c*—to the most refined expression—*Fc.*

Fc responses indicate an awareness of and acceptance of one's own affectional needs as well as the needs and feelings of other people. The affectional needs are experienced in terms of desire for approval and response from others. The infantile craving for contact has become controlled and refined, although retaining a passive flavor. It is believed that this condition occurs only when the basic security needs have been reasonably well satisfied.

An optimal number of Fc responses would indicate tactfulness, awareness, sensitivity. An overemphasis might mean too great a dependence on others. Underemphasis on or lack of Fc implies lack of acceptance of affectional needs if shading is avoided or denied, or lack of capacity for such needs if there is no sensitivity to shading.

cF responses also represent a relatively crude and immature need for closeness, a longing for dependence on others. Sometimes these responses represent sensuous feelings revealing a craving for sexual contact.

c indicates an infantile, undifferentiated, crude need for affection of an essentially physical contact variety.

FK Scores: When a person gives an FK response, he sees the blot as having depth and perspective with some objects closer to him and others farther away. FK indicates that the individual is making an effort to understand and to tolerate his anxiety. The FK score, therefore, if sufficiently large, is related to good adjustment, especially in response to psychotherapy. The absence of FK is not necessarily significant.

KF and K Scores: KF and K responses use shading to give a diffuse, unstructured, but three-dimensional effect to the blot material. KF and K are related to anxiety created by the frustration of affectional needs, against which frustration the individual has not erected adequate defenses. Since all persons have some anxiety due to frustration of the need for affection, some K or KF responses may be expected. Giving more than three K responses, however, indicates more than usual worry about affectional needs.

Fk, kF, and k Scores: In giving a k response, a person is using the shading to put three dimensions into the material, but his effort only results in the suggestion of a two-dimensional plane. The X ray and the topographical map remain flat, although there is an intellectual suggestion of three dimensions.

Fk, kF, and k seem to indicate the existence of anxiety regarding affectional needs that the individual tries to cover up by intellectu- alizing. The individual who gives *Fk*'s rather than *kF*'s or *k*'s may be somewhat better able to control his anxiety by intellectual means.

Hypotheses Related to Color Scores (Chromatic and Achromatic)

Color scores, in general, relate to the extent and nature of the in- dividual's responsiveness to stimuli from the environment. It is gen- erally taken for granted that these stimuli are in the area of inter- personal relationships and that, therefore, the responses to color are to be interpreted to show how the person reacts to the emotional im- pact of relationships with other people.

The five colored cards are emotionally challenging, and the sub- ject's reactions to them provide a great deal of information as to how this emotional challenge is met.

The following discussion is limited to the implications of each of the various color-scoring categories insofar as they can be considered in isolation.

FC Scores: In producing an *FC* response, the subject accepts the challenge of integrating the color into a concept of definite form. *FC* responses indicate a controlled but ready responsiveness to emotional impact. This controlled responsiveness implies that a person can react in an appropriate way to the emotional demands of the situation, that he can get along smoothly with other people. *FC* has been found to be one of the most dependable signs of good adjustment. Forced *FC* responses, or $F \leftrightarrow C$, reflect a certain tension in social relationships. Arbitrary *FC* responses, or F/C, indicate that the individual responds in a superficial, situation-determined manner to emotional impact. His own feelings do not get involved. An *FC*− response usually indi- cates breakdown in reality testing in connection with emotional con- tact.

CF Scores: In producing a *CF* response the subject does not at- tempt to integrate color with definite form. *CF* responses represent a somewhat uncontrolled but nevertheless appropriate and genuine re- activity to social stimuli. The stimulus influences the individual to such an extent that he becomes impulsive. The *CF* score thus may be viewed positively as showing spontaneity and negatively as indicating inadequate control. The positive or negative implication of the *CF* score must be judged from the rest of the record and particularly from the FC to CF and C balance. Forced CF responses, $C{\leftrightarrow}F$, like forced FC responses, are a sign that the individual is making an effort to involve himself emotionally, although he is unable to do so and still retain control. Arbitrary CF responses, C/F, imply that although the reaction to emotional stimuli is on an impersonal and superficial level, the control attempted is unsuccessful, perhaps because the individual is too wrapped up in his own problems.

C Scores: The C response is completely color-determined, ignoring form considerations. Each C scoring category represents a different way of handling color, as follows: (1) Pure C, or crude C responses, for example, "blood" to all red areas, indicate explosive, uncontrolled emotionality. Often the presence of C is a pathological sign. (2) Color-naming responses, C_n, indicate an unsuccessful attempt on the part of the individual to manipulate an emotional situation with magic rather than by realistic means. (3) Color description responses, C_{des}, are at a higher level than C_n responses. The subject acknowledges color; he usually cannot integrate it with his concepts, but he produces other concepts. The very descriptions indicate a strongly intellectual approach to emotional situations. (4) In producing color symbolism responses, C_{sym}, the subject finds an appropriate concept but fails to integrate color with the form of the blot. Color symbolism responses are interpreted in the same way as the C_{des} response, except that C_{sym} may indicate an even greater aesthetic and intellectual investment.

FC', C'F, and C' Scores: Generally, the use of shading as achromatic color is interpreted as a toned-down response to color. If C' responses occur in records that have many chromatic responses, this seems to be a simple extension of receptivity to color, implying a rich varied reaction to all kinds of stimuli presented in the blots. However, C' responses in a record with few chromatic responses seem to indicate a toned-down, hesitant responsiveness to external stimuli.

Content Scores

The content scores generally reveal the breadth of a subject's interests, and sometimes their nature. A wide range of content usually goes with good intelligence; a concentration of scores with animal content and few other categories goes with mediocre or defective intelligence. A concentration of scores in such areas as nature, anatomy, or art objects may indicate special interests or special defensive attitudes. It is considered optimum if the $A\%$ falls between 20 and 35%, with at least 25% of the content not in H, Hd, A, and Ad categories, and with the remainder spread over at least three other content categories.

Further interpretative hypotheses with regard to content are considered in the section on content analysis, pages 153–56.

Popular-Original Scores

The popular-original responses, $P-O$, reveal the subject's ability to view the world in the same way as most other people do, or in a different way from most other people. It is expected that most people will see about three of the ten popular responses. The occurrence of a large number of popular responses in a record (eight or more) indicates a strong need of the individual to think as other people do. The occurrence of a small number of popular responses in a record indicates an inability to see the world as others do. The continued inability to see the popular responses during the testing-the-limits phase is considered an indication of serious weakening of ties with reality.

Good original responses mean superiority and originality. A superior person tends to have twice as many O's as P's (provided there are at least five P's) and twice as many additional O's as main O's. Additional O's are considered particularly good indicators of superiority, since they indicate the ability to be original without losing contact with the matter-of-fact and the obvious. Too many O's (over 50%) may mean that the person is too erratic in his thinking. $O-$ responses show a weakness in reality testing.

Form-Level Rating

Form-level rating is the most important basis for estimating intellectual level and functioning. (This point is more fully discussed on pages 148–49.) The hypothesis is suggested that the highest form-level rating in a record be considered indicative of the individual's capacity, and that the average of all the form-level ratings be considered indicative of his general level of efficiency. The less the scatter in the form-level ratings, the better would be his functioning. Minus form-level responses represent more than a low level of intellectual functioning; also involved is a loosening of the ties with reality.

Additional Scores

The additional scores are usually interpreted as indicators of resources within the individual that he is reluctant to use for various reasons. Additional scores, therefore, should neither be neglected nor given equal weight with the main scores. To weight them for statistical comparison as one-half seems to be a happy compromise. In a rich record, the additional scores are merely another indication of superiority.

Interpretative Meanings of the Quantitative Proportions

Up to this point, the scores have been considered individually, although the necessity to relate one score to the other has been mentioned. The following section presents the first systematic steps necessary for relating the different scores as they must be related in developing a picture of the personality organization.

Proportions Relating to Inner Resources and Impulse Life

None of the following ratios may be interpreted unless there are at least three M responses.

$M:FM$ Ratio

If M is greater than two and exceeds FM (FM must be greater than zero), the need for immediate gratification is subordinated to the other values of the individual. This is generally a sign of maturity, for the individual shows the capacity to defer gratification without undue inner conflict. If M is greater than two and equals FM, it is indicative of a person who accepts his impulses readily; moreover, these impulses do not interfere with the picture he has of himself as a mature individual. When M is greater than two but less than one-half FM, the individual is ruled by immediate needs for gratification rather than long-range goals. This is suggestive of immaturity. The finding that M is greater than two and between one-half and one FM (for instance, M could be four and FM could be five, six, or seven) deserves particular attention. This ratio is frequently found within the normal range and indicates that instinctual gratification is more important than inner values to many persons in our culture.

The hypotheses suggested regarding the $M:FM$ ratio will require modification, particularly in the light of the *FC:CF* ratio. One example will suffice: impulsivity is suggested by the ratio $FM > 2M$, as indicated above, but this is true only when *CF* also exceeds *FC*, implying that the individual tends to act out his impulses. On the other hand, even when there are twice as many *FM* as *M* responses, but no dominance of *CF* responses, it cannot be said that the person tends to act out impulsively. This combination may indicate immaturity within the framework of socially acceptable behavior.

When *M* and *FM* are both few, the individual may be repressed if the F% is high, or he may show ego weakness if the form level is mediocre or poor.

M:(FM + m) Ratio

If *FM + m* is more than one and one-half times *M* (for instance, *FM + m* is seven or more, and *M* is four), it is indicative of tensions that are too strong to allow the individual to utilize his inner resources constructively. When *M* is approximately equal to or a little greater than *FM + m*, and there are not more than one or two *m*'s, the implication is that the individual is sufficiently in control of his impulse life to give himself stability.

Proportions Relating to Emotional Responsiveness to Environment

Sum C

Sum *C* indicates the degree of overt reactivity to outer stimuli, whether controlled or otherwise. Normal reactivity to emotional stimuli seems to require that Sum *C* be at least three. If it is less than three, there is too little responsiveness to environmental influences.

FC:(CF + C) Ratio

When *FC* exceeds *CF + C*, but the latter scores are still represented by a few responses, the individual is able to exert control over his impulses and emotions. Such a person is ordinarily able to respond appropriately and genuinely with both feeling and action to his social environment. If *CF + C* is absent, or nearly so, there is excessive control, and the socialized responses (represented by *FC*) tend to be superficial. The quality of the various types of color responses (*F↔C*, or *F/C*, or *C/F*, etc.) as well as form-level ratings should be used for modification of these hypotheses. If *CF + C* exceeds *FC*, there is evidence of weak control over emotional impulses.

Percentage of Responses to Cards VIII, IX, and X

The production of responses to the last three cards, which are entirely chromatic, indicates general responsiveness to emotional stimuli from the environment. This responsiveness may or may not be expressed in observable behavior. If the number of responses to the last three cards is over 40% of the total number of responses, it is hypothesized that the individual is stimulated by the environment; * if fewer than 30%, the individual may be lacking in responsiveness or may be inhibited under conditions of strong environmental impact.

Reaction Time to Chromatic Cards Compared with Reaction Time to Achromatic Cards

If the average reaction time to the chromatic cards exceeds that for the achromatic cards by more than ten seconds, this may indicate that the individal is disturbed by acute emotional stimuli. If, however, the individual is disturbed by the highly shaded cards (Cards IV, VI, and VII), and shows this by a prolonged reaction time, then it seems that disturbance results when the environmental stimuli touch on the area of affectional need. Careful analysis of the reaction time to each card is required, since a long reaction time may result from elements other than color or shading.

Proportions Relating to Introversive-Extratensive Balance

One object of Rorschach interpretation is to discover the role that the different areas of stimulation play in the life of a subject—their strength, and their importance in his general life situation. In this sense, and in this sense only, does the Rorschach terminology distinguish between people who are predominantly prompted from within (introverts) and people who are predominantly stimulated from without (extraverts). Since Rorschach's meaning of these terms is so different from the popular meaning, it is usual to use the terms introversive (rather than introverted) and extratensive (rather than extraverted) to make it clear that it is the Rorschach definition that is implied.

According to Rorschach usage, the markedly introversive person is one who has a well-developed imaginal function, either in terms of

---

* On the assumption that each of the ten cards is equally stimulating, the statistical expectation for three cards would be 30%. However, since Card X facilitates *D* responses, 40% is recognized as within the range of ordinary responsiveness to Cards VIII, IX, and X.

fantasy, long-range goals, or acknowledged impulses, while his responsiveness to and involvement with the outer world are reduced. He tends to restructure the world in terms of his own values and needs. The well-adjusted introversive person is not withdrawn or retiring; he is self-sufficient.

The markedly extratensive person, on the other hand, is one who is highly responsive to his environment, either in terms of overt emotional expression or affectional warmth of feeling, or a mere passive submission to forces coming upon him from without. He does not tend to restructure the world in terms of his own needs. The well-adjusted extratensive person is not passively reactive. He is creative in his relationship to objects and people external to him, and strives toward goals that he has staked out in the external world.

M:Sum C Ratio

The balance between the number of M responses and the Sum C indicates to what extent a person is stimulated from within or from without. If M is greater than two and exceeds Sum C, provided that Sum C is not zero, the individual tends to rely upon his inner life more than upon his environment for comfort or for stimulation. The opposite is true when Sum C exceeds M.

$(FM + m)$:$(Fc + c + C')$ Ratio

$FM + m$ responses indicate introversive tendencies not fully accepted by or available to the subject at the time. The achromatic responses indicate extratensive tendencies not fully accepted by or available to the subject at the time.

If this ratio is in the same direction as the M:Sum C ratio, it confirms and strengthens the impression given by the latter. If it is at variance with M:Sum C, the individual may be undergoing some kind of change in his development. Much would depend on which score or scores in the ratio are emphasized; for instance, emphasis on m or c would lead to the hypothesis of anxiety in the area of dependency needs, while emphasis on C' might indicate depression and withdrawal.

Percentage of Responses to Cards VIII, IX, and X

If the percentage of responses to the last three cards goes in the same direction as the other signs of introversion-extratension, it would seem that the indicated direction of balance is of such long standing that it might be termed "natural."

Proportions Relating to the Organization of Affectional Need

$(FK + Fc) : F$ Ratio

The optimum ratio of $FK + Fc$ to F is considered to exist when $FK + Fc$ is approximately one-fourth to three-fourths of F. For instance, if there are $2FK$ and $4Fc$, then F should fall between 8 and 24. This relationship implies that an individual possesses a healthy response to people, not being oversensitive or overdependent. If $FK + Fc$ exceeds three-fourths of F, the need for affection and response from others is overwhelming and may threaten the rest of the personality. If $FK + Fc$ is less than one-fourth of F, there tends to be a denial or repression or underdevelopment of the need for affection, which may constitute a major handicap in general adjustment.

Ratio of Differentiated to Undifferentiated Shading Scores

Where the undifferentiated shading scores $(K, KF, k, kF, c,$ and $cF)$ outnumber the differentiated shading scores $(Fc, Fk,$ and $FK)$, the affectional needs are so poorly integrated in the personality that a seriously disrupting influence can be considered to exist.

Ratio of Achromatic to Chromatic Scores— $(Fc + c + C') : (FC + CF + C)$

When the achromatic responses $(Fc + c + C')$ outnumber the chromatic responses $(FC + CF + C)$ by two to one, the individual's experience with outside stimulation has been so traumatized that he has withdrawn, for fear of being hurt. This is the "burnt child" hypothesis. The opposite situation, that is, when chromatic responses are twice the achromatic, suggests that the ability to interact with the social environment is optimum. If $CF + C$ is larger than FC, and together they exceed the achromatic scores by two to one or more, the individual tends to act out his emotions. Such an individual feels relaxed about his needs for approval and affection and therefore is not hampered in expressing his emotionality.

Proportions Relating to Intellectual Interest and Ambitions

Number of Responses, or R

The total number of responses generally (but not always) indicates the productive capacity of an individual, the more intelligent persons usually being the more productive. The average number of responses expected from normal adults ranges from 20 to 45. A small number of responses may indicate unproductivity because of limited capacity or because of disturbed emotionality. A large number of responses may indicate the rich productivity of an able person, or it may indicate a compulsive need for quantity.

$W:M$ Ratio

The $W:M$ ratio indicates how substantial an individual's intellectual ambitions are. When the ratio of W to M is approximately two to one, and the W's are good, this is taken as evidence that there is enough creative potential to fortify a real drive to intellectual achievement. The 2:1 ratio is considered optimum, but only when there are at least three M responses and approximately six W responses. When W is greater than twice M $(W > 2M)$, the level of aspiration is too high. Modification of this hypothesis might be necessary in the light of the form-level rating. If W is less than $2M$ $(W < 2M)$, the indication is that the individual has creative potential for which he has not found a satisfactory outlet.

$(H + A):(Hd + Ad)$ Ratio

This ratio gives an indication of the degree of an individual's criticalness. The sum of H and A scores is expected to be approximately twice the sum of the Hd and Ad scores. If $H + A$ is less than one-half $Hd + Ad$ there is a tendency to be exacting, critical, or meticulous. These tendencies may be associated with anxiety.

$A\%$, or Percentage of Animal Scores

The $A\%$ indicates the degree of stereotypy in an individual's thinking. The higher the $A\%$, the more commonplace are his thoughts, and the narrower are his interests. The optimum percentage is considered to be from 20 to 35%; $A\%$ of over 50% tends to be associated either with low intellectual capacity or disturbed adjustment.

Average Response Time

The average time per response is an indication of an individual's speed of perception; the faster the mental reactions, the more alert the individual tends to be. The expected average time per response is 30 seconds. An average response time of over one minute is an indication of slow mental processes, unless the longer time is spent in the elaboration of the response. The slowness in reaction may be due to poor mental capacity, or to emotional depression. An average response time of less than 30 seconds is quick and may be forced.

Proportions Relating to Constrictive Control

Two factors relating to control are $F\%$ and $(FK + F + Fc)\%$. The interpretations attached to $F\%$ have been considered elsewhere (page 133). Any $F-$ score is an indication that the effectiveness of an individual's control is in jeopardy because of weakness in reality testing.

$(FK + F + Fc)\%$ is another indicator of constrictive control. The normal range is between 50 and 75%. If the percentage exceeds 75%, the hypothesis of neurotic constriction, that is, lack of emotional spontaneity, is applicable. When $F\%$ is near 50%, but the $(FK + F + Fc)\%$ does not exceed 75%, the individual may be controlled and restrained but still able to live comfortably with other people.

Other control factors—$M : (FM + m)$ and $FC : (CF + C)$—have been discussed elsewhere in this book. (See page 14.)

Evaluation of Control, Inner Resources, Intellectual Approach, and Intellectual Level

We are now ready to study the more complex relationships among the scores. For instance, while the M:Sum C ratio is in itself significant, further nuances in interpretation are possible when the ratio is studied in relation to the $F\%$. A graphic portrayal of the distribution of the main and additional determinant scores, called a "psychogram," yields at a glance the information required to evaluate one determinant or to weigh groups of determinants one against the other. The initial hypotheses derived from the individual scores or ratios concerning such important factors as the kind of control, and the amount of spontaneity, can now be checked against these more inclusive relationships.

In similar manner, the single location score, the average form-level rating, or the number of original responses was used as the basis for an hypothesis concerning an individual's intellectual manner of approach and to evaluate his intellectual level. Each of these preliminary hypotheses can now be checked by the interrelationships among *all* the location scores, and among other scores, both quantitative and qualitative, that are related to intellectual functioning.

The Psychogram

The most important feature to observe in the psychogram is the shape of the distribution of the main determinant scores. Do most of the responses tend to cluster in the center, in the left half, or in the right half, or are they evenly distributed over the three main areas of the graph? Such an overview will provide a preliminary notion of the balance between the three major modes of perception. If the subject's perception has been influenced largely by his own imagination, his own needs and drives, the responses pile up on the left-hand side of the graph; if the subject's perception has been influenced largely by external stimuli, the responses pile up on the right-hand side of the graph; if the perception of the subject is largely rational, impersonal, unemotional, the responses tend to concentrate in the center of the graph.

As an illustration, let us consider a typical, healthy adult with average or slightly above average intelligence. He would probably give about 25 responses distributed as follows: $3M$, $4FM$, 1 additional m, no k, $1K$, $1FK$, $9F$, $2Fc$, no c, no C', $3FC$, $2CF$, and no C. This record shows what is considered an even distribution of scores. He gives the expected number of F scores ($F\% = 36$); there are some Fc and FK scores, and the $(FK + Fc) : F$ ratio is $3 : 9$, indicating good control and no rigidity. On the left-hand side of the graph the relationship between M and FM is $3:4$, which is satisfactory. There is no evidence of inadequate feelings toward the self or of tension (only one additional m). The presence of one K may be insignificant; to interpret this factor, we would have to see the K response and know to what card it was given. The right-hand side of the graph also indicates that this individual is responsive, seemingly spontaneous, without losing control; a person who is making a good social adjustment. The M:Sum C ratio $(3 : 3\frac{1}{2})$ and the $(FM + m) : (Fc + c + C')$ ratio $(4 : 2)$ do not markedly contradict each other, and indicate a person who is stimulated equally by inner promptings and outer reality. There are no evidences of anxiety (we have noted the absence of c, k, and C'). The fact that there is only one additional score would lead us to feel that the individual is making good use of his resources.

Thus far, we have considered only the quantitative aspects of the psychogram. Let us suppose that the form level, the type of FC and CF responses, and the kind of M responses, whether H or (H) or (A), were also shown. We could then be more specific about the subject's intellectual status (form level), his feelings toward people (M), and the genuineness of his social adjustment (FC and CF).

Manner of Approach

An examination of the distribution of location scores reveals the way an individual typically approaches everyday problems. One person may show a meticulous observation of details with a reluctance to draw general conclusions—for example, D and d emphasized, W underemphasized. Another person may start with a general survey of the situation and then turn to details—for example, initial W's followed by D's. A third subject may immediately jump to conclusions—poorly specified W's would predominate in the record.

Let us again consider our typical subject. He does not show a preference for any particular mode of approach. His location scores are distributed as follows: of his 25 responses, 28% are W's; 56% are D's; 12% are d's; and 4% are dd's. There is one additional W. On this basis, we can describe this person's manner of approach as showing the ability to see the more general while not overlooking the obvious. There seems to be a capacity also to pay unusual attention to minutiae, but not to such an extent that it detracts from his intellectual functioning. An analysis of the quality of the responses, especially the W responses, is needed to determine how these capacities are integrated, that is, whether the ability to note details is used to build up the wholes. The form-level rating of the W's, the D's, and the d's would further enable the interpreter to make specific observations concerning the quality of this person's intellectual approach.

Estimate of Intellectual Level

The evaluation of intellectual level requires the consideration of a number of factors: (1) form-level rating, (2) quantity and quality of M responses, (3) quantity and quality of W responses, (4) quantity and quality of O responses, (5) variety of content, and (6) succession.

Form-Level Rating

The form-level rating for each response, the average form-level rating for each location and determinant category, the scatter in the form-level ratings, and the average unweighted and weighted form-level ratings are all important in evaluating intellectual capacity and efficiency. It has been tentatively suggested that even one response with a form-level rating of 4.0 indicates very superior capacity; a rating of

3.0, superior capacity; a rating of 2.0, average or slightly above average capacity. Form-level ratings of 1.0 or less indicate below average and inferior capacity. The content of minus form-level responses sometimes provides important clues to difficulties in intellectual functioning.

A person who shows little scatter in his form-level ratings for the individual scores probably functions intellectually more smoothly than an individual who shows both minus and superior ratings in his record. When there is variation in the average form-level ratings for the several scoring categories, the categories in which the extremes occur should be noted.

More important than the form level rating for each individual response are the average unweighted form-level rating (FLR) and the average weighted form-level rating. When both the unweighted and the weighted average FLR's fall into the same range, the difference between capacity and efficiency may be considered to be relatively small. A marked discrepancy between the two ratings would indicate that important factors partly or completely interfere with intellectual efficiency.

An average weighted form-level rating from 1.0 to 1.4 indicates average or higher than average intellectual capacity. The range between 1.5 and 1.9, containing enough individual ratings of 2.5 or higher to compensate for all ratings of 1.0 or lower, indicates a superior level of intellectual capacity. An average of 2.0 or higher indicates very superior intellectual capacity, especially if there are sufficient ratings of 2.5 and higher to more than compensate for any inferior ratings.

Quantity and Quality of M Responses

The more *M* responses, the richer they are in quality compared with the usual responses, the more brilliant the subject's intellectual functioning. Lack of *M* in otherwise superior records (containing high form-level ratings and good *W*'s) is not a counterindication of superiority. Minus *M* responses represent a serious break in intellectual efficiency.

Quantity and Quality of W Responses

A high level of intellectual functioning is indicated by a fair number of *W* responses of good quality. This implies a high level of accuracy, specification, and organization of the *W* responses. A large number of undifferentiated whole responses indicates either (1) a low level of intellectual capacity or (2) emotional interference with efficient functioning. Lack of *W*'s in a record that contains good *D*'s indicates an overcautious approach rather than lack of capacity.

Quantity and Quality of O Responses

A large number of main and additional original responses that have good form level is characteristic of a high level of intellectual efficiency. Bizarre original responses indicate severe disturbance of intellectual function but not necessarily a low capacity.

A comparison of form level with the number of original responses offers clues as to the efficiency with which the individual utilizes his mental capacity. For example, high form level with few *O*'s might indicate a person of high intelligence who is not being creative or resourceful.

Variety of Content

Subjects of superior ability usually give at least 25% of their responses outside the categories of *H, Hd, A*, and *Ad*, and spread over at least three other content categories. Such a spread indicates a flexibility of interests that contributes to intellectual efficiency. A large proportion of animal responses (which are very easy to see in the blot material) indicates mediocre or defective intelligence.

Succession

Succession is determined by the order in which the location scores are given. An orderly succession is an indication of optimum intellectual functioning. A rigid succession is considered to indicate a limitation in efficiency. A loose or confused succession often indicates a weakening of intellectual control.

For a valid estimate of intellectual level, the interaction among the six aspects just discussed must be taken into consideration.

Sequence Analysis

Sequence analysis consists of a card-by-card, response-by-response process. There are no new interpretative hypotheses attached to the specific features revealed through sequence analysis. Its purpose is rather to confirm, modify, or discard the basic interpretative hypotheses as the dynamic aspect of the performance seems to demand. The test behavior, the language used by the subject, and the special qualities of the blot material are also taken into account.

The general method of sequence analysis cannot be easily described owing to the flexible character of this approach to interpretation. Only general considerations of this method, therefore, are outlined here. (For a more detailed discussion, see *Developments in the Rorschach Technique,* Vol. I.) Sequence analysis is demonstrated in the case material presented in Chapter Seven.

The following seven points may serve as a guide to sequence analysis:

1. It is necessary to have a knowledge of the type of response each card normally evokes. Familiarity with the cards and with typical responses constitutes a standard for judging a subject's performance.

2. The location scores should be examined in terms of succession, organization, and relationship to the blot material. Likewise, a study of the determinants used, in terms of succession, relationship to the blot material, locations, and content, is called for. A few of the numerous clues to the subject's personality that may be revealed through these analyses are illustrated below.

It is always important to pay particular attention to the first response to each card. The expected reaction is to give *W*'s to all the cards first. If a subject gives *W*'s first to most of the cards but not to all, the meaning of this should be ascertained. The determinants used in the first responses are also of significance since they reflect the readiness of the subject to use certain resources. Consider, as an example, a subject who tends to give *F* as the first response, followed by *M* or *FC* or *Fc*. This sequence suggests an inhibited control followed by a relaxation as the subject begins to feel at ease. The effect of the colored or shaded cards on the sequence of the determinants is the final item to be noted at this point.

3. The number of responses given to each card may suggest to the interpreter the kind of material that is stimulating or inhibiting to the subject.

The refusal to give a response to a card varies in significance with the card rejected. Card IX seems to be most frequently rejected, sometimes even by presumably normal people. Cards II, IV, and VI are also often rejected. The remaining cards are rejected occasionally by subjects who show strong resistance to the qualities of the particular card. The rejection of more than four cards by subjects over seven years of age points to a serious personality disturbance.

4. The variations in form-level ratings from card to card and from response to response should be examined. Lower than usual form-level ratings may give clues to the dynamics of a personality disturbance, if a disturbance exists.

5. Variations in reaction time and response time from card to card should be noted, considering how these time factors are related to the blot material, and to the location, determinants, and content of the responses. Long pauses may give clues to specific difficulty. Lengthened reaction time to the colored cards or to the shaded cards should be observed.

6. The sequence of reactions to the color of Cards II, III, VIII, IX, and X, and to the shading elements of all the cards, especially of Cards IV and VI, is of prime importance. There are three major considerations in analyzing color and shading dynamics. First, is color or shading used as a determinant? Second, if color and shading are not used or are used very little, what are the reactions to color or shading? Are the colored or highly shaded areas avoided, or is the color or shading denied even though the responses given suggest their use? Third, are there evidences of disturbance as a result of the color or the shading? Disturbances of this kind have traditionally been referred to as "color shock" or "shading shock." Consider this illustration:

> A subject gives two good whole responses, one *F*, and one *M* to Card I. Then he selects the black area in Card II (D_3) and III (*W*), both *F*'s, after taking more than one minute to respond in each instance. He then continues to give good wholes and details to Cards IV, V, VI and VII, a few of them *Fc* responses, followed by three anatomy responses to Cards VIII, IX, and X. In the inquiry he denies the use of color for his anatomy responses.
>
> This subject shows color avoidance, denial, and disturbance suggesting that he has serious difficulty in situations that are emotionally stimulating. This hypothesis is strongly indicated especially since he seems to be a sensitive and an alert individual.

7. A comparison should be made of the material that emerges during the inquiry or testing the limits with that produced during the performance proper. The general hypothesis is that the performance proper indicates the resources readily available to the subject, whereas the additional material that emerges in the inquiry represents resources available after the subject becomes more settled in the situation. Elaborating on main responses, or giving spontaneous additional

responses in the later stages, may indicate that the subject is suggestible or that he has become less defensive and therefore better able to use his resources. Or it may simply mean that he feels more at ease with the material and the examiner.

The seven brief comments given above should be considered merely as an introduction to the interpretative possibilities offered by sequence analysis.

Content Analysis

Rorschach interpretation, until recently, was based predominantly upon the structural elements of the test: the number of *W*'s, *M*'s, *P*'s, and so forth. The *qualitative* aspects of the responses have become an integral part of the interpretative process as a result of the work of Klopfer [4] and Beck [1]. The content of the responses—that is, what the subject sees in the blot material—is the most recent major factor to attract the attention of Rorschach workers (Brown [2], Goldfarb [3], Lindner [5], Phillips and Smith [6], and Wheeler [7]) . An analysis of the content of responses offers clues concerning the symbolic meaning of the subject's concept formations.

The significance of the most frequently occurring content has been briefly discussed elsewhere in this volume (pages 138–39) , primarily from a quantitative standpoint. Some qualitative aspects will be considered in this section. In addition, a selection of some of the less frequently occurring content including interpretative meanings is listed.

It may be well to reiterate that original concepts and repetitive concepts are particularly revealing. Also relevant is the question of the significance of the area selected in relation to content. Workers such as Wheeler [7] and Lindner [5] feel that content is not independent of location. For example, it has been said that the popular "crabs" of Card X does not have the same significance as would "crabs" to another area on this or any other card. Phillips and Smith [6], on the other hand, feel that content is largely a function of the individual and not of the stimulus. It suffices to say that the problems involved in the interpretation of content are many and that the meanings attached to the several contents offered here must be used with caution.

The hypotheses presented below are based on dynamic personality theory as well as clinical experiences. They are presented not as facts, but as working hypotheses, hunches, or guesses.

Human Figures

A few major points should be noted in the analysis of human figures:

Preoccupation with particular parts of the body may point to certain concerns or difficulties. Repeated perception of heads and faces may indicate a concern about intellectuality, or a feeling that biological activity is less worthy than intellectual activity. This type of perception is often found among people who use the defenses of intellectualization or compulsion. The perception of profiles may suggest that the individual is ill at ease with himself and others.

People who tend to see parts of the body that are directly or indirectly sexual in significance may be either trying to show that they are sufficiently mature to give such responses or attempting to cover up inadequate sexual relationships. For instance, it has been noted that paranoids often see buttocks and that persons deprived of adequate infantile oral satisfactions see breasts.

Problems in sexual identification are sometimes revealed by the content. If a subject is sexually confused, he may not be able to determine whether the human figures he sees in the blots are male or female.

The kinds of activities engaged in by the perceived human figures can be interpreted. People seen fighting, arguing, or attacking one another may reveal the subject's hostile feelings. People seen bowing, listening, or conversing may indicate the subject's feelings of submission. Laughing, dancing people may reflect the subject's actual contentment or may indicate a desire for contentment. Likewise, people perceived as ugly, beautiful, or menacing may be a projection of the subject's own feelings about people, even if these feelings are consciously repressed.

When human beings are seen in some form of guise—as monsters, clowns, ghosts, mythical figures, or figures with animal-like behavior —it may be an indication that the individual is not able to identify closely with real people. Witches, for example, have particular significance for revealing some of the qualities of the mother-child relationship.

Animal Figures

Animals are perceived by subjects of all ages, both normal and abnormal. These responses may represent potential adjustive techniques.

The meaning of perceiving various kinds of animals is rather speculative; however, there is some indication that seeing fierce animals, such as tigers and lions, may refer to certain aggressive tendencies in the individual that he is trying to handle in some way. Passive animals, such as cows or sheep, and domestic animals, such as dogs or cats, may show passivity and dependent attitudes.

Sexual Responses

Sexual responses may be of three kinds: (1) responses with obvious sexual symbolism, such as snake, totem pole, house; (2) responses given to areas usually associated with sex responses—for instance, bottom *D* in Card II, top *D* in Card VI, or bottom center *d* in Card VII; and (3) direct sex responses, such as mention of menstruation, intercourse, genital organs. The meanings attached to sex responses need to be studied in relation to other factors in the subject's Rorschach and with some knowledge of the subject's life history. It is impossible to say on the basis of the sexual responses alone whether the individual is avoiding sexual problems by naming them, whether he is worried about sexual problems, or whether as a result of being recently psychoanalyzed he feels a certain independence and strength in seeing sexual responses.

Anatomy, Geography, and Science Content

Anatomy, geography, or science responses are often given by subjects who are trying to show off intellectually. This is a way of covering up their real feelings. These responses may indicate feelings of intellectual inadequacy, especially when the responses avoid any commitment to definite form or specification. An accumulation of such responses has the same interpretative meaning even when the responses are given by specialists in these fields.

It is possible that anatomy responses may reveal that an individual has real concern about his body.

Miscellaneous Content

Masks may indicate an emphasis on role-playing to avoid personal exposure.

Emblems indicate attitudes toward authority—usually attitudes of submission.

Spiders may reveal attitudes toward the mother figure. The spider is considered to be the "wicked mother" symbol.

Letters of the alphabet or numerals are signs of a pathological condition, when given by adults.

Blood responses indicate strong, uncontrolled affective reactions.

Food may indicate dependency needs—the desire to be nurtured by others.

Maps indicate guardedness and evasiveness.

Teeth may be interpreted as indicating a resentful or aggressive attitude due perhaps to frustration of dependency needs. *Gums* may have the same connotation. The "teeth" response is given more often by children and adolescents than by adults.

Abstractions reflect feeling tone quite directly: a euphoric mood by "gaiety" or "spring"; dysphoric mood by "chaos" or "nightmare." These responses usually reflect superior intelligence.

This chapter has discussed the outlines of various interpretative procedures. The integration of data obtained by these procedures into a personality picture is demonstrated in the case studies presented in Chapter Seven.

References

1. Beck, S. J.; Beck, A. G.; Levitt, E. E.; and Molish, H. B. *Rorschach's Test, Vol. I: Basic Processes*. 3rd rev. ed. New York: Grune & Stratton, Inc.; 1961.

2. Brown, F. "An Exploratory Study of Dynamic Factors in the Content of the Rorschach Protocol," *J. Proj. Tech.*, 1953, 17, 251–279, 462–464.

3. Goldfarb, W. "The Animal Symbol in the Rorschach Test, and an Animal Association Test," *Rorschach Res. Exch.*, 1945, 9, 8–22.

4. Klopfer, B., et al. *Developments in the Rorschach Technique*, Vol. I. New York: Harcourt, Brace & World; 1954. Pages 376–402.

5. Lindner, R. R. "The Content Analysis of the Rorschach Protocol," in Abt, L. E., and Bellak, L. *Projective Psychology*. New York: Alfred A. Knopf, Inc.; 1950. Pages 75–90.

6. Phillips, L., and Smith, J. *Rorschach Interpretation: Advanced Technique*. New York: Grune & Stratton, Inc.; 1953.

7. Wheeler, W. M. "An Analysis of Rorschach Indices of Male Homosexuality," *Rorschach Res. Exch. and J. Proj. Tech.*, 1949, 13, 97–126.

Chapter Seven

TWO CASE STUDIES

Interview Material, Case of A. S.

Autobiographical Sketch of A. S.

I am 32 years old. My mother is a housewife, 62, and my father is a construction contractor and is 73. My relationship with my parents is very good, so long as I am not living with them. We think differently, are all very dogmatic, and therefore quarrel if we are together for more than two days. But, it's always good to see them again, and I do see them quite frequently.

I have two brothers: Freddie, who's 36, and Joseph, who is 26. Freddie is married, with two children. I'm not close to Freddie. When we were home together, he considered me a kid sister and a nuisance. Joseph is away at school studying physics. Although we do not spend a great deal of time together, our relationship is good.

I lived at home until ten years ago. My youthful days were very happy ones for me as I remember them. Although I was extremely overweight, I never lacked friends, and was always a popular member of the group.

Until high school years, the weight problem never concerned me. However, throughout this period, although I remained popular I did not have "dates" of the romantic type—naturally a great calamity to any teenager. I would diet sporadically, but remained very much overweight until I went to a small New England college.

I was always a good student, though not particularly interested in intellectual life. I was attending college as most other girls do—with the intention of marrying and raising a family shortly after graduation. Therefore, I spent a great deal of time having a good time during the college years. I met my first real boyfriend here and had my first tragedy in this area. After two years of courtship with plans for the future together, he broke off our relationship just before I graduated.

Upon graduation from college, I held a succession of jobs in the editorial field for three years. During the period I spent a two-month vacation in Europe with a girl with whom I had grown up. Upon our return, we decided to live in New York City, sharing an apartment together. When she married, less than a year later, I returned home to live with the family.

After giving up our jobs because we were simply "sick of it all," I and a fellow worker traveled around the United States for about a year. We spent the winter working as maids, waitresses, etc., in an elite hotel in Florida in return for room, board, a very small salary, and free time every afternoon which we spent water skiing. Here I had my second big romance, with a water-skiing instructor attached to the same hotel. This young man was everything that a girl's middle-class parents would *not* want to have for a son-in-law: not well-educated, a water bum, and, as I later found out, an alcoholic. However, he was *very* masculine. When I informed my parents of my marriage plans, they came scooting down to Florida to "size up" the situation. The resort season having come to an end, I returned home with my parents. I expected to marry my water-skiing instructor when he came to New York, but he never came, although his letters kept saying "in a few weeks." After working at a temporary clerical job for awhile, I returned to Florida to see him, and it was then that I learned about his alcoholism and a few other unsavory facts.

I returned home very much disheartened, and in a state of confusion as to what to do next. I decided to go to graduate school so that I could prepare myself for some profession. Being unsure of my motivation *and* my interest in chemistry (which had been my undergraduate major), I entered the science department. In the meantime I continued working as a secretary, and also continued living at home. I became extremely interested in my studies, and with the help of one of my professors, I was able to give up full-time working and give more time to being a student.

Again I was a good student, but now I was working hard to maintain that status. I had been out of school so long, and had forgotten most of what I knew about chemistry. I was therefore very unsure of my own abilities. This uncertainty concerning myself and my abilities still remains today.

Shortly after beginning studies again, I met a young professor at the University. We fell in love. But because he was of a different faith and, perhaps even more important, because he had some serious psychological problems, and he had some sexual difficulties, we never married. The objections have never been mine. We go through periods of not seeing one another, and at present I have not seen him for several months (the longest period yet). I suspect, however, that I am still "carrying the torch."

I have been living alone in New York with no intention of ever returning home to live.

I finished my course work for the Ph.D. in chemistry, and have been working on my doctoral dissertation. I started teaching, and am now an assistant professor at a junior college in New Jersey.

A. S. Described by Two Colleagues Who Have Known Her Professionally and Socially for About Three Years

A. S. is a person of superior intelligence. She dresses modestly and makes a very neat appearance. A. S. is a hard, conscientious worker, though not particularly creative. She is a loyal and dependable person, who is friendly and generous (gives gladly of herself in terms of time and energy).

She frequently expresses feelings of unworthiness, and has little confidence in herself. Her outlook regarding social, political, and moral issues is very conventional and uncompromising. A. S. is prone to hysterical outbursts, is verbally aggressive toward men, and apparently enjoys arguing vehemently with them. She is a very tense person (smokes incessantly, likes to consume liquor, and finds it difficult to control intake when at parties).

Other descriptive adjectives: good-natured to the point of being gullible, distrustful of men, argumentative.

Rorschach Protocol, Case of A. S.

CARD I

PERFORMANCE

3″

1. This looks like some family shield of two heads, some sort of animal. The whole thing looks like a crest of some sort. Shall I elaborate? Here are the heads of the animals. I don't know what would be in the center.

INQUIRY

1. *Location: W*
   S: The whole thing is a family crest.
   E: Show me the animal's head.
   S: Here is the nose, ears, the thing in the middle is just something decorative to hold the whole thing together. I like that—that is very good.

   Score: *W*   *F*   *Emblem*   1.5

COMMENT: The whole blot was included in the response, the shape being the sole determinant used. The basal rating of 1.0 was given for the concept "shield," which adequately fits the blot area, and additional credit was given for the specification of the animal heads.

CARD II

Good God! Is this the right way?
May I turn? (E. answered that she may do so, if she wants to.) It does not matter which way I turn? $\vee \wedge \vee \wedge$
This will take me a little while. $\vee \wedge$

45″

I can't possibly tell you what the whole thing looks like. I can only tell you about this part.

1. $\vee$ This looks like some kind of bug with antennae sticking out.

1. *Location: D_1*
    S. Instead of a bug, I think it is some kind of sea animal—in the crab family but not dangerous—it doesn't bite.
    E: What makes it look more like a sea animal?
    S: Bigger than a bug and it is broad this way and bugs usually are not.
Analogy Period:
    E: When you said this part looked like a crab did you think of the color?
    S: When I changed it to *crab* it was partially because it was red and because it was too broad for a bug.

Score: D   F,FC   A   1.0

COMMENT: This is a popular-level response to a large usual detail; therefore, a form-level rating of 1.0 was given. Although the subject said the response was changed to "crab" partially because of the color, this was elicited only after the analogy period; therefore an *additional FC* was scored.

2. These other two red things would be bugs—unicellular animals, very strange, nothing I have seen. I just can't make anything out of the black.

2. *Location: D_2*
    S: It is something you would see under a microscope, like amoeba or paramecium.
    E: What is it about this part that

makes it seem as if it is under a microscope?

S: Because of these darker portions, looks like structure of a cell, looks magnified. This larger siphon would take food in and smaller ones like excretory organs.

E: You said these "red things"—tell me what you meant by red things.

S: Looks like it is stained under a microscope.

Score: D   *Fc,F C*   *A.At*   1.5

COMMENT: The shading appears to be the primary determinant. Although the subject specified "red," this has been scored as an arbitrary use of color, as almost any color may be used for staining. The basal form-level rating of 0.5 was assigned to a response that is semidefinite in form. To this was added an additional credit of 0.5 for the use of the shading determinant, and another 0.5 for the specific organs named.

Add. Location: D_3's + d_1

S: (turned card and said spontaneously) I wish I could do something with this part (the black areas) —it is some sort of medical-book diagram of a male pelvic bone and this (small *d*) his—you know what. (E. supplied the word "penis.") Yes, his penis.

Score: W̶   *F*   *Sex*   1.0

COMMENT: The concept seems to fulfill the minimal requirements for accuracy of fit to justify a basal rating of 1.0.

CARD III

PERFORMANCE

He! He!

7″

1. These are two people playing a game together, involving this gadget (center red area) . I'll say it is a ball —it gives the impression of motion.

INQUIRY

1. *Location: W*
   E: Tell me more about how you see the ball and the people?
   S: It is one ball, going back and

forth between them, very unrealistic, doesn't really look like that.

E: Do these people look like men or women?

S: Neither; such a rough drawing, I couldn't possibly tell.

E: What about this part (the leg area)?

S: I can only see one leg because it is only a profile.

E: What about this part (lower center detail)?

S: Could be their hands and playing this game with some kind of racket, this part is the shadow.

Score: W   *M,Fm*   *H,Obj* $P \rightarrow O$ 1.5

COMMENT: These are the popular human figures usually seen on this card. An additional *Fm* has been scored for the ball in motion. To the basal form-level rating of 1.0 normally given for the popular response, 0.5 has been added for the organization involved in seeing them "playing a game." No additional credit has been given for the rackets, the ball in motion, or the shadow, since these concepts are too vague as far as form is concerned. Credit has already been given for the organizational element. Notice that the sexual specification of the figure has been avoided as well.

2. Two monkeys hanging from its tail —raccoons or monkeys.

2. *Location:* D_2's

S: Whichever it is which hangs from their tails.

E: Can you describe the monkeys for me?

S: Here are their tails, the heads.

Score: D   *FM*   *A*   1.5

COMMENT: The determinant *FM* has been used, as the hanging is not an involuntary action, but one that is attributable to monkeys. The basal rating of 1.0 was given for the concept of the monkeys, and additional credit of 0.5 was added for the specification of "hanging by their tails." If the subject had left "raccoons" as the response, this would have resulted in a minus form-level rating, because the action would be inaccurate for a raccoon.

CARD IV

PERFORMANCE

5″

1. Amphibious animal—if you call them that—it has wings, it can fly, also crawls along the ground, a prehistoric animal.

INQUIRY

1. *Location: W*
   S: Walking or crawling, the animal is on land now.
   E: Tell me about these parts (pointing to the lower extensions)?
   S: It does not have ordinary kind of legs, maybe it's asleep, it has closed eyes, sleeping position, got ears, too.
   E: Tell me what else about this gives you the impression of an amphibious animal?
   S: It has tough scaly skin—it's horny and horrible.

Score: W FM,Fc A 1.5

COMMENT: Stress has been placed on what the animal was doing, the texture of the skin having been mentioned only after some questioning; therefore, *Fc* is scored as additional. To the basal rating of 1.0 for prehistoric animal, which is general enough to be conceivable for this blot area, an additional credit of 0.5 was added for the specifications of eyes and ears. However, no credit was added for the wings because of the poor fit to the blot area, and poor proportion in relation to the size of the animal. The wings are irrelevant specifications.

CARD V

PERFORMANCE

1″

1. This is a bat but I don't know what these are (upper extensions). I don't think bats have things like that. I did not know it was split up the back either (pointing to the lower extensions).

INQUIRY

1. *Location: W*
   S: I am not awfully sure that bats have these things.
   E: Can you tell me more of how you see it?
   S: He's in motion, flying, because wings are outspread.

Score: W FM A P 1.0

COMMENT: In spite of the subject's criticism of the fit, the response remains the popular one for this card. No credit is added for the "flying," since it is part of the basic concept in this card and is as irrelevant for the form level as is the split up the back.

CARD VI

Oh, dear! My goodness! O.K.

8″

1. Just this part (upper *D*) is a bug,
   something like an ant—one of the
   social group which is a worker, trying to pull something. I think this
   is some kind of food for rest of ants.
   It's a bee because it has wings, a
   worker bee bringing up something
   edible for rest of clan.

1. *Location:* $D_1 + D_2$
   E: Tell me about the bee.
   S: Here is the bee, the mouth and
      the wings.
      I don't think bees eat leaves but
      it looks like a leaf or a piece of
      lettuce.
   E: What makes it look like a piece
      of lettuce?
   S: It's the shape and it has a vein
      up the middle. It is definitely a
      bee.

$$\text{Score:} \quad \left.\begin{array}{c} D \\ D \end{array}\right\} W \quad \begin{array}{c} FM \\ Fc \end{array} \quad \begin{array}{c} A \\ Pl \end{array} \quad \left.\begin{array}{c} \big\rangle Add. \\ \big\rangle O- \end{array}\right. \quad \begin{array}{c} 1.0 \\ 1.0 \end{array}$$

COMMENT: Since the subject apparently first saw each of the *D*'s
separately and then combined them, the bee and the lettuce leaf
have each been scored separately, and an additional *W* scored for
the combination. The basal form-level rating for the bee is 1.0,
since this is a popular level response for this area. The lettuce
leaf would receive a basal form-level rating of 0.5 as semidefinite
in form, to which would be added 0.5 for the specification of the
vein. The farfetched combination does not raise or lower the
form level. However it deserves an additional *O*−. The subject
is quite definite in making the upper *D* a bee, yet is just as definite about the lower part being some sort of food that it is pulling
—an act of which the subject is critical but which she is unable to
improve.

CARD VII

6″

1. Two dogs standing on their heads.

1. *Location:* D_4
   S: They look like poodles.
   E: What makes them look like
      poodles?
   S: The hair seems to be curly, not
      clipped yet.

$$\text{Score:} \quad D \quad FM,Fc \quad A \quad 2.0$$

COMMENT: The location has been scored D because the concept "two dogs" is merely a function of the symmetry of the blot and does not suggest any attempt to organize the two areas. Had any sort of relationship between the dogs been indicated, the scoring would have been W. The chief determinant appears to be the action of the dogs, but an additional Fc was given for the curly hair, a differentiated texture response. In this connection, it should be noted that the inquiry did not go far enough to establish whether or not the shading actually determined the curly hair. An additional question, such as "What makes the hair seem curly?" would probably have elicited the additional information. However, the subject has previously given some indication of the use of shading, and it has been assumed that the determinant in this case is Fc. A basal form-level rating of 1.5 was given for the specific concept "poodle," and additional credit of 0.5 was added for the position of "standing on their heads," which increases the accuracy of the match to the blot. It has been assumed that these are trick dogs and that this is not a bizarre response. Again, there should have been additional questioning during the analogy period to determine this fact.

2. V And this is a butterfly. Let me see if I can make something of the whole. (long pause)

2. *Location:* D_1
S: Here is the body and here the wings, the butterfly is on top of the flower, he's getting his pollen from the flower.

Score: D   FM,FK   A   1.5

COMMENT: The concept "butterfly" requires little imagination and was therefore given a basal rating of 1.0, to which was added 0.5 for the constructive organization. The "flower" was seen in the light gray portion of the central area in the middle of the card, so that the body of the butterfly was seen on top of the flower. The difference in shading was therefore used to see two different objects at a different distance from the eyes—therefore the additional FK.

3. This part looks like the Western Hemisphere, North America, South America, Central America, here the Pacific and Atlantic Ocean (white areas) just on the one side though. I can't make anything out of the whole.

3. *Location:* D_4
S: It is a little distorted here, but this part looks like North America, etc.

Score: D,S   F   Geo   1.0

COMMENT: Although the two oceans are implied in the concept "Western Hemisphere," and usually would therefore not be scored separately, an additional *S* score has been given in this case because the subject specifically pointed out and labeled these areas. A basal rating of 1.0 is indicated because the concept was specific and is a reasonably accurate match to the blot area. Had the subject merely indicated a continent, or given some similar reply, this would have been a semidefinite concept and been rated 0.5.

CARD VIII

PERFORMANCE   INQUIRY

That's very pretty.

   4"

1. These two are polar bears—pink ones.

     1. *Location:* D_1
        E: Tell me about the bears; you said pink ones, what do you mean?
        S: No, not pink, just painted pink, looks like a drawing by some kindergarten child.
        E: How do you see the bears?
        S: They are looking down at the water, sort of standing there.
        E: Do you see the water?
        S: No.

Score: D   F↔C,FM   A   P   1.0

COMMENT: Although the subject offered an explanation for the pinkness of the bears, this is still considered a forced use of color, since any attempt to explain the color of these animals is considered forced. Color has been given precedence in the scoring of this response because the movement was mentioned only after some questioning in the inquiry. The basal rating of 1.0 was given to a popular response.

2. This is a crab.

     2. *Location:* D_3
        S: I used this whole part but it's a very rough idea, something like a horseshoe crab, but these things are too long.

Score: D   F   A   1.0

COMMENT: The concept is considered accurate enough to warrant a basal rating of 1.0. The remark "but these things are too long" is a criticism of the card which, however, does not improve the form level and therefore is used as an irrelevant specification.

3. Some undersea growth—algae or something.

3. *Location:* D_4
S: Food for the crab but the crab is going away from it, not toward it.
E: What made it look like algae?
S: Just an association with crab.

Score: D   F   Pl   0.5

COMMENT: This is a vague *F* response suggested by the previous concept and has therefore been given a basal rating of 0.5, which is reserved for concepts that are vague or semidefinite in form.

4. ∨ This way a vase of flowers, this is the vase and these the flowers.

4. *Location:* W
S: A decorated vase, the outline is a little off. Not all here, the vase is painted, the rest is all flowers or could be one flower with petals (usual animal) ready to fall off.

Score: W,S   FC,CF,mF   Obj, Pl   1.5

COMMENT: The vase appears to be the dominant concept of this response, with the principal determinant score of *FC,* because it is painted. The additional *CF* was given for the flower, no specific flower having been mentioned, and the *mF* score was included to account for the falling petals. Although the subject made some effort to reconcile the concept with the blot area, the response is not convincing since the vase is unable to stand on its base but must hang. However, the organizational detail of the falling petals justifies raising the total concept from 1.0 to 1.5.

5. Right here is an iris.

5. *Location:* D_2
S: The shape and the color.

Score: D   FC   Pl   1.0

COMMENT: The scoring in this case is *FC* because a specific flower is mentioned which matches the blot area fairly accurately.

CARD IX

PERFORMANCE   INQUIRY

 6″

1. ∨ This right here is a carnation, 1. *Location:* D_5 + extension of D,S
 the pink thing with a green stem. E: Tell me more about the carna-
 ∧ ∨ ∧ (long pause) I don't know,   tion, how many do you see?
 I can't see anything. ∨   S: Just one, it's very rough. I really
              can't see anything.

  Scores: D   FC   Pl   1.0

COMMENT: A specific flower has been mentioned, and it matches the blot area adequately; therefore, the score is *FC* rather than *CF* and the form level is 1.0.

CARD X

PERFORMANCE   INQUIRY

Oh!

 5″

1. Little rabbit's face and he's crying, 1. *Location:* D_5
 I guess.   E: What makes you think he is cry-
              ing?
             S: To account for this business.
             E: What about this business?
             S: Green tears, modern art or some-
             thing.

  Score: D   FM,CF,mF   Ad   P,O−   1.0

COMMENT: The green tears warrant additional *CF* and *mF* scores but do not add to the form accuracy; therefore, the basal form-level rating of 1.0 for a popular response remains. An additional *O−* is given for the farfetched combination.

2. Wishbone, a turkey wishbone.   2. *Location:* D_{12}
             S: Just an association, whenever I
             think of a wishbone, I think of
             a turkey.

  Score: D   F A_{obj} 1.0

COMMENT: The scoring needs no explanation.

3. These are some kind of odd animals 3. *Location:* D_3
 sniffing up a tree, I don't know   S: They are yelling at each other,
 what kind, though. Let me see, they   tails here, hind legs, standing up
 have tails and horns and they don't   on hind feet.

like each other very well, they both
want the same thing up at the top.
∨ ∧

Score: D   FM→M   A   2.5

COMMENT: Although the response depicts animals in animal-
like action, the subject has used the word "yelling" in the inquiry, suggesting that she is possibly ascribing some humanlike
activity to these animals; therefore, the tendency to *M* has been
indicated in the scoring. To the basal rating of 1.0 for the animals, credits have been added as follows: 0.5 for the additional
specification of horns and tails on the animals; 0.5 for the organization of the concept, around the tree; and 0.5 for the animals
"standing up on hind feet," which adds to the fit to the blot area.

4. These are two mountain goats, moving very rapidly, gracefully, galloping off in opposite directions.

4. *Location:* D_6 + dark portion of D_{15}.
S: On top of their heads there is
darker hair, front legs out here,
and back legs way out here.

Score: dr   FM,Fc   A   2.0

COMMENT: The location score *dr* has been assigned because the
response combines the usual detail D_6 with a part of another usual
detail, D_{15}. The additional *Fc* score is for the use of shading indicated in "darker hair." The basal form-level rating of 1.5 for the
specific animal includes the determinant specification of galloping. Were these seen as mountain goats merely standing still, the
form-level rating would be minus, since the concept would be a
poor match for the blot area. An additional credit of 0.5 was
given for the darker hair.

5. These blue things are octopi.
(long pause)
Let me see, what are these things?

5. *Location:* D_1
S: The shape only.

Score: D   F   A   P   1.0

COMMENT: This is the usual popular response for this area. The
color was used only to identify the specific area and was not part
of the response.

6. These are just islands in the middle
of a lake, connected by a strip of
land.

6. *Location:* D_8
S: Simply the shape, the color is all
off.

Score: D   F   Geo   0.5

COMMENT: This, again, is a large usual detail, to which a basal rating of 0.5 was given for a response that is semidefinite in form.

> *Add. Location: D_{11}*
> S: I didn't say anything to this part —two collie dogs sitting down at their master's feet.
> E: Tell me more about it, what makes it look like a collie dog?
> S: The shape and color, the color is right too. I didn't say anything about these parts, either.

Score: D   FM,FC   A   2.0

COMMENT: This score was assigned a basal form-level rating of 1.0, and additional credits of 0.5 each were added for the specification that the dogs are sitting, and for the use of color.

TOTAL TIME: 22 minutes

Testing the Limits

M: Card II—could not see people.
   E: Why?
   S: I couldn't see why they should have red feet and red hats, and rest black—it's out of proportion.
   Then, spontaneously:
   S: I can see two animal heads here, they have their snouts together, why I don't know.

Card VI—∨
   S: Two people walking arm in arm, and one arm sticking out, two legs close together—it's a possibility.

Card VII—∨
   S: Little girls because heads are so large for their bodies, doing a dance, heads are thrown back, touching, here are their legs and arms, and their fannies stick out.

Card X—the red area
   S: Some kind of ghosts holding, shaking hands, facing each other.
   Subject could not find *M*'s in Cards I or IX.

Fc: Subject could easily see Card VI as a fur rug—only the bottom part.

Cards Liked Most and Least

Likes Cards III, VII, VIII most—"I like the pattern in Card III, found interesting things in Card VII, and I liked the color in VIII." Likes Card IX least—"I couldn't see much."

TABULATION AND SCORING SHEET

Card No., Response No. and Position	Reac. Time	W	D,d	Dd,S	Add.	Movement	Vista Depth	Form	Texture Ach. Color	Color	Add.	Main	Add.	Main	Add.
		LOCATION — Main Response				**DETERMINANT — Main Response**						**CONTENT**		**P — O**	
I ①	3″	W						F				Emblem			
II v ①	45″		D					F			FC	A			
②			D							Fc	F/C	A.At			
Add.					Wx							F	Sex		
III ①	7″	Wx				M					Fm	H	Obj	P→O	
②			D			FM						A			
IV ①	5″	W				FM					Fc	A			
V ①	1″	W				FM						A		P	
VI ①	8″		D⎫		W	FM						A			O-
②			D⎭						Fc			Pl			
VII ①	6″		D			FM					Fc	A			
v ②			D			FM					FK	A			
③			D	S				F				Geo			
VIII ①	4″		D							F↔C	FM	A		P	
②			D					F				A			
③			D					F				Pl			
④		W		S						FC	CF	Obj	Pl		
											mF				
⑤			D							FC		Pl			
IX v ①	6″		D							FC		Pl			
X ①	5″		D			FM					CF	Ad		P	O-
											mF				
②			D					F				A_obj			
③			D			FM→						M A			
④				dr		FM						Fc A			
⑤			D					F				A		P	
⑥			D					F				Geo			
Add.					D							FM	A		
												FC			
Total Time T=1320″		W + D + d + Dd + S = R				M + FM + m + k + K + FK + F + Fc + c + C′ + FC + CF + C = R						H 1		P 5	O 0
No. of Responses — Main		5 +18+ + 1 + =24				1 + 9 + + + + +8+2+ + +4+ + =24						Hd 0		O 0	1
No. of Responses — Add.		2	1		2	1	2	3	1	1	3	3	2	A 12		O- 0	2
Sum FLR		7.0	21.0	2.0		1.5	14.0		7.5	2.5	4.5		Ad 1			
Average FLR		1.4	1.2	2.0		1.5	1.6		0.9	1.3	1.1		1			

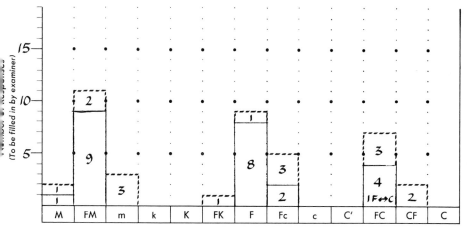

(To be filled in by examiner)

BASIC RELATIONSHIPS: Main Responses Only

Total Responses   R **24**

Total Time   T **1320** sec.

Average Time per Response   T/R **55** sec.

Average Reaction Time:

    Achromatic Cards (I, IV, V, VI, VII)   **4½** sec.

    Chromatic Cards (II, III, VIII, IX, X)   **13** sec.

$\dfrac{F}{R}$ **33** F%

$\dfrac{FK + F + Fc}{R}$ **42** %

$\dfrac{A + Ad}{R}$ **54** A%

(H + A) : (Hd + Ad)   **13 : 1**

Popular Responses   P **5**

Original Responses   O **0 + 3**

$\dfrac{FC + 2CF + 3C}{2}$ sum C **2.0**

M : sum C   **1 : 2.0**

(FM + m) : (Fc + c + C')   **9 : 2**

$\dfrac{\text{Responses to Cards VIII + IX + X}}{R}$ **50** %

W : M   **5 : 1**

II. SUPPLEMENTARY RELATIONSHIPS: Main + $\frac{1}{2}$ Add.

   M : FM   **1½ : 10**

   M : (FM + m)   **1½ : 11½**

   (FK + Fc) : F   **4 : 8½**

   (Fc + cF + c + C' + C'F + FC') :   **3½ : 6½**
       (FC + CF + C)

   (FK + Fc + Fk) : (K + KF + k + kF + c + cF)   **4 : 0**

   FC : (CF + C)   **5½ : 1**

III. MANNER OF APPROACH

	Main Responses			No. Add. Scores
	No.	Actual %	Expect. %	
W	5	21	20-30	2
D	18	75	45-55	1
d	0	0	5-15	0
Dd + S	1	4	< 10	2

IV. ESTIMATE OF INTELLECTUAL LEVEL

Capacity *Approaching superior*

Efficiency *Average to about average*

V. SUCCESSION

Rigid   ____

Orderly   ____

Loose   ✓

Confused   ____

VI. FORM LEVEL SUMMARY

Average Unweighted FLR **1.3**

Average Weighted FLR **1.4**

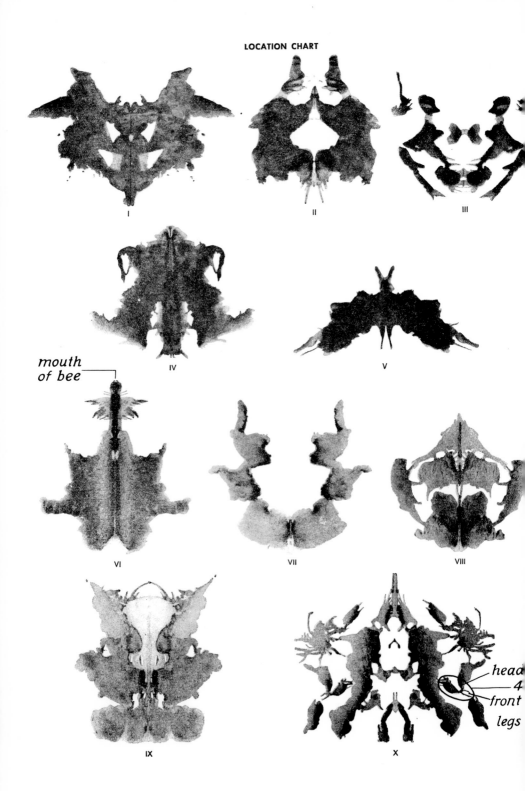

LOCATION CHART

I

II

III

IV

V

mouth
of bee

VI

VII

VIII

IX

X

head
4
front
legs

Quantitative Analysis, Case of A. S.

The Psychogram

The initial examination of the psychogram reveals an unusual combination, for an adult record, of extraordinarily few M responses $(1 + 1)$ together with a high number of FM responses $(9 + 2)$. (About three M responses are expected in a "normal" record.) Since there are so few M responses, the relationship of M to FM, and the $M:(FM + m)$ ratio, cannot be discussed in this case. However, other hypotheses may be tentatively applied.

The low M score suggests that A. S. may have some difficulty in interpersonal relations, perhaps because of a lack of empathy. It suggests also that in stress situations the subject can have little recourse to inner resources, that there may be an absence of a strong value system, and that, finally, there has been some difficulty in self-acceptance. It should be noted that, in spite of the paucity of M responses, low intelligence is contraindicated because of the additional M response indicating that potential capacity is not being used, perhaps owing to inhibition; also because of the additional m responses which may mean that tensions exist which are too strong to allow A. S. to utilize her inner resources constructively. Furthermore, the form-level rating of 2.5, achieved for the third response on Card X, must be taken into account in this connection.

The large number of FM responses suggests that A. S. has an awareness of her impulses to immediate gratification. However, it is quite likely that she has little insight, understanding, or acceptance of these impulses. Moreover, in view of the inadequate number of M responses, and the presence of only two additional CF responses, it seems reasonable to assume that frustration feelings may result both from the failure to act out these impulses and from lack of self-acceptance.

The over-all pattern of the psychogram shows that the responses bulk in the left half and in the center, with relatively few responses in the color area. This suggests that, although for the most part A. S. does not react freely to her environment, and her view of the world and her responsiveness are largely determined by her own needs, she does have the ability to view the world in a more impersonal, matter-of-fact way.

The proportion $(FK + Fc) : F$ of $4 : 8\frac{1}{2}$ indicates that the affectional needs are well-developed and are satisfactorily integrated in the personality organization. Therefore, they serve as a sensitive control function, permitting a healthy response to people without a vulnerable overdependence on them. The Fc score relates to an individual's recognition of his affectional needs of approval, belongingness, and response from others. A. S. shows a tendency to some emphasis on the Fc score, as indicated by the three additional Fc responses. It should be borne in mind, therefore, that there is possibly some sensitivity in this area, perhaps to the needs of others or to hurt from others. However, the proportion of differentiated to undifferentiated shading responses of 4:0, counting additionals as $\frac{1}{2}$, again supports the hypothesis that, on the whole, the affectional needs are adequately integrated within the personality organization.

The relationship of the achromatic surface responses with the chromatic surface responses, $(Fc + c + C'):(FC + CF + C)$, which yields the proportion $3\frac{1}{2}:6\frac{1}{2}$, suggests that A. S. has the ability to interact and respond positively in emotional situations. However, the forced FC response $(F \leftrightarrow C)$, suggesting some tension in social relationships, and the use of the two CF responses as additionals only, suggesting some hesitancy about actually expressing emotional responsiveness, indicate that A. S. may not fully utilize her ability. In this connection, the presence of the additional F/C score suggests that A. S. may modify her reactions by responding in a more superficial, behavioral way. The ratio of $FC:(CF + C)$, $5\frac{1}{2}:1$, tends to confirm the conclusion that A. S. may have possibly excessive control over her impulsive expression of emotionality, and that her socialized responses may have a superficial flavor. The Sum C of only two (three is the expected "normal" Sum C) indicates, again, that there is apparently too little overt responsiveness to environmental influence.

Introversive-Extratensive Balance

The three pertinent proportions to consider are: M:Sum C of 1:2, $(FM + m):(Fc + c + C')$ of 9:2, and the percentage of responses to the last three cards (VIII, IX, X) of 50.

The M:Sum C ratio of 1:2 suggests an extratensive balance, but interpretation of this ratio is necessarily qualified by the presence of only one M response. However, the indication is that this individual is most responsive to environmental factors. This may be an adjustment by a flight into reality in order to protect herself from the threat which the inner impulse life may present.

On the other hand, the second ratio, $(FM + m):(Fc + c + C')$, shows marked introversive tendencies. The apparent contradiction in orientation indicated by the two ratios may mean that A. S. is in a state of transition between introversion and extratension. It is also possible that the second ratio represents the direction in which A. S. is retreating. Another feasible supposition is that there exists a persistent secondary organization which has not been realized, but which remains as a source of conflict. In any case, such a discrepancy represents a conflict in tendencies within the personality, but the specific significance cannot be explained at this point.

Since half of the responses in this record occurred to the last three cards, it is indicated again that A. S. is stimulated to greater productiveness by environmental impact. However, this conclusion must be modified by the fact that six of the twelve responses were given to Card X, which lends itself to greater responsiveness because of its structure. It should also be noted that the relatively small amount of color actually used in the responses suggests that there is inhibition of overt expression to emotional reaction.

Control

In discussing the implications of the movement, shading, and color proportions, it has already been indicated that A. S. may be said to have "outer control," that is, control of emotional expression. The two additional factors to be considered in this area are the form responses of 33% and the total of form plus differentiated shading responses $(FK + F + Fc)$ of 42%.

The 33% of F responses (which is within the normal expected range of 20–50%) suggests an ability to view the world in an impersonal, matter-of-fact way, which should help A. S. to achieve a controlled adjustment. It suggests, also, that she has retained the ability to be responsive to her own needs and to react to emotional impact from outside. This hypothesis is substantiated by the $FK + F + Fc$ percentage of 42%. However, the tendency to suppress Fc responses shown by the three additionals suggests that there may be some difficulty in making close and warm affectional contacts, and that there may be some restraint in dealing with people.

Intellectual Estimate and Manner of Approach

The initial over-all impression with regard to intellectual estimate is that A. S. has average to above average capacity. However, the average unweighted form level of 1.3 and the weighted form level of 1.4, as well as the autobiographical materials, clearly indicate that A. S. is actually functioning on a better than average level. That her real capacity is in fact above average and approaches the superior is suggested by the fact that she achieves a form-level rating of 2.5 for one response, and a rating of 2.0 in three others, one of these an additional. Since it can be assumed that the presence of even one response of form level 2.5 is indicative of capacity between above average and superior (in the absence of any overtly contradictory material in the record), it seems likely that there are factors in personality organization that keep A. S. from realizing her full intellectual potential.

The combination 21% W, 75% D, 0% d, and 4% $Dd + S$ shows an overemphasis on D responses. The presence of 75% D shows an interest and an ability to differentiate perceptively, but relatively little interest in integration and organization. This common-sense approach may be an indication that A. S. feels insecure and may have some fear of losing her bearings if she does not stick close to the obvious. While A. S. has the ability to be intellectually critical, as indicated by her critical (mostly self-critical) remarks in her record, the presence of W, the 0% d, and the ratio of 13:1 for $(H + A):(Hd + Ad)$ show that on the whole her attitude is not a very critical one. The presence of 50% A responses reinforces the impression that A. S. tends to take a rather stereotyped view of the world, and that the range of interest is limited, perhaps because of disturbed adjustment.

The five popular responses, which is the expected average, indicate that the ties to reality are quite adequate; but the absence of main original responses and the presence of only three additionals suggest again that there is an inadequate use of capacity as well as some timidity. The W:M ratio of 5:1 (2:1 is the expected proportion) suggests a level of aspiration that is unrealistic and probably leads to feelings of frustration. However, it may also mean that A. S. does not feel free enough at the present time to direct her creative energies toward achievement of her goals. This is supported by the loose succession, which suggests some weakening of control because of emotional conditions, as well as the low number of M responses which were previously discussed.

Hypotheses

1. There is difficulty in interpersonal relations because of lack of empathy.

2. There is little recourse to inner resources in stress situations.

3. A strong value system is absent.

4. A. S. has some difficulty in self-acceptance.

5. There is some awareness of impulses, but little insight, understanding, or acceptance of them.

6. A. S. has feelings of frustration because of her lack of self-acceptance and her failure to "act out."

7. A. S. has the ability to view the world in an impersonal, matter-of-fact way.

8. The affectional needs are well-developed and integrated, serving as a sensitive control function.

9. There may be some undue sensitivity to the needs of others and to hurt from others, suggesting some restraint in contacts.

10. A. S. has the ability to interact and respond positively in emotional situations but does not fully utilize this ability.

11. The reaction to emotional stimulations may be in a superficial behavioral manner.

12. A. S. has control over the impulsive expression of emotionality.

13. Although A. S. is most responsive to environmental factors, suggesting a flight into reality adjustment, she shows marked introversive tendencies. This may be indicative of a state of transition, or of a direction of retreat, or it may be that the secondary organization is not realized and is a source of conflict.

14. A. S. is stimulated to productiveness by environmental impact, but her overt expression is inhibited.

15. A. S. has above-average to superior intellectual capacity, but the efficiency of functioning is average. This seems to be the result of inhibition and tension.

Sequence Analysis, Case of A. S.

As a rule, we become acquainted with the Rorschach information given by a subject by reading through the record even before we look at the quantitative summary. Naturally, any conclusions drawn from the sequence of responses have to be consistent with the other findings; the two procedures actually go hand in hand. Analyzing the sequence of responses, we relate this to other information available about the subject.

Card I

The one response that A. S. gives to Card I has the following characteristics: She immediately tries to organize the blot material into a whole response with a family shield. She goes beyond the very superficial approach such a concept frequently covers up by specifying in detail the animal heads, the nose, and ears. But she remains conspicuously ambivalent about the central figure, most frequently seen as a female. She says "the thing in the middle is just something decorative to hold the whole thing together."

A glance at the summary sheet shows us that there is no undue stress on a *W* approach; therefore, the concept *shield* is not an excuse for being unable to cope with the situation otherwise. She shows a concern with authority—and attitude toward authority is often revealed in the concept of emblems or shields. The question arises as to why can she not see the center detail, often seen as a female figure that "holds the whole thing together." Her feminine role, which she conceives of as a rather submissive one, has apparently not led to any satisfactory solution.

Card II

Card II provides us with as neat a description of "color dynamics" as we may wish. For 45″ she is very troubled and turns the card, saying: "This will take me a little while." Then she expresses her regret that she cannot give a *W* response. Finally, holding the card upside down, she interprets first the center red, and then, turning the card around again, gives a vague interpretation of "unicellular animals" to the top red. Only in the inquiry, when the total test situation has markedly changed, is she able to use the black part, in a most revealing manner.

This is a clear-cut case of subjective color disturbance. But also she reveals the strength of the color attraction for her, since she selects just the three red spots for her responses in the performance proper. However, the color comes through only hesitatingly. Only in the analogy period, after having given other clear-cut color responses on the last three cards, does she finally admit that the red helped her in seeing a crab, and it is "one which doesn't bite." Since a crab is red only after it's cooked, she's quite right. The struggle goes even further in the second response. First she flees from the hot color to the cooler shading in specifying the unicellular animals. Only when confronted with the

fact that she had called them "these two red things" in the performance proper does she admit that they may be "stained." Then she
turns spontaneously to the rest of the card, and combines in a somewhat doubtful anatomical response "a male pelvic bone and this his—
you know what." She is unable to use the word "penis" without help.
Even though such a combination of anatomical or dead animal objects
with live parts of the same organism has once been noted as suggestive of paranoid thinking, she is too much aware of the inconsistency
for us to worry about this pathological condition. However, it is not
farfetched to relate this response to the sexual difficulties with the
young professor mentioned in her autobiography. We should keep in
mind that the combination of the "not-dangerous" crab (which is frequently seen as a female organ) and the penis, which is attached to a
diagram of a male pelvis, may possibly be an indication that she plays
some part in contributing to the difficulty in their relationship. But
we know that even her friends describe her as argumentative with
men, which seems in contrast to her otherwise feminine and submissive approach to life.

It is clear from A. S.'s response to the first colored card that initially
she is not able to cope adequately with situations that are emotionally
tinged, but also that she has the capacity to make an adequate re-
covery.

Card III

Card III continues to add a great deal to the picture as it unfolds.
She starts with a usual popular response to the black area, with two
strange variations. On the one hand, she refuses to commit herself as
far as the sex of the two people is concerned, and uses a somewhat farfetched excuse for doing so ("rough drawing"). On the other hand,
she adds an original addition to the concept, namely, that the inner
center red is a ball in motion. It seems that these two variations are interdependent. What moves between these two people makes it more
difficult for her to say whether they are men or women.

The separation of the red spots from the black area gives people
who are uncomfortable with the color the opportunity to avoid using
it. Nevertheless, the fact that she sees two people "playing a game together" indicates that she is capable of warm, happy interpersonal relationships. She is responsive enough to the color to want to include
the red areas, but is yet unable to use the color in her responses.

Card IV

This card is the first of the strongly shaded cards and has two associations that are almost equally frequent. One is the "winged animal" and the other, using the shading, is an aggressive male figure such as a giant or gorilla. Her reaction is a strangely ambivalent one, "an amphibious animal" that "has wings" and "crawls along the ground." In the inquiry, she reveals further that the creature is "asleep," in a "sleeping position." The inquiry did not quite make it clear that the "tough, scaly skin" was based on shading, but we may safely assume that this was so.

Associations to this card are often interpreted as attitudes of the individual toward male authority figures, particularly the father. The prehistoric character of this strange monster may be related to the fact that her father is 73 years old and that one of her difficulties is the lack of differentiation of the father image in her, resulting in a confusion with regard to her feminine role.

Card V

Card V is immediately interpreted as the popular concept of a bat flying. It is not surprising that this essentially intelligent and well-controlled subject makes immediate use of the popular connotation to Card V. However, her insecurity about this concept is rather puzzling. The critical remark about the upper extension has some objective validity, but the remark concerning the lower extension, "I did not know it was split up the back either," seems to reveal a tendency on her part to be hypercritical of herself rather than putting the blame where it rightly belongs.

It may be interesting to observe that A. S. selects to use the concept "bat," which is something ugly, rather than "butterfly," which would represent a pleasanter, more optimistic approach.

Card VI

Card VI has two major characteristics: It is the most strongly shaded card, and the one card in which the blot material offers a striking contrast between top and bottom portions. She reacts to both these challenges by interpreting the top part and establishing an interesting connection with the bottom part. She also uses the shading aspect clearly for the bottom part and implicitly for the top.

The bee may reflect the image she has of herself as a hard worker (a fact noted by her supervisor). In addition, the "bee bringing up something edible for the rest of the clan" suggests that she feels an overwhelming sense of responsibility toward others.

This card frequently evokes both masculine and feminine sexual associations, either in direct or symbolic form. Apparently A. S. is not able to handle such material comfortably either overtly or in a more socialized manner, and so both sexual symbols are replaced by the oral symbolism of providing food.

Card VII

Card VII does not present any difficulties for A. S. since, after six seconds, she organizes the whole material into three concepts. The upper two-thirds are nicely specified as "two dogs standing on their heads." The shading is used for the curly hair. Then, with the card upside down, she uses the remaining third for the concept of butterfly. The only original addition to the butterfly is the fact that she sees it "on top of the flower. He's getting his pollen from the flower." Finally, she returns to the original location, and interprets the area quite carefully as a map.

Card VII often facilitates responses involving an adult female figure, which may reveal an attitude to the mother image. In addition, the bottom center detail is considered as symbolizing vaginal sexuality.

A. S., however, sees dogs standing upside down in the area used for the usual adult female figure, which may indicate an immature level of social development, possibly as a result of poor mother-child relationships. This in turn implies that there will be difficulty in adult heterosexual relationships (a fact clearly revealed in the autobiography).

The sensuous impact of the bottom center detail is sublimated in her response of the butterfly on top of the flower (the flower, given to the usual vaginal area, is a female symbol; at the same time A. S. refers to the butterfly as "he"). The carefulness with which the map is described also indicates uneasiness concerning sexuality. The map response reveals also that A. S. uses intellectuality as a defense.

The sequence of responses to this card clearly demonstrates the way she handles heterosexual relationships; first, there is an immature reaction, followed by a sublimation, and then an intellectualized withdrawal.

Card VIII

The appeal of the first all-colored card immediately evokes the remark, "That's very pretty!" This is followed by five responses in rapid sequence. She is obviously stimulated by the color and uses it with increasing intensity, but she also has difficulty with it.

The first response is the frequent response of polar bears, but she adds, "pink ones," and explains, in the inquiry, that it must be the "drawing of some kindergarten child." This represents a pathetic attempt to include the color that is automatically excluded by the concept of "polar bears." The second response refers to the top area, which she sees as a "horseshoe crab"—an aggressive symbol. The next response, "some under-sea growth, algae or something," is seen as "food for the crab, but the crab is going away from it, not toward it."

In the sequence of these three responses, it may be seen that A. S. is stimulated by the color but does not know what to do with it. Her first response shows a forced use of color, and the second, controlled aggression, and the algae is vague and also suggests withdrawal in the action of the crab. Such a reaction indicates a responsiveness to environmental stimulation but an inability to react spontaneously and freely.

Her next response shows an ability to recover in the face of emotional impact, and she uses the whole card to see a painted vase with natural flowers, a passive but pleasant concept. This response implies that she gives in to emotional challenges in a submissive way that creates conflicts for her. The final response combines a positive use of form with color, thus indicating a capacity to face emotionally stimulating situations after continued exposure.

Card IX

The positive reaction to color is continued in Card IX, which creates a good deal of difficulty for many subjects. She turns the card upside down and definitely identifies "the pink thing with a green stem" as a carnation. After this, however, the confusion of variegated forms and mixed-up colors becomes too much for her; she can't see anything and repeats in the inquiry, "I really can't see anything."

In responding in this passive manner to a card that often evokes responses such as "witches," "clowns," and "explosions," A. S. again demonstrates her tendency to withdraw in the face of emotionally threatening situations.

Card X

On Card X she continues with positive reactions. She moves quite freely over the card, picking six of the usual details and adding one in the inquiry.

First she picks up the popular rabbit's face, but adds the green tears, which she simply explains by calling it "modern art, or something." Then she sees the usual wishbone and gives it a definite specification, as belonging to a turkey. This is followed by the usual two top animals, described as "sniffing up a tree." Then come two mountain goats where the animal action reaches the height of expressiveness, "moving very rapidly, gracefully, galloping off in opposite directions." She adds a part of the adjacent detail, to give a good account of the head. Finally, she adds the usual octopi, and two islands, connected by a strip of land, and in the inquiry, the brown collies.

After the forced way of using color with the green tears of the rabbit, she avoids the color issue in the following five responses and only comes back to it in the additional response in the inquiry. This avoidance is facilitated by the use of obvious form-associations. In the inquiry to the last response, she states, "simply shape—the color is all off," but immediately makes her reconciliation with the color by seeing the collies where "the color is right, too." She concludes with an expression of regret that there was one more detail that she failed to include—like a child who has been trained to finish the plate of food put before it.

It should be noted that the one additional M in the entire record appears unexpectedly in this card, and that the humanlike behavior is attributed to animals. The one main M response, which appeared in Card III, depicted a pleasant cooperative relationship. In contrast, the action on this card is aggressive and hostile, as indicated by the animals' dislike of each other and their yelling at each other. These reactions suggest that A. S. may be basically hostile and aggressive but that she is unable to accept these feelings, and thus her energy is directed toward suppressing them. Her submissive, passive mode of behavior, noted throughout the record, is epitomized in the collies, which she sees as "sitting down at their master's feet."

Testing the Limits

When A. S. was directed to find human movement responses in the testing-the-limits period, she was easily able to give such responses to

Cards VI, VII, and X. It should be noted that the action depicted is friendly and cooperative.

It seems likely that A. S.'s inability to give more than one *M* response during the performance proper is a reflection of her insecurity in human relationships, but that she has the potential to form warm, lasting relationships.

Summary

The statement A. S. makes in her autobiography that "relationship with my parents is very good, so long as I am not living with them" puts into focus the defense mechanism to which she resorts in order to maintain a relatively adequate adjustment. She has neither wanted to nor been quite able to sever completely her relationship with her parents and, by extension, with the authority under which she grew up. Yet she is unable to ally herself with this authority, since she is critical of it. Her solution has been to remove herself to a safe distance so that she is not too easily hurt, and at the same time is close enough to maintain the contacts that give her pleasure and that satisfy her submissive needs.

That this adjustment is not working quite well enough is indicated most strongly in the effect it has had on her intellectual functioning. Although there is indication that her intellectual capacity approaches the superior range, she has not made full use of this capacity. While she does operate on an efficient level, she presents the picture her colleagues have noted of "a hard, conscientious worker, though not particularly creative." Her method of dealing with the conflicts created by her ambivalent feelings (for example, toward her parents and other authority and the necessity for conformity) has been to inhibit the overt expression of her feelings and to busy herself, instead, with the obvious, routine matters to allow little time left to think. She has a great deal of difficulty in facing unpleasant truths, and since she does not have a strong value system on which she can rely, she resorts to a superficial, "socialized" manner of dealing with problems.

The same mechanism of detachment is again evident in her interpersonal relationships. She has a warm, positive feeling about people and is aware of their needs. At the same time, her self-esteem is very low and she is unable to understand or accept her feelings of hostility or aggression, although she has some awareness of them. On the rare occasions when she permits herself to "act out," it is in a negative manner (for example, the argumentative quality that has been noted), which is contrary to her submissive tendency. Her reaction has therefore been one of controlling the spontaneous expression of her feelings, and this, in turn, has resulted in some restraint in her contacts with others. She presents a pleasant, friendly façade, but does not let people get too close to her for fear of being hurt by them. In addition, another purpose is served by not permitting herself free expression of her feelings: she is able to keep from awareness the objectionable nature of some of these feelings and therefore to avoid dealing with the conflict that arises if she becomes critical of anyone or anything.

The professional career and the total adjustment of A. S. fully justify calling her a normal subject. However, it is quite apparent that she is not using her capacities, both intellectual and emotional, to the fullest, and so is denying herself a great deal of the pleasure of living. She has some awareness of this lack, and it therefore seems quite likely that if the stresses in her life are kept to a minimum she will be able to achieve the greater self-realization of which she is capable.

Interview Material, Case of A. L.

Autobiographical Sketch of A. L.

I am 28 years old. I have no brothers or sisters. Ours was a very happy home with close ties between parents and child. Interest in science developed in junior high school. But I spent most of my spare time in athletics at a nearby park. I was somewhat backward socially until college.

I received my bachelor's degree in Electrical Engineering from a large college. I worked as a junior engineer in Washington, D. C., until I was inducted into the Army. I immensely enjoyed the freedom and independence of living away from home (in Washington). Then I was assigned to a training station at Ft. Monmouth, New Jersey. I spent the next year in Okinawa. Almost completely divorced from the military, our station was located right in an Okinawan village. I really came to love these people, and the oriental attitudes toward life made a lasting impression upon me. After returning home, I was steeped in the Orient, and even thought about returning there. The impersonal, busy, city life of New York was almost unbearable after my idyllic year overseas. That had been the happiest year of my life.

Getting back into the routine, I went to work for an electronic laboratory. I helped design the radiation monitoring instruments for an atomic submarine. The next year I returned to graduate school working as a graduate assistant. After a year of study I received the master's degree, and started work at an instrumental laboratory in Long Island. The same year I got married to a friend of an army buddy of mine. We now have two children, a girl 22 months old, and a boy 9 months old. Needing more room, we have just bought a home in Long Island.

Life History as Revealed in Interview with Examiner

A. L. wants no more children. The two he has are very sweet and cute. His wife, too, seems to be a gentle, soft-spoken little woman. She was a secretary before her marriage. When the children are about ten years old, she wants to go back to work, preferably as a clerk in a school so that she can have the same hours as the children.

When asked how he gets along with his wife, A. L. replied: "We share very well. She is the boss with the children, but otherwise, we share."

A. L.'s father was a textile designer and was always pretty well off. His family visit him once a week. He says he was spoiled as a child. A. L. said: "I am a very unambitious guy since I have a wife, house, and babies. I am aware of the financial demands but I am not interested in making more money. I don't like a position of administration which involves responsibility. I like the work I am doing now—like to be left on my own. I am not anxious to change my job although in my present job there is little opportunity for advancement. I have had a little trouble with one guy who was a boss of mine, but he is not my boss any longer. I recently received an increase in salary but not in rank. I'm interested in 'researchy' kind of work."

A. L.'s wife contributed the following: A. L. recently returned from the hospital. She said he was very unhappy when he came home because he found his wife sick with pneumonia and so he could not be fussed over as he would have liked. She also stated that A. L. likes to eat, especially home cooking. She would like to see him go on and study for a Ph.D. in physics, since he is interested in doing research. She feels he cannot get ahead in his present job or in any other, especially if he wants to do research, without a Ph.D. A. L. replied that he felt he did not have the "fortitude" to study now, nor could he take on the "responsibility."

Observations of a Female Friend Who Knew A. L. for About Ten Years

Warm, thoughtful person, unspoiled. Reserved, sensitive, easily repelled by loudness, crassness, etc. Devoted to those close to him; respected by friends. Wholesome, rational approach. Scientific interests; also aesthetically attracted to things oriental. Not aggressive.

Rorschach Protocol, Case of A. L.

CARD I

PERFORMANCE

INQUIRY

2″

1. Some sort of an insect, body and head and feelers, it is clearly defined, things on either side might be wings but actually shape is not too close.

1. *Location: W*
   E: Tell me how you see the insect.
   S: The body is this part (center) and head (top) and this and this (d_3) are the feelers. The wings are the pieces up here (top and side) and don't quite fit in. Whether alive or dead I don't know; could be either one —not important to me.
   E: What kind?
   S: I guess I never saw what a bat looks like. When I said insect— maybe I thought of a moth—I don't know what a bat looks like. Might be a mouse with wings— has a little short stubby tail. I don't know about this spot (center white) as if worn off. It doesn't look like animal's natural markings; looks like artificial things.
   E: What can it be?
   S: Might be anything by itself. I don't know.

Score: W   F   A   P   1.5

COMMENT: The response is within the range of the popular response usually given to this card. The specifications of body, head, and feelers are essential for the concept and do not help to raise the form level, but the "short stubby tail" raises the form level to 1.5. The remaining remarks are typical critical description which are irrelevant as far as form level is concerned.

CARD II

PERFORMANCE   INQUIRY

3″

1. This looks like two puppy dogs.
nose to nose, the red gadgets outside, I don't know what they are.

1. *Location:* W̶ (Subject does not include lower red center details.)
E: Tell me more about the puppies.
S: Oh ya! These are busts of puppy
dogs—up to chest—the head is
very clearly shown, ears (usual) ,
the nose is darker than rest of
body—very furlike texture to the
gray. Actually resemblance to
puppy dogs still here—the appendages which go up do not belong to puppy dog.
E: Can you tell me anything else
about the dogs?
S: These dogs are gray dogs.

Score: W̶   *Fc,FC′*   *A*   *P*   2.0

COMMENT: Additional form-level credits of 0.5 for organization
and 0.5 for the "darker nose" and for the texture were added to
the basal rating for a popular response. The "red gadgets" are
used merely to delineate the areas and are therefore not part of
the response.

2. Winged horse Pegasus comes to my
mind.

2. *Location:* D_2
S: Like ad of the Flying Red Horse,
Socony ad.
E: Where is the head?
S: No head, just impression of
wings and the red made me think
of the ad.

Score: D   *FC,FM*   *(A)*   *O*   2.0

COMMENT: An additional determinant score of *FM* was assigned
since the subject's response "winged horse" does imply movement.
The basal form-level rating of 1.5 takes into account the originality of the response; the meaningful use of color raises the concept
to 2.0.

3. Red item at bottom with two tentacles sticking out, looks like a crab
to me.

3. *Location:* D_1
E: What do you mean by the "red
item"?
S: I suppose I thought of lobsters
which are red, maybe some crabs
are red, too. The red object here

reminds me of a horseshoe crab, has long legs sticking out. Here the color—I don't think I ever saw a red horseshoe crab but nevertheless that is what it reminds me of.

Score: D   FC   A   1.5

COMMENT: The form-color combination appears to be the principal determinant in this response. The "long legs sticking out" raises the form level to 1.5.

Add. Location: d_1
S: I don't know what to make of this part. Looks like a male sex organ to me, penis and testicles.

Score: d   F   Sex   1.5

COMMENT: The response fulfills the minimum requirement, but additional credit of 0.5 is given for "testicles."

CARD III

PERFORMANCE

INQUIRY

4″

1. Looks like two people standing like this, attitude somewhat comical, maybe two magicians, might see on stage, holding something.

1. *Location:* W
   E: Tell me how you see the people?
   S: Struck me as being men because of dress; these look like lapels, shoes look like high-buttoned, pointed toes. A cowboy or a woman might wear shoes like these.
   E: What is the something they are holding?
   S: Might be a pitcher of water if they were magicians. The dark lapel-like clothing suggests formal dress. The shoes don't go with the formal dress. The shoes look like boots. The gray underneath the pitcher might be fire the pitcher is being warmed over.

Score: W   M,FC′,Fm   H   P   3.0

COMMENT: This is the popular response for the black area on this card. Additional credit of 0.5 each for the specifications of the lapels (including the *FC′*) and the shoes has been added to the basal form-level rating of 1.0. Further credit is given for the organizational element and another 0.5 for the pitcher and the fire.

2. The red item in the middle, completely different from the rest of the picture, looks like a pair of lungs.

2. *Location: D₁*
   E: Again you said "red item." What do you mean?
   S: Yes, the red made it look like lungs—a pair of lungs in a medical book (used color).

   Score: D   FC   At   1.0

COMMENT: The form-color combination is a popular level response and is scored 1.0.

3. Red items on the side and behind their heads—one on left in particular looks like some other internal organ, the kidney.

3. *Location: D₂*
   S: Some internal organ I've seen in a biology book. I think the color might have influenced me. This particular color of red makes it look like internal organ—also because connected with shape.

   Score: D   FC   At   1.0

COMMENT: The form-color combination is a popular level response.

Add. Location: D₂
   S: The red items on the outside might also be a musical instrument like a ukulele—the little projections on top might be the screws used to adjust string tension (not the color).

   Score: D   F,Fm   Obj   O   1.5

COMMENT: As an original response he earns a basal rating of 1.5 which is reinforced by the remark about string tension *(Fm)*.

4. Section on the bottom looks like a face with blinders over either eye.

4. *Location: D₃*
   E: Tell me more about the face?
   S: Looks like a human face; somewhat comical, teddy-bearish face. The mouth is the white section on the bottom. The nose is little white section here—the dark line

representing the nose. The dark area, they're blinders. I'm not sure what I meant by blinders, either dark glasses or what you put on horses. If glasses, the white area would be white shaggy eyebrows and these glasses would be over eyes. White area might be upturned horns.

E: What about the horns?

S: Like a devil's. The rest of the face seems kindly but upturned sections might be horns.

Score: D,S   FC',Fm   Hd   O   3.0

COMMENT: The additional *S* location score was given for the use of the white space for the mouth, nose, and eyebrows. An additional *m* score was given for the "comical expression." A basal form-level rating of 1.5 was assigned for the concept of "human face" with adequate specification. Added are credits for the blinders or dark glasses and for the eyebrows and horns. The expression varying between comical, teddy-bearish, devilish, and kindly represents a typical "double projection" and adds another credit.

CARD IV

PERFORMANCE   INQUIRY

Ye Gads!

5″

1. These bottom sections look like boots.

1. *Location:* D_2

S: When I see a boot, I think of Italy, the toe here and the heel here.

E: Are you thinking of a map or of a boot?

S: Could be either a boot or a map of Italy. When you look at map of Italy it looks like a boot. Also, when I see a boot it makes me think of Italy. In the boot itself —the change in color—I think it detracts from its appearance as a boot. I wouldn't expect this sharp change in color, also wouldn't expect this projection sticking out at heel.

Score: D   F   Obj   1.0

COMMENT: This is a popular response. The statement about Italy is merely an irrelevant comment as far as form level is concerned.

2. And this part looks like a dragon's head, eyes and shaggy eyebrows and maybe these are horns.

2. *Location:* D_1
S: This thing in center down here looks like what I imagine ancient or middle age dragons were supposed to look like—eyes and horns coming out, maybe tusks and forked tongue or a tongue of fire coming out at bottom. Half top, half front view of it.
E: What are these (projections)?
S: These upper projections remind me of horns.

Score: D   F,Fm   (Ad)   2.5

COMMENT: A basal form-level rating of 1.0 was given for "dragon's head," which is an adequate fit for this area. This was increased 0.5 for the additional specifications of the eyes and eyebrows. Further credits were added for the tusks and the tongue of fire, which has a symbolic rather than an animal movement quality, and therefore the additional *Fm* score was given.

3. At top—very wrinkled face and brows, nose, eyes, slanty eyebrows.

3. *Location: dr*
S: Sort of satanic in expression, wrinkles in forehead, these (extensions) might be horns and there is a cleft at top of head. I can see the slanty eyes and wrinkles in forehead.
E: What makes it look like wrinkles?
S: There the lines definitely look like wrinkles. It has a texture like the texture of an old wrinkled forehead.
E: Did you use these parts (side projections)?
S: These two projections (side) are unnatural for a head but unnatural projections might be horns if it were a devil.

Score: dr   Fc,m   (Hd)   2.5

COMMENT: The area used is neither a *D* nor a *d*, but an unusual combination of both; therefore, the *dr* score. Shading was used for the wrinkled forehead. An additional *m* score was given for the sinister quality implied in the specification of "satanic in expression." The basal form-level rating of 1.5 was increased to 2.5 by the specifications of wrinkles in the forehead and the satanic expression, another "double projection" reinforced by the "horns."

4. These earlike looking things, I can't make anything out of them, they don't look like ears.

4. *Location: S*
   E: Do you want to count this as a response?
   S: Sort of have earlike shape, the white opening but the rest no resemblance to ears. Rather obscure. I didn't notice it this time but I see what I meant. Elongated earlike shape, just the shape.

Score: S   F   Hd   1.0

COMMENT: This has been included as a response as the subject did not withdraw it but made it more specific, instead, by limiting the concept to the white space only.

Add. ∨ *Location: d_2*
S: This region around here looks like a female sex organ.
E: What makes it look like a female sex organ?
S: That's definitely the shading. The dark area hairlike and the white the structure around the opening.

Score: d   Fc   Sex   1.5

COMMENT: The shading specification merits an additional credit.

CARD V

PERFORMANCE

INQUIRY

3″

1. When you first handed it to me, it had a butterfly look. Looking at it closer, these extremities do not look like they belong to a butterfly, they have a pincerlike quality. Is it cricket to turn?

1. *Location: W*
   S: Wings, body, feelers, this bottom might not be part of butterfly.
   E: What do you mean by the pincerlike quality?
   S: Nothing.

Score: W   F   A   P   1.0

COMMENT: This is the usual popular response for this card. The "pincerlike quality" is merely a comment, as confirmed by the inquiry.

Add. Location: d$_2$
S: These things over here do not look like part of the butterfly. In fact, look like chicken legs. Drumsticks on a plate.

Score: d   F   Food   1.0

COMMENT: A popular-level response. "On a plate" is just added to indicate that the drumstick is cooked.

2. ⋁ Toes of a ballet dancer at very bottom.

2. *Location: d$_3$*
E: Tell me how you see the toes? Do you see the girl, also?
S: As if a girl was balancing—just the legs.

Score: d   M   Hd   1.5

COMMENT: This is a frequent response to this small detail and was given a basal form-level rating of 1.0 to which was added 0.5 for the specification of "balancing."

3. ⋁ This part very remotely looks like neck of a swan.

3. *Location: d$_1$*
E: Where is the body?
S: Here might be part of the body.
E: How do you see the swan?
S: The neck looks like it is on a live swan.

Score: d   F→FM   Ad   1.5

COMMENT: A tendency to *FM* is scored because movement was seen only after questioning. The swan deserves additional weight beyond the more usual "snakes."

CARD VI

PERFORMANCE

3″

1. From this region down, looks like a bearskin rug.

INQUIRY

1. *Location: W*
E: Which side of the rug do you see?
S: Furry side, here are the front and back legs.

E: What makes it look furry?

S: I think the irregular outline is important in making me think of that—also furry quality inside.

2. > ∨ Looking at it this way, looks like a head and neck of a tortoise. (pause) The winglike region around the neck looks out of place. Half turtle and half animal with wings. It would be quite a creature.

2. *Location: D_3*

E: Tell me just how you see this.

S: The way it is connected to bearskin plus the wings would make it quite weird. (Turtle and tortoise are the same to subject.) Top piece above whiskerlike quality has the shape of a head of a turtle, just the head. Looking at whole thing including the wing (top) looks like a winged creature. These look like whiskers but in wrong place—coming out of neck, eyes, and mouth of creature.

E: Tell me about the way it is connected?

S: The connection is in terms of this piece here—but I think of each one separately—not the two together.

Score: $\left.\begin{array}{c} W\!X \\ D \end{array}\right\}W \quad \begin{array}{c} Fc \\ F \end{array} \quad \left.\begin{array}{c} A_{obj} \\ Ad \end{array} \quad P\right\}O- \quad \begin{array}{c} 1.0 \\ 1.0 \end{array}$

COMMENT: The final remark of the subject describes the effort on his part to combine the first two responses, resulting in a fanciful combination that he abandons finally. The bearksin rug is scored in the usual way for a popular response to this card. The turtle head or winged creature does exceed the minimum basal rating, but loses the additional credit because of the forced combination.

3. < > ∧ All the irregularities in outline make it look like the shoreline —like land on a map.

3. *Location:* White space plus part of side area.

E: How do you see it?

S: On a map.

E: Describe it further for me.

S: Not just the edge but some region here, the white is the water, the land, the grey area.

Score: S,dr   F   Geo   0.5

COMMENT: Since the use of white space appears to be dominant in this response, S has been used as the primary location score. A basal form-level rating of 0.5 was assigned to a concept that is vague in form.

CARD VII

PERFORMANCE

10″ < ∨ This is the most difficult
    one I saw.

14″

1. These look like pieces of a jigsaw
puzzle.

INQUIRY

1. *Location:* part of usual D_3
    S: Just the shape. I can see how the
    pieces look like a jigsaw puzzle;
    this area, too (side extension).

Score: dr   F   Obj   0.5

COMMENT: This response is a very general one and almost equally applicable to any of the cards. Such a response avoids outright rejection and is, at the same time, quite evasive.

2. Two horns or bunny ears—look like
bunny ears, just the ears.

2. *Location:* d_2
    E: Tell me how you see the bunny
    ears.
    S: Ears sticking straight up. Not on
    a live bunny but on a little doll
    made with stiff ears.

Score: d   F,Fm   Ad   1.0

COMMENT: This is an adequate concept for this usual detail. The "stiffness" is especially reinforced but does not raise the form level.

Add. a. Location: D_1
    E: What about the rest of the card?
    S: Well, this bottom section might
    be a moth with the black as the
    body, the rest the outspread
    wings. This could be a live moth.
    E: What about the center area?
    S: Not too certain but moths might
    have hard black little bodies.

Score: D   FC′,Fc   A   2.0

COMMENT: Since this response was elicited only during the inquiry, it is scored as an additional response. The primary determinant is the achromatic use of color, with the texture effect of hardness receiving an additional score. The specifications of blackness and hardness increased the basal form-level rating from 1.0 to 2.0.

> *Add. b. Location:* W̶, S
> > ∨ S: These can look like legs. Something standing upright on legs, and these are arms out like that.
> > E: What is it?
> > S: I don't know what it is. It could be a big fat man in a peculiar ludicrous attitude.
> > E: Where is the head?
> > S: Not a distinct head. Head disappears on a very fat person. More waistlike region around here— (white is part of man) — legs planted wide apart.

Score: W̶,S   M   Hd   1.0

COMMENT: This response just makes a basal rating of 1.0. The stance as it is described would add an original quality to this response but is lost by the subject's inability to specify the man any further.

CARD VIII

PERFORMANCE   INQUIRY

4″

1. < This absolutely looks like a rat— also the one on the other side.

> 1. *Location:* D_1
> > S: Very clear.
> > E: Where are the legs?
> > S: One, two, three, and maybe the fourth leg is behind the third.
> > E: Tell me about the way you see the legs.
> > S: Poised on legs, very active.

Score: D   FM   A   P   1.0

COMMENT: This is the usual popular response for this detail. Had the subject not included any action in his response, the scoring would have indicated only a tendency to *P*.

2. This bottom coloration and shape looks like a human cell under the microscope, except no nucleus.

2. *Location:* part of usual D_2
   S: One cell overlapping the other. Color identical to a stained cell. Little before the time you gave this to me, at work I had looked at cell samples under a microscope.
   E: Anything else that makes it look like a cell?
   S: The delicate—the shading is what gives it the very thin slice look. This one is lying on top of this one. (Our company is diversified, we are working on an electric device for scanning slides.)

Score: dr   Fc,C/F   Bio   0.5

COMMENT: The use of shading is differentiated enough for *Fc,* even though the outline is semidefinite. The arbitrary use of color to mark off a subdivision in an object of indefinite form is scored *C/F* since any other colors could have been used for a microscope slide. The basal form-level rating of 0.5 which was assigned is reserved for such a semidefinite response.

3. Top formation which has the rib center has a definite insect look, but I don't know what kind of insect. The white could be the legs of a frog and the rest of the white might be a frog. It has the characteristic manner in which they hold their legs out.

3. *Location:* D_5
   S: The color had nothing to do with that.
   E: Is it an insect or frog?
   S: I can see the frog shape—can't see insect shape. The lines might have given me the impression of insect where you have divisions in body like that.

Score: S   FM   A   1.5

COMMENT: The subject deliberately specified only the white space in his response. It is not clear whether insect and frog are used synonymously or whether he changed his response from insect to frog, but the scoring remains the same in either case. An *FM* score is given for the action implied. A basal form-level rating of 1.0 was given for the frog, to which 0.5 was added for its stance.

4. ∨ Gray at bottom rather a nasty looking animal—a bat.

4. *Location:* D_3
   E: Tell me more about it.
   S: Well it looks like the top or

> front view of a bat with wings out like this. The little white areas might be eyes.

Score: *D,S*   *F*   *A*   1.5

COMMENT: The concept fits the blot adequately, but no additional constructive specifications were added beyond the eyes. The gray was used by the subject to identify the area and was not included in his response.

> *Add. Location:* Very top tiny detail. (See Location Chart.)
> S: Here a mouth or could be even a goatee on a person.

Score: *dd*   *F*   *Hd*   *O*   1.5

COMMENT: An original, clearly seen *dd*.

CARD IX

PERFORMANCE   INQUIRY

Nice colors!

< ∨

   5″

1. These two red items with lines in them, look like human hands, sort of half-closed fists.

1. *Location:* See Location Chart.
   S: Thumbs and fingers absolutely look like hands, semiclenched fists holding on to something.

Score: *dd*   *M*   *Hd*   2.0

COMMENT: The response fits this unusual tiny detail quite accurately. A basal form-level rating of 1.5 was based on the constructive details of thumbs and fingers, as well as the accurate shape, and additional credit of 0.5 was given for the indicated action.

2. If those are the fists, these might be a large winged animal, an eagle with human hands holding on to the green.

2. *Location:* D_6 plus part of D_9.
   S: That's what it looks like. The green itself does not particularly impress me as anything.

Score: *dr̄*   *FM→M*   *(A),Hd*   *O*   1.5

COMMENT: The determinant score of *FM→M* was used because the subject specified animal movement but indicated that the movement was centered in "human hands." A basal form-level rating of 1.0 for the eagle was increased by 0.5 for the action of holding on to something. The eagle with human hands may seem a somewhat fantastic concept save for the fact that many emblems do so delineate an eagle's claws, a symbolic fabulatory response. The "green" was obviously named to indicate the area, and was not included in the scoring.

3. Face of a moose.

3. *Location:* D_3

S: Real face of a moose, the brown color looks like a moose's eyes. Moose's head is sideways. These two brown projections are the antlers. One of them is going across. The darker shading in the antlers contributes to it. Looks like antlers although in the moose's face the shading in the brown has a furlike texture.

Analogy Period:

E: What do you mean by "shading in the brown?"

S: The color of the brown in the antlers. Shading does add to the furlike look of the face.

E: What about the color in the face?

S: A moose is brown. It's hard for me to say if I would see a moose if this part were blue. The tip here which looks like a nose is darker brown but the shading in the face gives it a furlike look.

Score: D   FC,Fc   Ad   2.0

COMMENT: Although this is a popular-level response, it was credited with a basal form-level rating of 1.5 because a specific animal was named. Credit for the detailed use of shading was added.

4. The reddish orange has a lobster-like quality.

4. *Location:* D_2

E: Anything else about it remind you of a lobster?

S: The color and these spinelike things that stick out make it look like a lobster. Definitely a lobster color.

Score: D   FC   A   1.5

COMMENT: A basal form-level rating of 1.5 includes the specific use of the color. (Compare Cards II and III.) No additional credit was given for the specification of the "spinelike" things, since this specification was already included in the concept of "lobster."

> *Add. Location: D,S* plus part of D_9
> (See Location Chart.)
> S: This area in here might be some sort of animal with two canine teeth sticking out. These two things here, region around eyes, sort of looking half down and half in front—eye region and cheeks.

Score: dr,S   F→FM   A   O   1.5

COMMENT: The specification of eyes and teeth constitute the original quality. The description of the "eyes sort of looking half down and half in front" gives the image a lifelike quality. It justifies the tendency toward animal movement score.

CARD X

PERFORMANCE   INQUIRY

3″

1. These are two little animals, none   1. *Location: D_4*
   that I know of but like I've seen in
   cartoons, small legs, large heads,
   have a grimace, angry, arguing with
   each other.

   Score: D   M   (A)   2.0

COMMENT: The determinant is *M* rather than *FM* because "arguing" is solely a human activity. Had they been seen as fighting, the determinant would have been *FM*. A basal form-level rating of 1.5 for the clarity of the animal figures was increased by 0.5 for the grimace.

2. Looking at an insect head-on, you'd   2. *Location: D_7*
   see large eyes like on a fly. These
   look like ears rather than antennae.

   Score: D   F   A   →P   1.0

COMMENT: The popular response to this is an animal head with long ears or horns. However, the subject said this was an insect but added long ears; therefore, the →*P* score.

3. Scorpions   3. *Location: D*$_1$

   Score: D   F   A   P   1.0

COMMENT: The scoring for this response is self-evident for the usual popular response.

4. Two leaves in the fall, reddish gold look. The yellow around the leaf is the sunlight through which you might see the leaf.

4. *Location: D*$_{10}$
   S: The little center is the leaf. The general field of pale yellow around it could be the sun falling on the leaf. The color and the shading in the leaf itself look very much like a leaf in the fall, particularly in this area (right) where there are highlights in it.

   Score: D   CF,Fc   Pl   Add. O   1.5

COMMENT: Had specific kinds of leaves been named to match the blot area, the score would have been *FC*. The additional *Fc* was scored for the transparency effect indicated by seeing through the sunlight. The basal form-level rating of 0.5 for a vague response was increased by 0.5 for the use of color and by 0.5 for the organization.

5. ∨ This object looks like those I've seen in physiology of sex books—male or female, but if female, here are the two ovaries leading into the urethra.

5. *Location: D*$_{12}$
   S: Just the shape.

   Score: D   F   At   1.0

COMMENT: The specification of the ovaries and the urethra increased the basal form-level from 1.0 to 1.5. However, the confusion of urethra and uterus weakened the concept and therefore reduced the rating to 1.0.

   Add. Location: D$_{12}$
   S: Could also be a chicken wing bone except knobs on end. I

don't know. I guess chicken bone
has these.
E: Anything else?
S: That's about it.

Score: D   F   *Food*   1.0

COMMENT: The response is on a popular level.

6. > Looks like little puppy. The red
objects were the first thing that
caught my eye but can't assign anything to them.

6. *Location:* D_{11}
S: Tail here, head looking sideways, foot.
E: Tell me more about it.
S: Sort of stretched, shaggy hair because feet are not clearly defined
and because of irregular edge,
the reddish color reminded me
of Irish setter which has long
hair.

Score: D   *FM,FC,Fc*   *A*   2.5

COMMENT: The *FM* determinant takes precedence over the *FC*
in this response, since the subject spontaneously noted the movement and the shading and the color were added in the inquiry.
The basal form-level rating of 1.5 was given for the specific concept of Irish setter, and additional credits of 0.5 each were added
for the use of color and shading and for the action.

TOTAL TIME: 20 minutes

Testing the Limits

E: Can you see people doing something in this card (VII) just as
you did in Card III?
S: I really can't (the subject could not see people in any position of
the card beyond the vague figure) .

Cards Liked Most and Least

Likes Card X most—"I like nature very much and also animals,
also the puppies here (Card II) ."

Likes Card IX least—"rather frightening figure."

TABULATION AND SCORING SHEET

Card No., Response No. and Position	Reac. Time	W	D,d	Dd,S	Add.	Movement	Vista Depth	Form	Texture Ach. Color	Color	Add.	Main	Add.	Main	Add.	F
I ①	2"	W						F				A		P		1.
II ①	3"	Wˣ							Fc		FC'	A		P		2-
②			D							FC	FM	(A)		O		2-
③			D							FC		A				1.
Add.					d			F					Sex			1.
III ①	4"	Wˣ				M					FC'	H		P		3.
											Fm					
②			D							FC		At				1.
③			D							FC		At				1.
Add.					D			F					Obj		O	1.
											Fm					
④			D	S					FC'		Fm	Hd			O	3.
IV ①	5"		D					F				Obj				1.
②			D					F			Fm	(Ad)				2-
③				dr					Fc		m	(Hd)				2-
④				S				F				Hd				1.
v Add.					d				Fc				Sex			1.
V ①	3"	Wˣ						F				A		P		1.
Add.					d			F					Food			1.
v ②			d			M						Hd				1.
v ③			d					F→			FM	Ad				1.
VI ①	3"	Wˣ							Fc			A obj		P		1.
v ②			D }	W				F				Ad		}	O-	1.
③				S	dr			F				Geo				0-
VII v ①	14"			dr				F				Obj				0-
②			d					F			Fm	Ad				1.
Add. a				D							FC'		A			2-
											Fc					
v Add. b				Wˣ							M		Hd			1.
				S												
VIII < ①	4"		D			FM						A		P		1.

	Total Time T =	W + D + d + Dd + S = R				M + FM + m + k + K + FK + F + Fc + c + C' + FC + CF + C = R						H		P		
No. of Responses	Main	+ + + + =				+ + + + + + + + + + + =						Hd		O		
	Add.											A		O–		
Sum FLR												Ad				
Average FLR																

TABULATION AND SCORING SHEET

Card No., Response No. and Position	Reac. Time	W	D,d	Dd,S	Add.	Movement	Vista Depth	Form	Texture Ach. Color	Color	Add.	Main	Add.	Main	Add.	FLR
②				dr					Fc		C/F	Bio				0.5
③				S		FM						A				1.5
v④			D		S			F				A				1.5
Add.					dd			F					Hd	O		1.5
⚡v①	5"			dd		M						Hd				2.0
②				dr		FM→					M	(A)	Hd	O		1.5
③			D							FC	Fc	Ad				2.0
④			D							FC		A				1.5
Add.					dr						F→		A	O		1.5
				S							FM					
⚡①	3"		D			M						(A)				2.0
②			D					F				A			→P	1.0
③			D					F				A		P		1.0
④			D							CF	Fc	Pl			O	1.5
v⑤			D					F				At				1.0
Add.					D						F		Food			1.0
>⑥			D			FM				FC		A				2.5
											Fc					

		W + D + d + Dd + S = R				M + FM + m + k + K + FK + F + Fc + c + C' + FC + CF + C = R						H	O	P		FLR
Total Time T = 1200												H 1	0	P 7	1	
No. of Responses Main		5 +18 +3 +5 +3 =34				4 + 4 + + + +14 +4 + + 1 + 6 +1 + =34						Hd 5	3	O 3	4	
Add.		2	3	3	3	4	2	3	6		6	5	3	1	1	A 14 2 / O− 0 1
Sum FLR		8.5	28.0	4.0	7.0	3.0	8.5	6.5			16.0	6.0	3.0	9.0	1.5	Ad 5 0 / 63.0
Average FLR		1.7	1.6	1.3	1.4	1.0	2.1	1.6			1.1	1.5	3.0	1.5	1.5	1.5

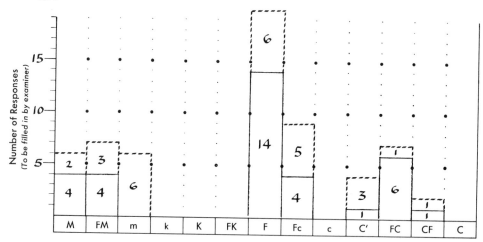

Number of Responses
(To be filled in by examiner)

	M	FM	m	k	K	FK	F	Fc	c	C'	FC	CF	C
top (dashed)	2	3					6				1		
bottom	4	4	6				14	5		3	6	1	1
								4		1		1	

I. BASIC RELATIONSHIPS: Main Responses Only

Total Responses	R	**34**
Total Time	T	**1200** sec.
Average Time per Response	T/R	**35** sec.

Average Reaction Time:

Achromatic Cards (I, IV, V, VI, VII)   **5** sec.

Chromatic Cards (II, III, VIII, IX, X)   **4** sec.

$\dfrac{F}{R}$ **41** F%

$\dfrac{FK + F + Fc}{R}$ **53** %

$\dfrac{A + Ad}{R}$ **56** A%

(H + A) : (Hd + Ad)   **15:10**

Popular Responses   P **7**

Original Responses   O **3**

$\dfrac{FC + 2CF + 3C}{2}$ sum C **4.0**

M : sum C   **4 : 4.0**

(FM + m) : (Fc + c + C')   **4 : 5**

$\dfrac{\text{Responses to Cards VIII + IX + X}}{R}$ **41** %

W : M   **5 : 4**

II. SUPPLEMENTARY RELATIONSHIPS: Main + $\frac{1}{2}$ Add.

M : FM   **5 : 5½**

M : (FM + m)   **5 : 8½**

(FK + Fc) : F   **6½ : 17**

(Fc + cF + c + C' + C'F + FC') : (FC + CF + C)   **9 : 8**

(FK + Fc + Fk) : (K + KF + k + kF + c + cF)   **6½ : 0**

FC : (CF + C)   **6½ : 1½**

III. MANNER OF APPROACH

	Main Responses			
	No.	Actual %	Expect. %	No. Add. Scores
W	**5**	**15**	20-30	**2**
D	**18**	**53**	45-55	**3**
d	**3**	**9**	5-15	**3**
Dd+S	**8**	**24**	< 10	**7**

IV. ESTIMATE OF INTELLECTUAL LEVEL

Capacity   *Superior*

Efficiency   *Approaching superior*

V. SUCCESSION

Rigid   ———

Orderly   ✓

Loose   ———

Confused   ———

VI. FORM LEVEL SUMMARY

Average Unweighted FLR **1.5**

Average Weighted FLR **1.8**

LOCATION CHART

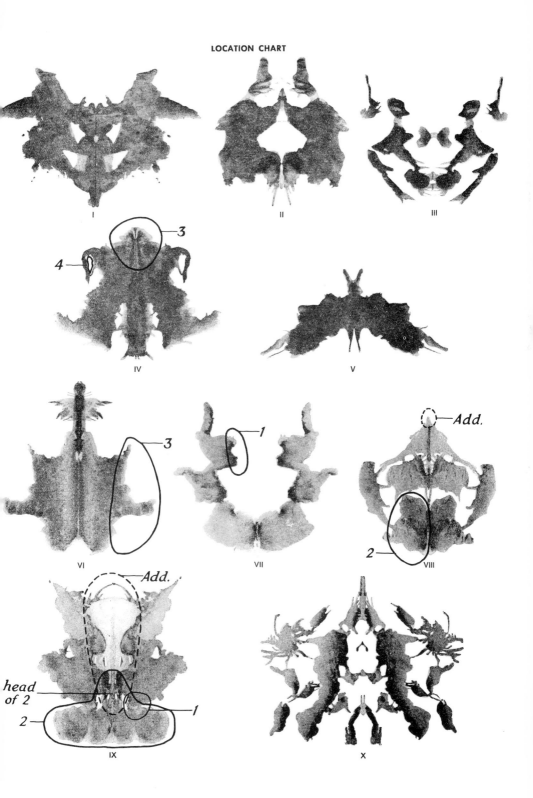

Quantitative Analysis, Case of A. L.

The Psychogram

An initial examination of the psychogram shows a good distribution of responses, with the majority on the right side. This pattern suggests that A. L. is able to react rather freely to his environment, but may be hampered by tensions from utilizing his inner resources to the fullest extent.

A. L.'s four M responses of good form level indicate not only that he has the ability to use his imaginal processes to enrich his perceptions of the world, but also that he has superior intellectual potential. A further examination of these M responses suggests, however, that there is some interference with his level of functioning. Only one of the main M responses is a true human figure; two of the others are Hd's; one is scored (A); and both of the additionals are scored Hd. It therefore seems likely that an inordinate degree of self-criticism and intellectual reservation hamper A. L. from realizing his creative potential. This is borne out by an examination of the $(H + A):(Hd + Ad)$ ratio of $15:10$ where the combination of $Hd + Ad$ is more than one-half $H + A$. This ratio indicates an overcritical attitude.

It may be that A. L.'s critical, exacting, and meticulous handling of the material is his method of defense. The limited number of H responses also poses some question as to the degree to which A. L. can establish empathic interpersonal relationships.

Although A. L. does acknowledge to some extent his need for immediate impulse gratification, indicated by the four main FM responses, the three additional FM's suggest that he is not very ready to face these needs.

An examination of the m score again shows A. L.'s attempt at suppression. There are no main m responses, but the six additional m's suggest the existence of strong tension and conflict. That he is rather ambivalent in this regard is indicated by the easy emergence of these responses as additionals. These responses reveal a feeling of helplessness combined with circuitous attempts to deal with threatening environmental forces.

The $M{:}FM$ ratio of $5{:}5\frac{1}{2}$ indicates that A. L.'s impulse life is not in conflict with his value system. Accompanied by a reasonable number of CF responses, this ratio would be a sign of mature spontaneity. Since there is only one main CF response, A. L. appears unable to react freely to his environment and therefore his attention becomes focussed upon himself. In addition, as has already been noted, he has difficulty in accepting his impulse life and is seeking escape in fantasy.

The $M:(FM + m)$ proportion of $5:8\frac{1}{2}$ $(FM + m$ being more than one and one-half $M)$ indicates again that the inner tensions may be too strong to permit A. L. to utilize his inner resources for a constructive solution of everyday problems.

At first glance it appears that A. L.'s affectional needs are well integrated in his personality structure, serving as a control function and not interfering unduly with his ability to interact with others. This conclusion is supported by the relationship of $FK + Fc$ to F, the ratio of $6\frac{1}{2}:17$ falling within the limits of one-fourth to three-fourths F, and by the relationship of achromatic to chromatic responses, $(Fc + c + C'):(FC + CF + C)$ being $9:8$. The absence of K and FK responses suggests that there is no undue anxiety in this area, but it is also conceivable that such anxiety is being kept from awareness through the erection of defense mechanisms. This latter possibility is supported by the Fc's $(4 + 5)$ which reveal his awareness and acceptance of his needs for approval and response from others. Furthermore, the large number of additionals indicates that there may be some sensitivity in this regard. It would therefore appear that A. L. reacts quickly to any clouding of the emotional atmosphere and that he can be hurt easily. In an attempt to protect himself from such exposure, he limits his interactions.

A. L.'s reluctance to expose himself is demonstrated to some extent by the right side of the psychogram. His ability to give $6 + 2\ FC$ responses shows that he is emotionally responsive to external stimuli, that he can respond with appropriate feelings and actions to the emotional demands of situations, and that he can usually make pleasant, gracious responses in social situations. However, the relationship of $FC:(CF + C)$ of $6\frac{1}{2}:1\frac{1}{2}$ indicates that his control over the impulsive expression of emotionality is perhaps excessive and that his socialized responses may be superficial. This may be because he is unable or unwilling to allow himself strong emotional reactions. The presence of the additional C/F response suggests that he is not always successful in maintaining this sort of control, perhaps because he is too wrapped up in his own problems. A. L.'s tendency to react in a superficial, overcontrolled manner to environmental stimulation is seen also in the large number of popular responses. He gave $7 + 1\ P$'s, where the expected average is five, demonstrating his tendency to overconventionality and to seeing the world in an obvious, agreed-upon way. His large number of animal responses (41%)—where the optimum expected is between 20 and 35%—also illustrates his tendency to take a rather stereotyped view of the world. However, the average FLR of 1.5 for Fc shows that there is a great deal of successful effort involved in his manipulations of the environmental situation.

Introversive-Extratensive Balance

The three factors to be considered are the relationships of M:Sum C and $(FM + m):(Fc + c + C')$ and the number of responses to the last three cards. The M:Sum C ratio of 4:4 (the 1:1 ratio occurs frequently) does not by itself indicate any particular tendency. However, both the ratio of 4:5 for $(FM + m):(Fc + c + C')$ and the production of 41% of the responses to Cards VIII, IX, and X show an extratensive tendency. This does not mean that A. L. is necessarily actually reacting to environmental stimulation at the present time, but it does indicate that his greatest potential responsiveness is to the emotional implications of the environment. In view of the neutral balance of M:Sum C, it is probable that this responsiveness takes the form of a passive submission to forces coming upon him from without. He seems to accept reality as he finds it, regardless of whether he perceives it clearly, and tends to do little restructuring. Although he is easily stimulated by environmental forces he is reactive rather than striving. The high FLR rating for M, together with the relatively good rating for Fc, may indicate that A. L. works very hard and fairly successfully on this careful balance between extratensive and introversive tendencies.

Control

An examination of A. L.'s control functions suggests that he tends to utilize a constrictive or suppressive control in dealing with his feelings, emotions, and impulses. This conclusion is based on three factors: Firstly, the combination of $FK + Fc$ is 38% of F responses, falling within the limits of one-fourth to three-fourth F. Secondly, the 53% $FK + F + Fc$ does not exceed 75% of the responses. And finally, the 41% of F responses falls within the 20 to 50% limits considered optimal for adjustment. However, the form level of these responses is not of uniformly good quality, and the six additional F responses seem to indicate a tendency to overemphasis in this area. Such a combination represents an adjustment at the expense of close affectional relationships, emotional involvements, and adequate utilization of creative potential. In other words, the control aspects of adjustment are being emphasized at the expense of the creative aspects.

Since A. L. produced four M responses, he would seem to have sufficient inner resources to provide an inner control function. The content of these responses indicates a tendency to use these inner resources to control through intellectual criticism, and the $M:(FM + m)$ ratio of $5:8\frac{1}{2}$ indicates that strong tensions are impeding the full utilization of these resources.

A. L.'s overt behavior, or outer control, appears to be one of controlled responsiveness, a socialized responsiveness which may be superficial. This can be seen in the relationship of $FC:(CF + C)$ of $7:1\frac{1}{2}$; when CF is absent or nearly so. The implication is one of socially skilled expression with minimal involvement.

Intellectual Approach, Efficiency, and Potential

A. L. gave only 15% W responses, which is below the expected range of 20 to 30% of this scoring category. This underemphasis on W responses suggests that he has little interest in seeking relationships between the separate facts of his experience; he cuts himself off from achieving an organized view of the world. Further examination of these five W responses shows that four are actually W's, indicative of intellectual criticalness. It may be, therefore, that A. L.'s ability to make generalizations is impeded by his tendency to be overcritical.

Since A. L.'s ability to handle both large and small and usual details comes within the expected average (54% D responses and 9% d), the underproduction of W's can be ascribed to an overuse of unusual details and white spaces. A. L. has used these locations in 24% of his responses, whereas $Dd + S$ is expected to fall below 10%. This suggests that his reluctance to draw general conclusions from detailed observations stems from a need to defend himself against feelings of insecurity by clinging to limited areas of certainty.

In general, A. L. does not seem to be functioning at the intellectual level of which he is capable. The average unweighted form-level rating of 1.5 indicates above-average intellectual functioning. However, the fact that he achieved a form-level rating of 3.0 for two responses suggests that he has the potential for superior functioning but that there is some interference preventing him from using his potential to the fullest. This is confirmed by the underproduction of original responses, and by the $W:M$ ratio of 5:4, indicating that he has creative potential for which he has not found an adequate outlet. In addition, the large number of popular responses (7 + 1) and animal responses (41%) both indicate a view of the world with a stress on the obvious, conventional, agreed-upon approach to situations. Such restriction could be an indication that A. L. finds it necessary to limit achievement in order to hold on to other values.

Hypotheses

1. A. L. has superior intellectual potential, but is not functioning at the level of which he is capable.

2. A. L.'s exacting, critical attitude may be an expression of defensiveness.

3. The extreme self-criticism and intellectual reservations appear to be associated with anxiety.

4. A. L. does not willingly accept his needs for immediate gratification.

5. A. L. attempts to keep his feelings of tension and conflict from awareness, but is not completely successful. The result is a feeling of helplessness at times.

6. A. L.'s impulse life and value system are not in conflict, but only because his relationships with his environment are carefully controlled. The resulting self-absorption could find release in psychosomatic symptom formation.

7. The affectional needs appear to be well integrated in the total personality structure. However, A. L.'s awareness of these needs is accompanied by an extra sensitivity in this regard which "tones down" his interactions.

8. The feelings of anxiety surrounding the affectional needs are kept from full awareness through the erection of defense mechanisms.

9. A. L. has a limited ability for empathic relationships.

10. A. L. is emotionally responsive to external stimuli and is able to respond appropriately and in a socialized manner.

11. There is an excessive control over spontaneous expression of emotionality, and the socialized responses are therefore superficial. This control is sometimes not too successful, because A. L. becomes too wrapped up in his own problems.

12. A. L.'s greatest potential responsiveness is to the emotional implications of the environment. This responsiveness takes a passive form so that his attitude is reactive rather than striving.

13. A. L. utilizes a suppressive, constrictive control in dealing with his feelings and impulses. This is at the expense of close affec-

tional relationships, emotional involvements, and adequate utilization of creative potential.

14. A. L. tends to view the world in an overconventional, obvious way. He shows little interest in achieving an organized view of the world, but he shows a marked ability to find a limited constructive view of his own.

15. The ability to make generalizations is hampered by A. L.'s overcritical and perfectionist approach.

Sequence Analysis, Case of A. L.

Card I

The beginning of A. L.'s record is hardly outstanding for a person with superior intelligence. It is, rather, an expression of his cautiousness. He gives just the usual popular concept, with some reservations, and adds only the "short stubby tail" to give it a little more interest. The statement, "I guess I never saw what a bat looks like," seems to be a strange comment to make after specifying "insect" for the entire blot. Since A. L. denies that he knows what a bat looks like, the combination of mouse and wings, a good description of a bat, suggests that A. L. is reluctant to commit himself unless absolutely certain. The comment regarding the white spot may be an indication that A. L. is critical of unimportant details. Further confirmation will be needed before taking the symbolism of the mouse and tail as an indication of A. L.'s lack of sexual aggressiveness.

Card II

A. L. immediately becomes more assertive under the impact of color and gives a fairly detailed response to the achromatic area. This is followed by his reference to the Socony advertisement and, finally, by his interpretation to the lower red area, which is frequently seen as a female sex organ. Only at the end of the inquiry is he capable of seeing a male sex organ in the usual top center detail area. This may correspond to the "stubby tail" afterthought in Card I. It should be noted at this point that A. L. seems to find it necessary to account for all the separate parts of the blot. The one little area not used in his three main responses was then used for his one additional response.

The response of the "puppy dogs, nose to nose" is warm and friendly but also reveals a childish quality. The response crab "with two tentacles sticking out" given to the area where female sex organs are usually seen suggests that he feels females are aggressive.

His reaction to color is difficult to assess. Although he is not obviously disturbed by it, apparently he has a strong need to include it in his concepts.

Card III

He closely follows his performance on Card II, starting out and finishing up with superior responses that reach a form level of 3.0. In between, he uses the red areas for two anatomical concepts.

A. L.'s need to account for the red areas in this card results in tension as indicated by the response of lungs and kidney. Such anatomical concepts suggest somatic concern or a tendency to be hypochondriacal under stress. However, he is able to recover and uses a pleasanter concept ("ukulele") when he is not bound to the use of color.

The initial response to this card where he describes two people, "maybe two magicians," is the first human response A. L. makes. However, the fact that they are magicians removes them somewhat from reality, and seeing them "on stage" removes them even further from possible contact. Although these figures are clearly identified as "being men," A. L. makes the statement that a woman might wear shoes like those. This suggests that he sees women as aggressive and ready to take over the male role.

The qualification that it "might be a pitcher of water if they were magicians" is unwarranted since a pitcher of water could be appropriate no matter what kinds of people are seen. Thinking of this nature may interfere with the capacity to be logical or to appraise situations objectively.

The very elaborate response at the end of Card III seems to be of great significance to him. The "somewhat comical, teddy-bearish face" changes from a humorous, playful quality to a sinister one of a devil. This suggests that A. L. has ambivalent feelings toward people, seeing them as friendly and warm but, at the same time, also dangerous. The horse blinders on a human face may indicate self-derogation.

In addition, A. L. again accounts for all parts of the blot, and his tendency to be critical is clearly illustrated in such meticulous specifications as "the little projections on top might be the screws" of the ukulele, and "the nose is little white section here—the dark line representing the nose."

Card IV

Card IV brings out a number of specific points. First of all, it clarifies A. L.'s attitude to the shading. He uses shading quite effectively in small doses, indicating that he is reluctant to accept his affectional needs without hesitation. He starts with the boots, then becomes quite involved with the dragon head, but still says, "I don't think shading had anything to do with it," in spite of the elaborate specifications in which he gets involved. Only his third response, a "wrinkled face," with its many-sided expressive qualities, brings in the use of shading. After a short interlude with the earlike shapes, he adds the usual vaginal response, emphasizing the shading qualities. He is very careful not to let his dependency needs overwhelm him. However, once he becomes more familiar and at home with the blot material, he is able to utilize the shading qualities of the blot in his response.

Card IV is sometimes referred to as the "father card" because of the frequency of responses such as "giant" or "gorilla"—often revealing thereby the father-child relationship. A. L.'s responses "boots," "a dragon's head," and "very wrinkled face," plus such qualifications as "horns," "tongue of fire," "satanic expression," contain the suggestion of a feeling of hostility toward male figures and consequently toward himself.

The frequent reference to eyes, ears, and nose, particularly evident in this card, suggests that A. L. may have deep-seated feelings of insecurity, and is rather distrustful of the world around him.

It is likely that A. L.'s tendency to be critical, which has already been noted and is again evident in this card (for example, note the several comments regarding the exact fit of the blot areas) is his method of dealing with the insecurity he feels.

Looseness in thinking, as in Card III, is again evident in A. L.'s vacillation between map of Italy and boot as well as the "half top, half front view" of the dragon's head. It is possible that when A. L. makes an effort to suppress disturbing material, tensions build up which interfere with logical processes. However, once the disturbing material comes out, as in the clear and unequivocal additional sex response (noted also in Card II), he can then bring himself to face the disturbing factor and to deal with it effectively.

The reaction to this card further corroborates A. L.'s need to account for all areas of the blot including the white space (for example, "ears").

Card V

The first response to Card V, the usual butterfly, is somewhat marred by his concern with the "pincerlike quality" of something he cannot reconcile with a butterfly. The next response picks out a small detail after the card is turned around and he is able to give it a movement quality, and then he finally is able to get at the detail of the "pincerlike quality" and does a pretty good job of seeing it as a neck of a swan with part of the body. In other words, even though he has marked resistance to the phallic-assertive qualities, he is able to deal with it in a constructive way. However, the aggressive quality seen in a benign concept like butterfly suggests that A. L. may sometimes have the feeling of being caught even in pleasant, non-threatening situations.

In contrast to his responses to Card III, where he sees women as aggressive, here he is able to assign a feminine role to the female (as noted in his response "toes of a ballet dancer").

Since A. L.'s compulsive need to account for all parts of the blot is satisfied by his initial response, he seems to be less pressured, less critical, and more logical than in other instances. Nevertheless, some immaturity is still evidenced by the additional response of "drumsticks on a plate."

Card VI

Card VI, with its extremely marked phallic quality, brings to the fore his difficulty with the male role. He does first pick out the usual bearskin rug, but he does not know what to do with the top part. Turning the card around, he finally sees the head and neck of a tortoise but has marked difficulty in reconciling it with the existing bearskin, especially since the phallic part is also embellished with wings and whiskers, "but in the wrong place."

The threatening quality of this card for him, plus his compulsive need to use all of the blot material, produces confusion in his thinking and results in a strange response.

In A. L.'s reaction to this card, his critical attitude, previously noted, begins to emerge as a positive quality which enables him to maintain an awareness of the reality of the situation. Even though he cannot quite keep himself from giving a strange response, he realizes that this "would be quite a creature."

His third response, which is evasive, vague, and neutral, can be interpreted as a safe retreat from a dangerous situation.

Card VII

This card combines softness and shading with a distinct vaginal resemblance at the center bottom section, and thus very often brings out some aspects of the mother-child relationship. The long delay and the evasive nature of his first response immediately express his disturbance over the card.

He sees "pieces of a jigsaw puzzle," and then two horns, or bunny ears, and he emphasizes "just the ears." "Bunny" is a childish term (he could have said "rabbit"), and putting the ears on a doll further emphasizes the childish quality.

The traumatic nature of this card is further seen in A. L.'s not attempting to use all parts of the blot during the performance proper, which has been characteristic of his reaction to the other cards. Interestingly enough, he avoids using the parts which are usually seen as two women or two children. The emphasis on stiffness in the second response acknowledges the phallic qualities in a guarded way.

Most interesting are his two additional responses. Ascribing "hard black little bodies" to moths suggests that he sees females as controlling figures who wield "an iron fist in a velvet glove." His second addition shows a peculiar and, for this ordinarily quite precise man, a symbolically significant attempt to overcome the conflicts which the card had aroused. He now uses the whole card including the white space to see "something standing upright on legs" which "could be a fat man" without a distinct head. He tries to get out from under his mother—the "moth with the hard black body"—by asserting his male role, but his critical faculty is lost along with his head.

Card VIII

A. L. reacts quickly to this card, in contrast to Card VII. It would appear, therefore, that the first all-colored card does not present any particular difficulties due to color. He immediately turns the card sideways and identifies the usual portion as a rat, a particularly antisocial, aggressive animal. This is the first time that A. L. gives such an overtly unpleasant initial response to a card. Such an atypical reaction could result from the leftover disturbances created by Card VII, or from the effect of the emotional impact produced by the color. A. L. apparently cannot cope with hostile feelings, and in his second response he seeks an escape by using his professional experience, which he even acknowledges in the inquiry. It should be noted that A. L. describes the "human cell" with precision and clarity. This suggests the possibility that when he takes the human factor out of emotional situations, he is able to think more clearly, more objectively, and with some perspective.

His next concern is with the top white space which he sees clearly, but his negativism prevents him from discarding a response (the insect) of which he himself is critical. The negativism in A. L.'s personality (suggested before by his overcriticalness, and his use of white space) is now more evident.

Although A. L. made a point in Card I of never having seen a bat, he now very definitely gives a "nasty" bat as a response, suggesting that under continued emotional stimulation, A. L. is able to give direct expression to hostile feelings. In the inquiry, however, he reverts back to the more typical evasive pattern and changes an essentially aggressive "mouth" to a "goatee," which is a more benign concept.

Card IX

Card IX, with its puzzling influx of color and shading, is difficult for many people, and consequently is sometimes rejected. Because A. L. has a compulsive need to respond, he quickly makes the socialized comment, "nice colors," but then gives several responses which indicate that his feelings were quite the opposite. His hostile feelings are clearly evident in the initial response of human hands with "half-closed fists," but the hostility is somewhat lessened since the fists are holding on to something. Nevertheless, his hostility breaks through finally in full force in the additional response at the end of the inquiry when he has "two canine teeth sticking out."

The combination of an eagle with human hands is quite commonly used in emblems; nevertheless, this kind of symbolism seems to occur when he feels overwhelmed by inner tensions with which he is unable to cope.

The previously noted compulsive quality in A. L.'s personality is again evident in his need to account for all parts of the blot even if only by a comment concerning the green area or by the thinly disguised color-naming in the lobster response. Such behaviors suggest that A. L. is insecure and attempts to alleviate these feelings by accounting for all aspects of his environment. However, he does this by sacrificing orderly thinking.

Clearly positive signs in A. L.'s personality emerge in the handling of this card. In the middle of this emotionally charged card, A. L. is able to describe the moose's head (popular level response), using shading and color very well. He also demonstrates that with continued exposure he is able to deal more directly with the elements of a situation. Whereas the initial reaction to the Rorschach material showed such qualities as cautiousness and evasiveness, he is now able by Card IX to handle the stimulus material in a more straightforward manner (for example, the lobster response is directly attributed to the color, and the canine teeth are just "sticking out" with no elaborate attempt at rationalization).

Card X

A. L.'s reaction to Card X is a continuation of the more direct handling of the blot material that was begun in Card IX. His hostility is more overt and also more adequately handled in relation to the blot material. He first sees two animals arguing, followed by an insect head-on, and then the scorpions. Now that A. L. has dealt with these disturbing areas, he relaxes and gives an extremely poetic response ("two leaves in the fall"). His critical, meticulous characteristics now serve to enhance the quality of this response.

A. L. next gives an indirect sex response which shows a great deal of confusion regarding sexual identity as well as female anatomy. However, after this confused response, he shows the capacity to recover, and gives a well-described response involving movement, color, and shading.

Again, it should be noted that A. L. mentions "large eyes" and "ears rather than antennae" (#2) and "head looking sideways" (#6) — specifications suggesting his distrustful attitude toward the world around him.

Testing the Limits

It is interesting that the card which A. L. liked the most (Card X) was not only one which had some pleasant clear concepts, but more significantly the one where overt anger was expressed. A. L. seems to have very little awareness of his negative feelings, since reasons given for liking this card most were "nature" and "animals." On the other hand, Card VII, which gave A. L. the most trouble, was overlooked as the one liked least. Instead, Card IX was selected, the card which was greeted with the comment "nice colors." Although the reason for disliking the card was "rather frightening figure," the actual content of the responses given to this card had no frightening qualities. Apparently A. L. is rather frightened by emotional stimulation and his reaction to it.

Summary

A. L. presents the picture of a reasonably well-adjusted person who has achieved all the typical middle-class goals—a satisfying job, a wife, a home, and children. However, this adjustment is characterized by a passivity that helps A. L. keep his interpersonal involvement to a minimum, and that aids him in avoiding disturbances.

A. L. is an anxious, insecure, and somewhat angry individual who has little insight into the true nature of these feelings. However, he does have some feelings of being ineffectual and he is self-critical. He is unwilling to take on responsibility and tries instead to limit the areas within which he operates. He disavows either professional or academic ambition, and even limits his role within his family. A. L. offers not very convincing rationalizations for his attitudes, but is thus able to cope with the world without becoming overwhelmed by it. Because of an underlying feeling of helplessness he can but passively watch, listen, and criticize.

A. L.'s uncertainty about the world around him, and his reluctance to become deeply involved in it, is actually an extension of his serious reservations about himself, particularly his masculine role. By clinging to immature attitudes, he is not only able to achieve some of the childhood gratifications that he still seeks, but, more importantly, he is able to avoid coming face to face with the questions and doubts he has about himself that are quite frightening to him.

A. L. is a person of superior intellectual potential but is not at the present time functioning freely at the level of his capabilities. He is also a person who is capable of warm, positive interpersonal relationships, and of a good deal of creativity. This ability comes out in his autobiography when he speaks about being settled for a year in Okinawa. He says: "Almost completely divorced from the military, our station was located right in an Okinawan village. I really came to love these people, and the Oriental attitudes toward life made a lasting impression upon me. After returning home, I was steeped in the Orient, and even thought about returning there. The impersonal, busy, city life of New York was almost unbearable after my idyllic year overseas. That had been the happiest year of my life."

He is able to make good judgments and arrive at sound conclusions when the implied threatening aspects of a situation are removed, either by closer examination or continued exposure. But all his efforts are currently focussed on avoiding even the possibility of threat, and in so doing, he does not allow himself to explore the actual situation or to expand his own horizon. The precarious balance he thus achieves is at the expense of his potentials.

It seems quite apparent that A. L. could benefit from therapy and could thereby realize a fuller, more mature life.

Appendix

THE CASE OF TONY

TONY was referred to the Bureau of Child Guidance while he was in the fourth grade, because he was retarded in all his school subjects. When the Rorschach was administered, he was ten years and three months of age. He was born in Puerto Rico, but entered the first grade of school in this country. He does not have a language handicap. He lives with both parents in New York City and has two siblings. When he was six years old, his Binet (Form L) IQ was 86. His attendance at school is excellent, but his work is very poor. He is practically a non-reader. He wants to participate in school activities and always volunteers to answer questions but then finds that he cannot answer them. He is interested in drawing and making things out of pipe cleaners.

Rorschach Protocol

Tony's Rorschach record, together with the scoring and comments, follows:

CARD I

PERFORMANCE   INQUIRY

5″

1. An eagle—the inside is an eagle.   1. (Q.) This ain't the eagle.

   Score: W   F   A   1.0

   COMMENT: The eagle is considered a main response since the subject, only upon questioning, made the comment, "This ain't the eagle"—a kind of half-hearted rejection.

                                             Add. Pebbles falling (*dd*), this ruins the whole thing. Looks like it's cracking and split here (points to center line). (The last comment refers to the eagle.)

Score: dd   mF   Pebbles   0.5

COMMENT: This has been scored as an additional response since it was given during the inquiry.

2. And these here look like two mountain bears.	2. They call them mountain bears 'cause they climb. They're slipping off the mountain, they're trying to hold on. They were having a fight and they're slipping. (Q. What happens?) I don't know.—They'll hang on. The good man shall win.

Score: W   FM,Fm   A   1.5

COMMENT: A *W* location score was assigned since the subject specified that the bears were engaged in a joint activity. Both the *FM* and *Fm* scores are given to represent the apparent conflict Tony experiences between "slipping off" and "trying to hold on."

CARD II

PERFORMANCE   INQUIRY

6″

1. Looks like a—like skeletons dancing.	1. Red head, red feet—like dancing. You could describe that easily—like clapping hands together. (Q. Tell me more about it being a skeleton.) Well, a human being wouldn't be dressed in black, right? You remember when you told me about the head (referring to the verbal absurdity on the Stanford-Binet). This is like it. There's one thing I can't get out of seeing—this line right here (*dd* in upper white space). They look like they are doing a dance.

Score: W   M,FC   (H)   2.0

COMMENT: The entire blot, including the red areas, is used to see humanlike figures in human activity. Bright color as well as achromatic color has been taken into account in the additional

FC score. Achromatic color does not have to be scored separately under these circumstances. However, one might want to add an *FC'* score to account for the symbolic significance of the black used to signify the skeletons. The form-level score of 2.0 was determined as follows: 1.5 for human figures; 0.5 for specific activities of dancing and clapping; 0.5 for organization; −0.5 for the specification, "skeletons," which spoils the human figure. The subject's comment about "this line right here" should have been clarified.

CARD III

PERFORMANCE   INQUIRY

3″

1. Not again! Another skeleton with a—

2. Bow tie in the middle.

3. They're eating something in this pot with flames coming down.

1. And here's the same thing, but this is a different kind of skeleton. These are women. There's the flames going down behind them and bow tie in the middle, and they're roasting something down here (points out usual figures; points to chest protrusion and says, "It's a girl, of course").

2. (D_1)

3. (Q. Explain about the flames.) Like coming out of the fire. That's the death flames (D_2) coming out of the pot and going up. They're cooking. It's like Hallowe'en.

Score:	1.	W		M	(H)	P	1.5	
	2.	D	W	F	Obj	P	1.0	$O-$
	3.	D		CF,mF	$Flames$		0.5	

COMMENT: The first response is the usual popular human figures seen in action. However, the form-level rating is 1.5 because of the specification of the "chest protrusion." The bow tie, although part of the first response, is scored separately because it is poorly integrated in the response and also because it is a popular response. The flames have been scored as the third response since they are seen as a separate detail at first. The *mF* score was assigned since the flames are very clearly seen in movement and are semi-definite in form. Since an attempt was made to combine all the elements into an organized response, an additional *W* score was given. An additional *O*− score was given because of the bizarre quality of the organization.

CARD IV

PERFORMANCE   INQUIRY

5″

1. That looks like a beast. (laughs) All these are ugly.

    1. Here's the eagle—no, the beast. Here's the big claws (upper side projections) and big feet. Sitting on a mountain (center bottom). Looks like a ghost to haunt you. Looks like he has a cracked skull (upper center line). Every picture I see is a skeleton.

Score: *W*   *FM→M,Fc*   *A→(H)*   2.5

COMMENT: To see an animal in action in the whole card calls for an *FM* score; but changing it to a ghost or skeleton warrants the →*M* score. The additional *Fc* score is for the "cracked skull." The form-level rating of 2.5 includes: 1.0 for the beast; 0.5 for the additional specification of claws; 0.5 for the activity of sitting; and 0.5 for the particular specification of the "cracked" skull.

CARD V

PERFORMANCE   INQUIRY

4″

1. Looks like the back of a certain—I don't know what you call it—an eagle! The back of an eagle.

    1. I said before that it's an eagle, but it looks like an animal. But I can't describe the animal. A little insect, a grasshopper, butterfly. You never saw one? I was in camp and saw one. (Q. Tell me about it.) It has wings and down here (d_3) grasshopper things (meant antennae). (Q. Any particular way?) Of course it's facing that way, like it's mashed against it—is flat. If you took a butterfly it looks like it, but this is a grasshopper.

Score: *W*   *F*   *A*   *P*   1.0

COMMENT: The usual popular response is given to the whole blot. The remark, "like it's smashed against it," is not given an additional m score because it is not a spontaneous comment and came out only after much questioning during the inquiry.

CARD VI

PERFORMANCE	INQUIRY
6″	
1. That looks like a skeleton cat.	1. Like a skeleton cat $(D_2 \vee)$. Looks like it's upside down.

Score: D   F−   A.At   −1.0

COMMENT: Although the inquiry is not entirely sufficient to score the form level of the main response accurately, it does seem that Tony attempts to use "skeletons" as a way of making form discrepancies seemingly disappear, and therefore the −1.0 score.

> *Add.* Down here $(\vee)$ looks like skeletons dancing. Can't we forget skeletons and put them to human beings, old ones? Skeletons get me scared and I dream at night. (Heads, hands, and feet were specified by the subject. He saw two skeletons.)

Score: D   M   (H)   2.0

COMMENT: The form-level rating of 2.0 for the additional response is derived as follows: 1.0 for the human figure; 0.5 for the additional specification of hands; and 0.5 for the dancing.

CARD VII

PERFORMANCE	INQUIRY
6″	
1. That looks like two elephants sitting on top of this mountain.	1. (Upper two-thirds, D_4, used for the elephants; the bottom third, D_1, for the mountain.)

Score: W   FM   A   2.0

COMMENT: The inquiry is insufficient for scoring form level. However, it would be possible to assign a score of 1.0 for the elephants and 0.5 for sitting on the mountain, and perhaps also another 0.5 for the trunks, probably seen as raised. This would make a total of 2.0.

> *Add.* This looks like a butterfly (D_1).

Score: *D*   *F*   *A*   1.0

COMMENT: The subject changes his first concept of mountain for this area to a butterfly—a much more definite concept.

CARD VIII

PERFORMANCE   INQUIRY

Oh! nice! What is it? $> \wedge$

10″

1. Two foxes on a mountain, that's all. Hey, they make nice pictures (covers all of blot but the animals). What is it without the rest—looks like something. These pictures are crazy. All these pictures are crazy. How did you get them? Did you buy them just for me?

1. Two foxes, you know, (D_1) that eat chickens, birds—on a hill climbing (indicates remainder of card). They lost their tail.

Score: *D→W*   *FM*   *A*   *P*   1.0

COMMENT: The usual popular animal in action response is scored with a →W indicated because the response includes the total center area of the card for the "mountain." The remark, "They lost their tail," is an irrelevant specification as far as the form level is concerned.

CARD IX

PERFORMANCE   INQUIRY

8″

1. Over here, the white part looks like the world.

1. This is nothing. I don't even know what it looks like. Don't look like nothing. Before I said it looks like a world, but it ain't.

COMMENT: The response as originally given was rejected during the inquiry and therefore not scored.

Add. (looks and points to the blue in upper *S* area) The blue is the world—that's all it could be.

Score: *S→dr*   *FC−*   *Geo*   −1.0

COMMENT: The new response given during the inquiry is considered an additional response. The *FC−* score is given for an inaccurate response.

CARD X

PERFORMANCE	INQUIRY

9″

1. Here looks like a spider, two spiders.   1. (D_1)

   Score: D   F   A   P   1.0

   COMMENT: This is the usual popular response to this area.

2. A wishbone. Let's see, I better not   2. (D_{12})
   say any more.

   Score: D   F A_{obj} 1.0

   COMMENT: A common response to the area, but not popular.

3. Looks like a bee—too much to say.   3. (D_{15})
   I give up—too many things.

   Score: D   F−   A   −1.0

   COMMENT: The concept "bee" is a poor fit for this particular
   area; therefore, the F− score and the −1.0 rating.

4. This looks like a lung.   4. $(D_9$—Subject denies color.)

   Score: D   F   At   1.0

   COMMENT: The concept "lungs" fits the area fairly well; therefore, the 1.0 form-level score. Color was not used.

5. This looks like a territory.   5. (D_{11})

   Score: D   F   Geo   0.5

   COMMENT: A vague concept of indefinite shape is scored F and
   receives a form-level rating of 0.5.

6. Here it looks like a bird biting on   6. (D_4)
   this animal, whatever it is.

   Score: D   FM   A   1.5

   COMMENT: Since the bird is engaged in "biting," the basal form-
   level rating of 1.0 was raised to 1.5.

TOTAL TIME: about 15 minutes

TABULATION AND SCORING SHEET

Card No., Response No. and Position	Reac. Time	LOCATION W	D,d	Dd,S	Add.	DETERMINANT Movement	Vista Depth	Form	Texture Ach. Color	Color	Add.	CONTENT Main	Add.	P–O Main	Add.	FLR
①	5"	W						F				A				1.0
Add.					dd						mF		Pebbles			0.5
②		W				FM					Fm	A				1.5
①	6"	W				M					FC	(H)				2.0
①	3"	Wx				M						(H)		P		1.5
②			D		W			F				Obj		P	0–	1.0
③			D							CF	mF	Flames				0.5
①	5"	W				FM→						M Fc	A→	(H)			2.5
①	4"	W						F				A		P		1.0
①	6"		D					F~				A.At				–1.0
Add.					D						M		(H)			2.0
①	6"	W				FM						A				2.0
Add.					D						F		A			1.0
①	10"	D→		W		FM						A		P		1.0
	8"															
Add.					S→						FC–		Geo			–1.0
					dr											
①	9"		D					F				A		P		1.0
②			D					F				A obj				1.0
③			D					F~				A				–1.0
④			D					F				At				1.0
⑤			D					F				Geo				0.5
⑥			D				FM						A				1.5

Total Time T = 900

	W + D + d + Dd + S = R	M + FM + m + k + K + FK + F + Fc + c + C' + FC + CF + C = R	(H) 2	2	P 5	
No. of responses Main	7 +10+ + + =17	2 +5+ + + + +9+ + + + +1 + =17	Hd 0		O 0	
Add.	2 2 2 1	2 3 1 1 2	A 9	1	O– 0	1
Sum FLR	11.5 5.5	3.5 8.5 4.5 0.5	Ad 0			19.5
Average FLR	1.6 0.6	1.8 1.7 0.5 0.5				0.93

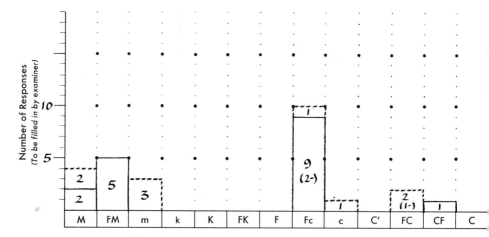

	M	FM	m	k	K	FK	F	Fc	c	C'	FC	CF	C

Number of Responses (To be filled in by examiner)

M: 2 / 2
FM: 5
m: 3
Fc: 9 (2-) / 1
c: 1
FC: 2 (1-)
CF: 1

I. BASIC RELATIONSHIPS: Main Responses Only

Total Responses   R _17_

Total Time   T _900_ sec.

Average Time per Response   T/R _53_ sec.

Average Reaction Time:

Achromatic Cards (I, IV, V, VI, VII)   _5_ sec.

Chromatic Cards (II, III, VIII, IX, X)   _7_ sec.

$\dfrac{F}{R}$ _53_ F%

$\dfrac{FK + F + Fc}{R}$ _53_ %

$\dfrac{A + Ad}{R}$ _53_ A%

(H + A) : (Hd + Ad)   _11:0_

Popular Responses   P _5_

Original Responses   O _0_

$\dfrac{FC + 2CF + 3C}{2}$ sum C _1.0_

M : sum C   _2:1.0_

(FM + m) : (Fc + c + C')   _5:0_

$\dfrac{\text{Responses to Cards VIII + IX + X}}{R}$ _41_ %

W : M   _7:2_

II. SUPPLEMENTARY RELATIONSHIPS: Main + $\frac{1}{2}$ Add

M : FM   **3 : 5**

M : (FM + m)   **3 : 6**

(FK + Fc) : **F**   **½ : 9**

(Fc + cF + c + C' + C'F + FC') : (FC + CF + C)   **½ : 2**

(FK + Fc + Fk) : (K + KF + k + kF + c + cF)   **½ : 0**

FC : (CF + C)   **1 : 1**

III. MANNER OF APPROACH

	Main Responses			No. Add. Scores
	No.	Actual %	Expect. %	
W	7	41	20-30	2
D	10	59	45-55	2
d	0		5-15	0
Dd+S	0		< 10	3

IV. ESTIMATE OF INTELLECTUAL LEVEL

Capacity _High average_

Efficiency _Below average_

V. SUCCESSION

Rigid   ✓

Orderly _____

Loose _____

Confused _____

VI. FORM LEVEL SUMMARY

Average Unweighted FLR _0.93_

Average Weighted   FLR _1.05_

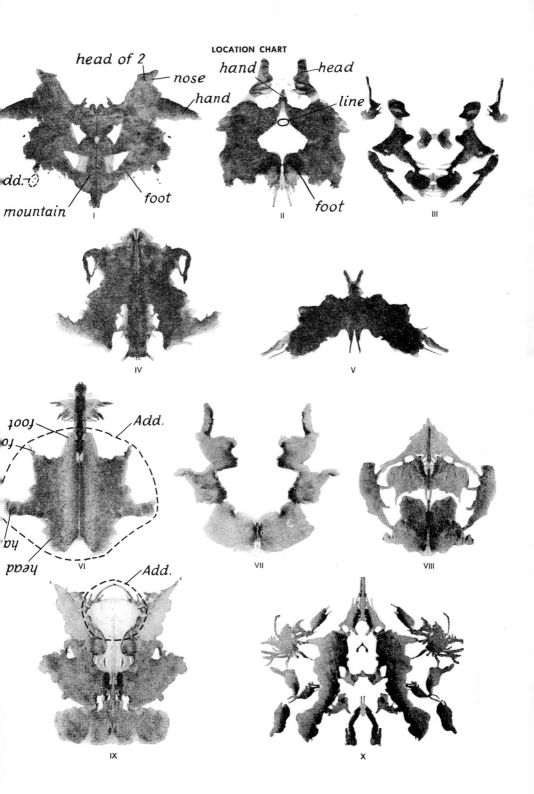

LOCATION CHART

head of 2

nose

hand

dd.

mountain

I

hand

head

line

foot

II

III

IV

V

foot

to

Add.

ha

head

VI

VII

VIII

Add.

IX

X

Thematic Apperception Test Record*

CARD I

Looks like he's sad, and he's looking at a picture or something. I think it is, can't say any more. (Q. Tell me a story about it.) Looks like he's thinking of something. Something is peculiar about this picture. Looks like he's sad. Must be a sad picture. If I could of saw the picture it would be different. It could be anything. I can't see anything that's going to happen.

CARD 6GF

The man is yelling at her and she's sitting down and she's like angry. Looks like he's drunk—laughs—looks like he's angry at her. I could say he's drunk or something. She's angry at him or he's angry at her. Looks like he was drinking too much and he came in the house yelling at her and they had a fight. They make up, that's all. That's what always happens every time.

CARD 6BM

There's like somebody that died and they're sad, both of them. And they're in church, any kind of church, not very special. She's looking out the window. Looks like it's snowing. The man took off his hat, that's how I know he's in church cause why would he take off his hat in the house. (G. Who died?) Don't ask me. I can't go into the story. They're thinking about the wife with two children alone, the cousin's wife.

CARD 8BM

Eh Gad! Over here there's a gun, and here there's two men operating on this man. They're gonna have to cut his stomach open, and the boy is standing beside. The two men are scared to do it and the boy feels sorrow for his father—say it's his father. He's thinking about his poor mother, how sorry she'll be. He got shot, we even see the gun. They're going to cut him open, that's all. They'll take the bullet out and patch him up.

---

* The sequence is that in which the cards were presented to Tony.

CARD 7BM

The man is talking to the child about being bad and the child doesn't care and he ain't listening to him. He hits teachers with apples. The teachers get me so mad I try to throw books at them—and it looks like the kid is mad about something. And say the father's name is Bill. Looks like the father is smiling and the son is unhappy about something—like they want to put him in a home cause he was bad and doesn't listen. That's all. (Q. What happens?) He gets worse. He runs away then they go looking for him, then they capture him, then they put him into an orphan home, and from all the whippings he tries to run away again, but this time the moth-aunt wanted to take Billy out of the orphanage. They took him out. They made up but the father didn't. Everytime he would see him he (the father) would yell, and the son would spit at him.

CARD 5

This looks like a lady sneaking into a house to take something. It looks like she's a tomboy and it looks like a child, cause you could see by the pants, looks like pants. Can't say nothing else about it. (Q. Try to tell a story.) —It looks like a mother, but—O.K.—The mother was very wicked to her children. Everytime she would make the children go to the forest the children did not like her but they would stay with her, but she was very wicked. One day daddy said, "Do you want to go away to a cottage?" It's very deep into the forest and there's a big tree. They set out with some crumbs to eat. They came to the cottage. They went in. There were three chairs, three bowls. They went upstairs. There was a big bed, a medium sized bed, and a small bed. There was one closet. The closet was empty. They went downstairs to the living room. There was a big and a little chair. They sat down near the table. They saw one bowl, two bowls of soup. They ate the daddy soup and the mother soup. They went upstairs to sleep and then the next morning they set out to catch fish. They caught a fish and they set home. They got home, they cooked the fish, and it was very good. They had a stove but they were very careful with their matches.

CARD 3BM

Yikes! What the devil is this! (Peers closely at gun.) If I only could see what that darn thing is. What is that! Looks like a gun. This boy looks like he killed somebody. The gun is on the floor and he is scared. He is on the floor crying. (Q. Finish the story.) I don't know. I give up. He gets arrested and put in a home. Oh come on, let's stop!

CARD 14

This I can't see nothing. Looks like this boy is stealing something. He's going to this dark house. Something tells him that he will be put into a home. He doesn't care—he—somebody woke up. They saw the shadow. He ran away, and they called the police. The police searched the whole country. Then they found the boy and put him in the home. He ran away, then went to jail, from jail to prison, from prison to an orphanage, where people are guilty or not, and he was guilty—no, he was not guilty. They let him free and he started all over again doing bad things. Then he got a record and they put him in a home again, where they hit the bad children. He made a break for it. He had a rifle and he shot one policeman, then they put him in a home again. No, not a home again. Then they put him in jail for another year, and then from jail they put him into the home and he escaped, and he went to the mountains, and the police found him, and put him in a home where they whip you hard. His folks didn't feel a bit bad cause he was bad at home, but his aunt felt sad. She took him out of the home. Then he made up for being bad. But his father and his mother never even saw his aunt and never went near her and never saw the son.

CARD 9BM

I could start with architecting. These men are architectors. They finished a very hard workman job. They saw a comfortable spot. They went there and slept. It looks like a boy was sneaking up. He stole one of the carpenter's tools. The carpenter woke up and went after him. He called the police. Oh, not back to the homes! That'll be all—the architectors called the police. The police captured the boy. The boy went to the home. In the home he got a beating. From the home he went to jail cause he shot a policeman. He stayed for years. They wanted to hang him. They did not. He tried and tried to make up. His family hated him for it, everybody in his family. His aunts hated him, but he had a friend and he bailed him out. From that day on he went being like bad, cause you could see like a boy sneaking up.

CARD 2

This girl and boy and mother were living on the farm. The boy was John. The girl was Suzy. The mother was Aunt Clara—was Aunt Clara—cross out mother, just say Aunt Clara. It was a very early start. The girl started to school. The boy started to plow the field. The mother just stood thinking about her husband in World War II. The girl liked going to school. She had a nice teacher, but one of the teachers liked to have her. She would give a hundred dollars to have her in her class. That's all.

CARD 4

It looks like this man stole something from him. Well, this man wanted to kill him but his wife will not let him. But when he went home his wife called the police and they took the thing away. He had a gun, but his gun was loaded with blanks. He just used it to scare people when people bothered him. They gave it to his wife and his wife saved it for him, and he lived happily ever after.

Bibliography

SELECTED REFERENCES ON ADMINISTRATION, SCORING, AND INTERPRETATION

ABT, L. E., and BELLAK, L. *Projective Psychology.* New York: Grove Press; 1959.

ALLEN, R. M. *Introduction to the Rorschach Technique.* New York: International Universities Press, Inc.; 1953.

——. *Elements of the Rorschach Interpretation.* New York: International Universities Press, Inc.; 1954.

AMES, L. B.; LEARNED, J.; MÉTRAUX, R. W.; and WALKER, R. N. *Child Rorschach Responses.* New York: Paul B. Hoeber, Inc.; 1952.

——. *Rorschach Responses in Old Age.* New York: Paul B. Hoeber, Inc.; 1954.

AMES, L. B.; MÉTRAUX, R. W.; and WALKER, R. N. *Adolescent Rorschach Responses.* New York: Paul B. Hoeber, Inc.; 1959.

ANDERSON, H. H., and ANDERSON, G. L. *Introduction to Projective Techniques.* New York: Prentice-Hall; 1951.

BECK, S. J. *Rorschach's Test, Vol. II: Variety of Personality Pictures.* New York: Grune & Stratton, Inc.; 1945.

——. *Rorschach's Test, Vol. III: Advances in Interpretation.* New York: Grune & Stratton, Inc.; 1952.

——. *Rorschach Experiment: Ventures in Blind Diagnosis.* New York: Grune & Stratton, Inc.; 1960.

BECK, S. J.; BECK, A. G.; LEVITT, E. E.; and MOLISH, H. B. *Rorschach's Test, Vol. I: Basic Processes.* 3rd rev. ed. New York: Grune & Stratton, Inc.; 1961.

BLUM, L. H.; DAVIDSON, H. H.; and FIELDSTEEL, N. D. *Rorschach Workbook.* New York: International Universities Press, Inc.; 1954.

HALPERN, F. *Clinical Approach to Children's Rorschachs.* New York: Grune & Stratton, Inc.; 1953.

HARROWER, M.; ROMAN, M.; VORHAUS, P.; and BAUMAN, G. *Creative Variations in the Projective Techniques.* Springfield, Illinois: Charles C. Thomas; 1960.

Journal of Projective Techniques (formerly *Rorschach Research Exchange*), Vol. I (1936) to present.

KLOPFER, B.; AINSWORTH, M. D.; KLOPFER, W. G.; and HOLT, R. R. *Developments in the Rorschach Technique, Vol. I: Technique and Theory.* New York: Harcourt, Brace & World; 1954.

KLOPFER, B., AND OTHERS. *Developments in the Rorschach Technique. Vol. II: Fields of Application.* New York: Harcourt, Brace & World; 1956.

LEDWITH, N. H. *Rorschach Responses of Elementary School Children.* Pittsburgh: Univ. of Pittsburgh Press; 1959.

PHILLIPS, L., and SMITH, J. G. *Rorschach Interpretation: Advanced Technique.* New York: Grune & Stratton, Inc.; 1953.

PIOTROWSKI, Z. A. *Perceptanalysis.* New York: The Macmillan Company; 1957.

RAPAPORT, D.; GILL, M.; and SCHAFER, R. *Diagnostic Psychological Testing, Vol. II.* Chicago: Year Book Medical Publishers, Inc.; 1946.

RICKERS-OVSIANKINA, M. A. *Rorschach Psychology.* New York: John Wiley & Sons, Inc.; 1960.

RORSCHACH, H. *Psychodiagnostics: A Diagnostic Test Based on Perception.* (Trans. by Lemkau, P., and Kronenberg, B.) New York: Grune & Stratton, Inc.; 1951.

SARASON, S. B. *Clinical Interaction, with Special Reference to the Rorschach.* New York: Harper & Brothers; 1954.

SCHACHTEL, E. G. "Dynamic Perception and the Symbolism of Form," *Psychiatry,* 1941, 4, 79–96.

——. "On Color and Affect," *Psychiatry,* 1943, 6, 393–409.

——. "Subjective Definitions in the Rorschach Test Situation and Their Effect on Test Performance," *Psychiatry,* 1945, 8, 419–448.

——. "Projection and Its Relation to Character Attitudes and Creativity in the Kinesthetic Responses," *Psychiatry,* 1950, 13, 69–100.

SCHAFER, R. *Clinical Application of Psychological Tests.* New York: International Universities Press, Inc.; 1952.

——. *Psychoanalytic Interpretation in Rorschach Testing.* New York: Grune & Stratton, Inc.; 1956.

SHERMAN, M. H. *Rorschach Reader.* New York: International Universities Press, Inc.; 1961.

SMALL, L. *Rorschach Location and Scoring Manual.* New York: Grune & Stratton, Inc.; 1956.

Index

A (see animal figure responses)

abstract concept responses, 90
  analysis of, 156

abstract movement responses (see inanimate movement responses)

accuracy
  and form level, 95–96, 100–01
  interpretation of, 133–34

achromatic color responses, 78, 84, 119

achromatic color scores
  interpretation of, 137, 138, 142, 143–44
  tabulation of, 123, 124, 125

action (see movement)

Ad (see animal figure responses)

additional scores, 50
  interpretation of, 129, 140, 152–53
  tabulation of, 121–23

administration of test, 26–46

affectional needs, 18
  evaluation of, 135–37, 142, 144

affective characteristics (see emotional control; emotions)

Ainsworth, M. D., 24n.

alphabet response, 156

analogy period in testing, 29–30, 41–42

analysis (see content analysis; interpretation; sequence analysis)

anatomical responses, 87, 88
  analysis of, 155

animal figure responses, 40, 87–88, 124
  analysis of, 154–55
  interpretation of, 145, 150

animal movement responses, 37–38, 43, 71–72, 111–12

animal movement scores
  interpretation of, 134–35, 140–41, 143, 147
  tabulation of, 121, 124–25

anxiety, 18
  evaluation of, 136–37, 143, 145, 147

approach to problems, 18
  evaluation of, 130–32, 148

architectural responses, 90

art concept responses, 90

At (see anatomical responses)

atmosphere in testing situation, 26–27, 29

Bartlett, F. C., 5–6

basic relationships (see relationships)

Beck, Samuel J., 6, 153

behavior of subject, 15–16, 26–28
  interpretation of, 130, 151

Binet, Alfred, 4

bizarre responses, 93, 94, 100–01, 104
  interpretation of, 150

blocking, 33

blood responses, 82, 117, 156

botanical responses, 89

Brown, F., 153

C (see color responses)

c (see shading responses)

cards, Rorschach, 3
  description of, 8–12
  illustration of, 54–64
  location of responses on, 35–36 (see also Location Chart)
  perception of, 14–15
  popular responses for, 54–63, 91–93
  position in which held, 32–33
  presentation of, 27–28, 30–31 (see also administration of test; scoring)

case studies, 20–23, 157–87, 187–223, 224–37

C'F (see achromatic color responses)

CF (see chromatic color responses)

chromatic color responses, 43, 78–83, 117–19

chromatic color scores
  interpretation of, 137–38, 140–44, 147–48
  sequence analysis of, 152
  tabulation of, 121, 123, 124–25

cognition (see intellectual level)

color responses, inquiry regarding, 38–39, 41–42 (see also achromatic color responses; chromatic color responses)